Kitnay Aadmi Thay?

Diptakirti Chaudhuri has been a salesman for more than twelve years now—having sold soaps, soft drinks, oils and newspapers all over India.

His obsessive love for movies is a hereditary disease, which was nurtured during his engineering and MBA college days.

When not watching or reading about movies, he writes about them on his blog, Calcutta Chromosome (http://diptakirti.blogspot.com) or discusses them on Twitter (@diptakirti).

He has published a book for children on the 2011 cricket World Cup. This is his second book.

He lives in Gurgaon with his wife, a son and a daughter. None of them shares his obsessive love for the movies. Yet.

Kitnay Aadmi Thay?

Completely Useless Bollywood Trivia

DIPTAKIRTI CHAUDHURI

westland

westland ltd

Venkat Towers, 165, P.H. Road, Maduravoyal, Chennai 600 095

No. 38/10 (New No.5), Raghava Nagar, New Timber Yard Layout Banglore 560 026

Survery No. A - 9, II Floor, Moula Ali Industrial Area, Moula Ali Hyderabad 500 040

23/181 Anand Nagar, Nehru Road, Santacruz East, Mumbai 400055

4322/3 Ansari Road, Daryaganj, New Delhi 110 002

First published by westland ltd 2012

Copyright ©Diptakirti Chaudhuri 2012

All rights reserved

10 9 8 7 6 5 4 3 2 1

ISBN: 978-93-81626-19-1

Typeset by Four Words Inc.

Printed at Gopsons Papers Ltd

Acknowledgements

Without IMDb and YouTube, this book couldn't have been written. Those diligent souls who enrich these sites with meticulously tagged info and videos are mankind's gift to God.

The readers of *Calcutta Chromosome* were generous with their encouragement, exhortations and embellishments. Even the name of the book was 'crowd-sourced' from the readers of the blog.

A special word of thanks to Brajesh Bajpai, who was convinced that I had to write this book. More than I was myself.

Udayan Chakrabarti read the very first draft of this book and loved it enough to criticise it mercilessly.

Pavan Jha shared his amazing knowledge and perspective of Hindi films and improved the book with his suggestions.

Arnab Ray (a.k.a. Greatbong) was a 'senior' with his sage advice about book-writing and book-marketing.

Akanksha Sharma, Abhishek Kanodia and Rahul Fernandes *jo Hindi ka bahut gyan rakhte HAIN* corrected most of the dialogues in the book.

With his glowing recommendation, Bishwanath Ghosh found this book a home in Westland.

Prita Maitra of Westland was the calming oasis of reason and expertise in the chaotic madness of this book.

Aradhana Bisht of Westland was most helpful in putting the finishing touches.

Dyujoy and Drishti Chaudhuri made me realise there are fun things beside movies. Writing this book with them around me was the most fun I've ever had.

I owe the last decade of my life to Trishna Chaudhuri for suffering me patiently (and sometimes, not-so-patiently). Maybe one day, she will learn to suffer bad Hindi movies too.

Kurt Vonnegut said that every book should be written to please just one person. I wrote this book to please two. Nilendu Misra and Shivaramakrishnan Krishnamurthy have been my sounding-boards, doppelgangers and co-authors for many years now.

And finally, this book is dedicated to the biggest Bollywood fan I know, someone who has not lost track from Rishi to Ranbir, from *Stardust* to *Zoom*.

Her name is Reeta Chaudhuri—*'jo khush kismati se meri maa hai...'*

Introduction

This book is for Bollywood fans.

If you love **Disco Dancer**, if you feel choked (or even better, cry) when Amitabh dies in **Deewaar**, if you know when Hrithik met Suzanne, if you have film magazines from a decade back — this book is for you.

This book is about the favourite pastime of Bollywood fans.

Which are the ten best death scenes? Seven best sequels? Anupam Kher's eight best performances? The twelve best comedies of all times? The whole parlour game of making lists—and fighting endlessly over them—is what this book is all about. Currently, blood is being shed in college canteens, on internet discussion forums, over a drink, to decide the ten best Gulzar-RD partnerships. This book is not intended to stop those battles but to fuel them.

(BTW, none of the above lists appears in this book.)

This book is about getting more people to join in the game.

This book is incomplete. But before you ask for your money back, I can assure you it is more fun this way. It presents you with names on a list and you are supposed to come up with more. Scribble in the extra names on the margins. Call up your childhood buddy in Alwar and ask him how many films he remembers in which Amitabh played a Sikh. Feel superior if an obvious title is missing.

Enjoy!

0

Opening Credits

'Movies should have a beginning, a middle and an end.'—Georges Franju

'But not necessarily in that order.'—Jean-Luc Godard

Lights, Popcorn, Action: 10 Opening Credits

*A*s you struggle to open the slightly oily packet of chips, the lights go off, making the already difficult job of locating the seal impossible. You also stop tugging at the polythene and concentrate on the list of people who are going to fill your next three hours—and maybe the rest of your life—with meaning.

No amount of pre-release hype or music-channel song promos can bring about a surge of adrenaline as a rocking opening credits sequence does. And while some do it with mirrors, Bollywood does it with a mix of cool devices.

Pre-credit Backstory Compression[1]

One of the most popular devices—till the 1980s—was an attempt to knock off the socio-historical context of the film, motivation of the hero and the emergence of the key characters before the titles so that the 'real' story can begin. It took economy of expression to a completely new level and said more in these 22 minutes than in the next 222!

There were many filmmakers who employed this device but nobody did it better than Manmohan Desai.

---

[1] Acknowledgements are due to Rajorshi Chakrabarti, who defined this concept in his essay 'Perchance to Dream' published in the anthology *The Popcorn Essayists* (edited by Jai Arjun Singh). The book cannot be recommended enough.

In his biggest hit, he separated a family of five in a matter of eight minutes. The father got into a gun-battle with a smuggler and escaped with a crate of gold biscuits. The mother was rendered blind by the falling branch of a tree. Their three sons were picked up by a Hindu police officer, a Muslim tailor and a Christian priest but not before all of them had left tons of identifiers to pick up years later.

Years passed and we came to an accident site where a blind flower-lady was hit badly and urgently needed blood.

A Christian do-gooder took her to the hospital. A Hindu police inspector was at the hospital to lodge the case. A Muslim qawwali singer was also there, flirting with a lady doctor. All of them were found to be the same blood group as the blind lady and they were all co-opted to donate some blood.

As the transfusion started, a doctor asked them their names. And as the titles came on, they told us. **Amar Akbar Anthony**.

Hit song

One of the most popular 'previews' of a Hindi film is always the music. And no better way to promote it than to put it right upfront when the audience is settling down and the stars of the film are being announced.

An Evening in Paris had one of the best title tracks, in which Shammi Kapoor wooed Parisian blondes in the glittering streets of the city while Mohammed Rafi belted out the hit number. Well-known landmarks zoomed past us as Shammi jumped up and down on the Champs Élysees while wide-eyed Frenchmen tried to grasp the exotic notion of an Indian dancing in their midst.

Another great title track was from **Maine Pyar Kiya**—though it did not feature the lead pair. Instead it showed two figures in silhouette doing a sexy (as sexy as Rajshri allowed them) dance routine to the tune of the title track and who swore that incredibly beautiful things happened to them only because they fell in love. The superhit song also had impeccable pedigree because it was lifted from Stevie Wonder's *I just called to say I love you*!

Music, Video

Apart from the hit music from the film, titles often have customised music—usually played to a set of mood-setting visuals. R.D. Burman had perfected the art of creating rocking title music by putting together a medley of the film's tunes.

The Greatest Film Ever Made opened with a jailor getting off a train and on to a horse, accompanied by the trusted manservant of a thakur. We did not know this when the movie started but the entire title sequence staked out the rocky, rugged terrain that was going to be the setting of the movie. As the two riders moved from outskirts to villages, the tune—which started on a grand scale—slowly moved into incorporating a melody more suited to a regular village scene. We soaked in the atmosphere that was so germane to the film and the music that was going to be the beat to which the film would unfold.

Ramesh Sippy and R.D. Burman collaborated again five years later with **Shaan**—one of the grandest Hollywood-style thrillers of India. And the titles paid homage to the biggest series of thrillers that exist, James Bond. A slithering female figure shimmied and sashayed on a scarlet screen as Usha Uthup's husky voice sang *Doston se pyaar kiya* and R.D. Burman deftly mixed the strains of that song with refrains of all the other songs of the film.

The Innovations

And sometimes, nothing works better than a quirky new thing. Filmmakers down the ages have come up with some nifty moves for those elements that would bring a smile, and kick off some roller-coaster (and some not-so-rollicking) rides.

The two cons in **Do Aur Do Paanch** devoted their lives to trumping each other. And the title sequence of the film was exactly about that.

Shot as a cartoon, it had animated versions of Amitabh Bachchan and Shashi Kapoor in the best Spy vs Spy traditions of *MAD* comics. The animation was done in the visual style of **Pink Panther** and was all about the duo tiptoeing through alleyways, cutting each other's climbing ropes, planting bombs or bomb-shaped diamond cases on each other. As the cast and crew appeared in star-bursts, the sequence ended with the duo being marched away to jail.

A completely obscure movie from the mid-'80s—**Jaal**—did an amazingly neat revelation of the credits. The entire title sequence was about Vinod Mehra getting released from jail and going around, sick and unwanted. The lead actors' names were painted in red on the walls of Central Jail. The next set of names was painted on the road which Vinod Mehra walked on. A co-passenger on a bus was reading a newspaper that had the names of the writers while a door (banged on his face) and a roadside signboard had the other crew members' names. And as a finale, Vinod Mehra stumbled into a kotha bearing the director's name on its walls!

Rohan Sippy's directorial debut was **Kuch Naa Kaho**, an intelligent take on the usual love story, although the Aishwarya-Abhishek starrer didn't do too well commercially.

Apart from the cool dialogues, the film had a super opening sequence with the names of the cast and crew of the film appearing on various parts of Abhishek's room and bathroom as he took a bath. The editor appeared on the edge of a pair of scissors, the lyricist on a CD cover, the composers on a music system while the financiers appeared on a credit card. The story-screenplay-dialogue guys were on spines of books while the publicity people were on a boldly coloured toothpaste tube! And Aishwarya was on the shower curtain while Abhishek was on a soap. And the two most important people—the director and producer—were written with a finger on steamed glass. Ironic—check. Creative—double check!

The titles of **Taare Zameen Par** were suffused with the magic of a child's hyperactive imagination. Created in the style of a child's drawing book, the titles floated between underwater scenes, octopus and fish blew blue ink which became outer space, planets jostled for space with spaceships, aquaria became playgrounds and delightfully creative things happened.

In the film, the titles happened on a bus ride from school to home—where the former was all about dictatorial teachers reading out poor marks and the latter was where the fears and insecurities of the parents took over. And the imagination of Ishaan Awasthi was such a beautiful refuge from both.

Before the camera focused on Chamanganj in Kanpur for the opening scenes of **Tanu Weds Manu**, we heard a radio announcement. Starting with static and interference of changing radio channels, it went on to an advertisement for Vicco Turmeric Ayurvedic Cream and started listing the people who had sent in song requests to a radio programme—anchored by the inimitable Ameen Sayani. The twist was that Ameen-bhai read out names of the characters in the movie. So, *Dilli se Manoj Sharma urf Manu, Kanpur Uttar Pradesh se Tanuja Trivedi urf Tanu* and all their friends (including *Lucknow se Raja Awasthi* and *Azamganj se Pappi Tiwari*) requested for the song that played on the radio of a household getting ready to receive a would-be groom for their daughter.

The song was from **Bawarchi**—*Bhor aayi gaya aadhiyara...*

Achha, ab picture chalu karo re...

1

Movies, Masti, Magic

'I lost it at the movies.'—Pauline Kael

Some of the best movies exist only in our imagination. Some movies are inspired by the strangest of things. And movies, in turn, inspire many things. Movies are long or short. Even their names are uniquely long or short.

◆ Imagining Things: 10 Best Movies to Have Not Been Made
◆ Geet Gaata Chal: 10 Songs that became Movies
◆ Meta: 10 Films within Films
◆ Lambooji / Tinguji: 10 Movie Titles of Extreme Length
◆ Utterly Butterly Bollywood: 30 Amul Ads

Imagining Things: 10 Best Movies To Have Not Been Made

Of course, an earlier list could have been one that is everyone's favourite—the Ten Favourite Movies of all time. Bollywood. Hollywood. Regional. Whatever.

But instead of going with that old favourite, we could do an interesting twist and come up with a list of Hindi films that were 'launched' but never made.

They had flashy mahurats. They had more stars than the Andromeda galaxy. They had storylines rivalling epics. They had everything going for them—except they never got made. Dates and egos, deaths and eccentricities got in the way of these brilliant films, which may well have re-written box-office history.

Ek
Just when we had finished gasping at **Devdas**' budget (allegedly ₹ 50 crore), Ram Gopal Verma announced a film on international terrorism called **Ek** around the same time with a budget of—hold your breath—₹ 100 crore way back in 2003.

Amitabh Bachchan, Nana Patekar, Ajay Devgn and an international cast were supposed to zoom across the major world capitals in a saga involving the Al Qaeda, CIA and RAW.

When a journalist gasped at the budget, RGV pointed out that the budget was actually only $20 million and a top star like George Clooney or Julia Roberts got that kind of money for a single film. The logic was sound but no producer—neither Warner Bros nor Ramsay—came forward to pick up the tab. And after **RGV Ki Aag**, they probably never will.

64 Squares

'Two players. One alive. One dead. A game unfinished' was the tantalising line on the poster doing the rounds of Bollywood discussion forums.

A game of chess with a dead man could have infinite possibilities and Vidhu Vinod Chopra felt that his first English language film—starring Amitabh Bachchan and Anupam Kher—should explore the emotions of two people across a chessboard. Amitabh and Anupam Kher have acted together in several films but none of these really pit them *against* each other, and this movie would have been the first time.

Initially titled **Chess**, it was subsequently called **Move 5** and finally **64 Squares**. No details are available on the Vinod Chopra Films' website but sources say it is back in development.

Galti Se / Jaan Boojh Ke

The film, which eventually released as **My Wife's Murder**, was intended with a twist quite unique to cinema in general, not only Indian cinema. Ram Gopal Verma intended to make two films, both of which start identically, about a man and his nagging wife. After the initial mood setting, the wife dies in both the films. But in the first one, the husband kills her accidentally, while in the second, it is a planned murder. The plots diverge from there and you never know where they end. He intended to release both the films (with identical casts) on the same day and invite the audience to sample one or both.

But when the film released in Telugu (where the husband kills the wife *jaan boojh ke*) and had a controversial tagline ('Ever Wished Your Wife Was Dead?'), it sparked off an avalanche of protests, and the Hindi version was a tame *Galti Se* version.

Bajirao Mastani

When Sanjay Leela Bhansali announced this film, there was a lot of banter on whether Salman would still have his faux-American accent while playing the Maratha chieftain. Nevertheless, a Maratha warrior's affair with a courtesan promised to be a great story. Sanjay Leela Bhansali directing a period film added to the allure. And if there was anything missing, then the casting ping-pong made up for it.

After the success of **Hum Dil De Chuke Sanam**, it was Salman Khan and Aishwarya Rai. Then, Sallu beat up Ash and she walked off. Kareena agreed to sacrifice her multi-crore fees to work with Bhansali. Salman stayed on. Bhansali got engaged in **Black** and to pacify Salman, he gave him a walk-on part in **Saawariya**. In the meantime, Kareena had walked off. When last heard, Salman had screamed 'I am not Bajirao' and sauntered off.

Allwyn Kalicharan

At one point of time, Anurag Kashyap had an impressive body of critically acclaimed works, none of which had released. When **Black Friday** eventually got a release, Anurag was hailed as the greatest thing to happen to Bollywood by no less than Danny Boyle.

But even before that, he launched a sci-fi film with Anil Kapoor in the lead. The film was supposed to be about a cop in a dystopian Delhi of the future (apparently called Hastinapur) and those in the know swore that the city never looked as apocalyptic as it did in this film. The name itself was a twist on the famous refrigerator brand and a pun on the West Indian batsman—explained by a backstory.

Anil Kapoor pulled out of the film and producers felt no one would 'understand' the film, leading to a shelving of the project.

Time Machine

After the super success of **Mr India**, Shekhar Kapur consolidated his post-**Masoom** reputation as a director of intelligent, commercially successful films. Extending the mildly sci-fi theme of an Invisible Man, he launched **Time Machine**—starring Aamir Khan and Raveena Tandon. No film on time travel can ever be boring and this was slated to be a cracker.

Except that Shekhar was a brooding director and Aamir Khan was slowly upping his perfectionist gear as well. So, the scenes took a lot of time getting canned, made worse by the fact that Shekhar also had international ambitions.

In the end, Aamir started doing just one film a year (or less). Raveena got married and had a kid. Shekhar got an Oscar nomination and did not want to make masala films.

And India still awaits a rocking film on time travel.

Apparently, Aamir has acquired the rights of the film from Shekhar Kapur and is on the lookout for a director to helm the project and for actors to replace the original cast.

Tara Rum Pum

Shekhar Kapur could well be the poster-boy of unfinished classics. Some time after the ascent of A.R. Rehman in Hindi cinema, he realised that the Mozart of Madras was the ideal composer to help him create a fresh, new musical starring a fresh, new face. For the latter role, he zeroed in on Preity Zinta and it was rumoured that this would be her first lead role (after the supporting success of **Dil Se**). It all fizzled out in the end.

Yash Raj Films produced a film of the same name starring Saif Ali Khan and Rani Mukherji but with no connection to this film.

Kalinga

Dilip Kumar returning to tinsel-town to direct a multi-starrer was massive news. It was backed by Sudhakar Bokade who had produced films like **Prahaar** and **Saajan** and was a big name in the mid-1990s. Sure, there were apprehensions about Dilip Kumar's legendary perfection and eccentricity but Bokade had produced Nana Patekar's debut directorial venture, **Prahaar**, without a hitch.

The shooting continued amidst uneasy rumours before the producer ran into financial difficulties with flops like **Sauda** and **Sapne Saajan Ke** and the film was quietly shelved.

Occasionally, there have been declarations by Dilip Kumar that he would complete the film since it would otherwise be a blemish on his career, but no tangible progress has been seen. And the IMDb.com forlornly lists Jackie Shroff as the only cast member.

Aakhri Mughal

This was supposed to be Abhishek Bachchan's launch vehicle. Directed by J.P. Dutta, it was the tale of Bahadur

Shah Zafar's relationship with his son. Apparently, the rights were with Kamal Amrohi once upon a time and he had wanted to make the film with Amitabh Bachchan, after seeing him in **Zanjeer**. It did not happen then. It did not happen with the son.

With all star sons getting launched in all-singing-all-dancing-all-muscle-flexing roles, a debut like this would have been very different (to the point of being risky). But then, so was Abhishek's actual debut film—**Refugee**—with the same director.

So, what was it? Was it the budget? Was it the beard AB Jr had to grow? We'll never know.

Dus

Mukul S. Anand had a really short career but he managed to establish his reputation as a maker of extravagant entertainers. He worked with some of the top stars of his time and at the time of his untimely death, he was working on a major terrorist saga titled **Dus**.

Salman Khan, Sanjay Dutt, Raveena Tandon and Shilpa Shetty were the lead players. It was about a terrorist group led by Raveena Tandon (in her first negative role), who capture intelligence officer Sanjay Dutt and brainwash him. His partner, Salman Khan, goes in to save him, assisted by Shilpa Shetty. Parts of the film were shot and even a promotional video was released but with the maker's demise, the film was never completed.

Why was it called **Dus**, though? Sanjay and Salman were both part of an anti-terrorist cell called Force 10.

A terrorist plot was also central to **Dus** *(directed by Anubhav Sinha) that released in 2005—which starred Sanjay Dutt, Abhishek Bachchan, Zayed Khan and Shilpa Shetty.*

Honourable Mentions

There were at least two movies that were launched with Amitabh Bachchan and Madhuri Dixit in the lead. And both of them had an amazing third lead.

There was Tinnu Anand's **Shanakht** with AB, MD and Rajnikanth. And there was Inder Kumar's **Rishta** with Aamir Khan as the third star.

But some jinx prevented this dynamite duo from having a release together (unless you count the *Makhana* song in **Bade Miyan Chote Miyan**). But with her comeback, we still live in hope.

Geet Gaata Chal:
10 Songs That Became Movies

Qayamat Se Qayamat Tak, **Daag—The Fire** and **Dilwale Dulhania Le Jayenge** started three different trends.

QSQT was the first film to have a hugely popular abbreviation. **Daag** was the first film to have an appendage—The Subtitle. And **DDLJ** was the first film to start the trend of taking its title from a popular song. It would be better to clarify that these are probably not the very first movies to do so but definitely the inflection point because after these, each particular trend picked up like a rocket.

A list of film titles that went on to become songs in other films could be a never-ending one. Therefore, to keep the list manageable, a better idea would be to look at some of the famous examples. And some of the special ones.

The film that was ostensibly the 'tipping point' of the song-as-film trend, **Dilwale Dulhania Le Jayenge** (released in 1995) took its name from a song in **Chor Machaye Shor** (1970). It was one of the few films—if not the only one—which credited a person (Kirron Kher) for 'title idea'.

One of the earliest examples—in 1960—was a film called **Mud Mud Ke Na Dekh**, obviously inspired by the famous dance number from **Shree 420** (1955). Incidentally, this one (**MMKND**) is probably Prem Chopra's first movie.

The movie, which has the maximum number of songs which went on to become film titles is Subhash Ghai's reincarnation drama **Karz**—with five of its songs made into films at last count!

Paisa Yeh Paisa, Main Solah Baras Ki, Dard-e-Dil and **Ek Hasina Thi** are moderately successful films, based on songs from the blockbuster. Of course, Farah Khan's **Om Shanti Om** is the best known of the lot as it went on to become a monster hit giving credits and paying tributes to the original maker and star all the way.

Koi Mil Gaya (2003) took its name from the song in **Kuch Kuch Hota Hai** (1998). Both films have won the Filmfare Award for Best Film—as of now, this is the only combination.

Hum Hain Rahi Pyar Ke (1993) was the first time a film title taken from a song (from **Nau Do Gyarah**) won the Filmfare for Best Film. It narrowly beat the trendsetter (**DDLJ**) by two years.

No winner of Filmfare Best Female Playback awards has been made into a film yet. On the other hand, four songs that won in the Best Male Playback Singer category have been turned into films—**Dil Toh Baccha Hai Ji** from **Ishqiya, Na Tum Jaano Na Hum** from **Kaho Naa Pyaar Hai, Papa Kahte Hain** from **QSQT** and **Roop Tera Mastana** from **Aradhana**.

The pair of **Na Tum Jaano Na Hum** and **Kaho Naa Pyaar Hai** indicates that there was only a two-year lag (thirty months, to be precise) between the original song and the movie that emerged from it. This is quite amazing since it takes almost that much time to shoot a standard Bollywood movie. Of course, **Kaho Naa Pyaar Hai** was such a big hit that there was a scramble for everything connected to that film—hero, heroine, director, composer and even the song names.

However, the leader in the short-distance category is **Dil Toh Baccha Hai Ji** from **Ishqiya** in which the superhit Gulzar-Vishal musical output went from song (in January 2010) to film (in January 2011) in twelve months flat. Beat that!

Since we have a short-distance winner, maybe we could try to identify the long-distance winner as to which film and its original song had the maximum gap between them.

Almost forty years after **Jis Desh Men Ganga Behti Hai** (1960) played the song **Aa Ab Laut Chalen**, Raj Kapoor's son Rishi made a film of the same name (1999).

Now this 39-year difference is not conclusive considering that at least two decades of difference can easily be taken as the norm. For example, **Jhoom Barabar Jhoom** (2007) was 33 years after **5 Rifles** (1974), **Kabhi Alvida Naa Kehna** (2006) was 30 years after **Chalte Chalte** (1976) and **Ta Ra Rum Pum** (2007) came 28 years after **Baton Baton Mein** (1979).

So, there might be a longer time-gap lurking somewhere out there...

One hit song from **Baton Baton Mein** has inspired two movies from its words—**Kabhi Khushi Kabhie Gham / Ta Ra Rum Pum**, which has been replicated by another hit song from **Karz**—**Ek Hasina Thi / Ekk Deewana Tha**.

To go one step deeper, we can now get a double-layer song-to-film transition. That is, a song being made into a film of which there is a song, which is made into another film. Kamal Amrohi's **Pakeezah** (1971) had the famous **Chalte**

Chalte, which was duly made into a film five years later and it catapulted Bappi Lahiri into gold-encrusted stardom. And **Kabhi Alvida Naa Kehna** (from a **Chalte Chalte** song) was made thirty years later.

Sudhir Mishra's first film, **Yeh Woh Manzil Toh Nahin**, featured what is probably Mirza Ghalib's most famous ghazal—*Hazaaron Khwaishein Aisi*—and that song became a film he directed in 2003.

He subsequently wrote a film about the love story of a screen-writer and an actress set in 1950s' Bollywood, naming it after the next line of the same ghazal—*Bahut nikle mere armaan*. When it was pointed out that people might mistake the film for a sequel to **Hazaaron Khwaishein Aisi**, he changed the name to yet another hit song—**Khoya Khoya Chand** (from **Kala Bazar**).

A song from a 1960 film becoming a film in 2007... forty-seven years is probably the longer time-gap we were talking about three paragraphs earlier!

Meta: 10 Films Within Films

*T*here have been many films that have films being made as part of their stories. Some of them are the centre piece. Some are relatively peripheral. And when you look at the biggest films that got 'made' in other films and the magnificent cast and crew they had, you wish some of them actually got made.

Om Shanti Om is probably the biggest tribute to the crazy world of Bollywood. Starting from the late '70s to present day, it simultaneously spoofed and saluted the whole gamut of filmi people—starting from masala directors to award-hungry stars. Needless to say, there was a procession of films that flitted in and out of the film.

To start with, we had **Dreamy Girl**—Shantipriya's grandest hit, ripped off from the Hema Malini film of (almost) the same name. The film had, among other things, a typical filmi song (*Dhoom tana*) that also featured Sunil Dutt.[2]

There was another film called **Maa Bharti** being made in the film, starring Shantipriya, which had a fire scene and she had to be rescued by Om. This scene is reminiscent of Sunil Dutt-Nargis' real-life love story on the sets of **Mother India**, where Nargis was rescued from a fire

---

[2] The song featuring Sunil Dutt was taken from the film, **Amrapali** and Deepika Padukone was morphed on to the scene.

by Sunil Dutt. As you would have figured out, **Maa Bharti** is a literal translation of the real-life title!

At a present-day Filmfare Awards function, we had the full roster of Best Actor nominees, all of them were made fun of quite mercilessly—Abhishek Bachchan in **Dhoom 5**, Akshay Kumar in **Return of Khiladi** and Om Kapoor in two identically filmed, identically written, identically scored films called **Phir Bhi Dil Hai N.R.I.** and **Main Bhi Hoon Na**.

And, of course, we had the film for which there was the shedding of so much blood, sweat and tears—literally. The film that was launched, then abandoned and then finally resurrected in a different avatar—**Om Shanti Om**.

Vidhu Vinod Chopra's second feature film, **Khamosh**, was a murder mystery unfolding during a film shoot in Pahalgam. Amol Palekar and Shabana Azmi were the lead stars in this typical masala film called **Aakhri Khoon**, which had a bathing scene, a rape, a suicide, promises of undying love between Niloufer and Vijay-babu, and bombastic dialogue. Some of the details were real (Shabana as the three-time National Award-winning actress) while some were not (Soni Razdan getting murdered).

And some of them were deliciously self-referential. The director (played by Sadashiv Amrapurkar) kept repeating throughout the film, 'Arre, my next film **Shakuntala** will be a classic. This is just a thriller.' His screen name was Chandran. It could well have been Vidhu Vinod Chopra![3]

---

[3] Vidhu Vinod Chopra's next film was indeed a classic–**Parinda**.

On location for **Aakhri Khoon**

Hrishikesh Mukherjee's double-Amol, single-Utpal, mustachioed comedy—**Golmaal**—had Deven Varma playing himself as the hero's friend. And when Amol Palekar landed up at the film studios to pick up a set of kurta-pajamas, there was a quick succession of filmi snippets. Amitabh Bachchan appeared as himself (shooting for **Jurmana**) and asked Deven Varma about the latter's films. Deven revealed that he was working for a 'mythological mystery suspense drama' called **Parvati Ka Pati Kaun?**

In fact, the idea of twin brothers with and without a moustache came ostensibly from a film Deven was working in. Not to mention a series of filmi in-jokes about kurta sizes of various stars, long shooting times for films, and girl students seeking autographs (in uniforms straight out of **Guddi**)![4]

---

[4] Both **Jurmana** and **Guddi** were also directed by Hrishikesh Mukherjee.

Luck By Chance, Zoya Akhtar's debut set in the film industry, had a long list of film stars in real and fictitious roles playing their parts in many films within the film.

The centre piece of the film was a film called **Dil Ki Aag**, from which the lead Zafar Khan (Hrithik Roshan) dropped out and triggered off a chain of events that brought newcomer Vikram Jaisingh (Farhan Akhtar) into the limelight. The film was produced by industry veteran Romi Rolly (played with panache by Rishi Kapoor) whose flop-actor brother was making his directorial debut. The story of the film—a sister of the heroine murdered by the anti-hero—seemed very close to **Baazigar**, another film which made a newcomer a star and as the film's director proudly proclaimed, 'The original was a hit in the US!'.

On the other hand, Farhan's love interest and struggling actress, Sona Mishra (Konkona Sen Sharma), was unable to break into the big league as the biggest film she had acted in was a B-grade potboiler—**Teer aur Talwar**, a poster of which hung from her wall.[5]

As the evocatively shot title sequence (featuring junior artistes and crew members) came to an end, we saw the director's name appear next to a film called **Kismet Talkies**. *That was supposed to have been Zoya Akhtar's debut film's title!*

In **Bollywood Calling**, Nagesh Kukunoor took a pointed look at the mainstream cinema of the country. Om Puri starred as the hapless producer—and then, reluctant director—of a typical multi-starrer masala mix called **Maut: The Death**. The title itself was a swipe at the craze for double-barrelled names in the industry.

---

[5] Some of the other posters visible in the film were decidedly tongue-in-cheek as they showed Sanjay Kapoor in Clint Eastwood-style films called **The Good, The Bad and The Worst** and **For A Few Rupees More!**

If the standard Bollywood formula of long-lost brothers growing up on two sides of the law was not enough, this film literally imported another complexity in the form of an American actor (since one of the brothers was born to a foreign mother)! Add to that a portly Navin Nischol playing a dacoit leader, the American actor having a terminal disease and the usual vagaries of tinsel town, and you don't worry about the film you are watching but about the film they are making in the film you are watching.

Jaya Bhaduri in her debut (Hindi) role played **Guddi**, the ultimate movie fan—a Meera to *Dharmendra-rupi Krishna*, as she explained in a hilarious scene. To bring her face-to-face with the realism of the glamour factory, her uncle (Utpal Dutt) and hapless fiancé (Shamit Bhanja, in a role originally meant for Amitabh Bachchan) brought her to Bombay. She met Dharmendra, saw the dust and grime of the studios, the heroism of the villains (Pran) and the villainy of the heroes. And during her trip, she saw a plethora of films being shot.

Antara Mali's tale in **Main Madhuri Dixit Banna Chahti Hoon** was the story of a million girls across the country who want to make it big in the film industry but don't know how.

In a super-real atmosphere peopled by a film secretary (Govind Namdeo), wannabe-heroes perpetually on the brink of stardom, and a sympathetic husband (played by scene-stealer Rajpal Yadav), Chutki's break came in the form of a title role in **Roshni**—in which she co-starred with Dev Anand, Anil Kapoor and Sachin Tendulkar(!), among others. Except that, the debut vehicle was a B-grade classic with duplicates of all the stars.

And despite the derision of the city audience, the film ended on a note of hope—how Chutki's performance had been appreciated in this mess of a film, how the film had done very well in small centres and how more offers were coming in.

The film also demonstrates the power of Madhuri Dixit as an icon of hope in the 1990s. After all, there isn't a film that says, '_Main Amitabh Bachchan Banna Chahta Hoon_'.

In Sudhir Mishra's **Khoya Khoya Chand**, the film industry of the 1950s came alive and we could identify hundreds of faces, traits, settings, words and music.

The talented writer-director's (Shiney Ahuja) rise in the film industry and his tempestuous love affair with a heroine (Soha Ali Khan) evoked immediate comparisons with the lives of Guru Dutt and Waheeda Rehman. The slimy leading actor (Rajat Kapoor), the friendly assistant director (Saurabh Shukla) and many other characters added to the authenticity. The film that was being made for an important part was **Ishq Aur Jung**, which opened with a majestic premiere at Regal Cinema. And the background of the industry ensured that there were many passing mentions of films and actors throughout.

Andaz Apna Apna kicked off its relentless laughathon with Prem (Aamir Khan) meeting Juhi Chawla, playing herself.[6]

In the totally unreal sequence, Aamir appeared as a cyclist and gave a lift to the stranded actress. Within a

---

[6] During a stray discussion at the offices of Wah Wah Productions, there was a 'notice' of a forthcoming film **Jungle Mein Oye Oye** and Mehmood mentions a new film starring Prem (Salman Khan) called **Dracula Ki Mohabbat**. Deadly!

blink, they were in love and Aamir was invited to her film set as her 'special' guest. The film starred Govinda and seemed to be called **Pehra** (shown on the clapstick). It also seemed to have only one line of dialogue—*Aa gale lag jaa*—which was used by Govinda as a cue to hug Juhi, egged on by the director ('*Govinda, chipakke chipakke!*').

Again, the film packed in jokes about Shah Rukh's K-k-kiran, filmstars' lack of punctuality and even one about Aamir's fussiness when it comes to choosing films.

Ram Gopal Verma set his first Hindi love story in Bollywood, where a chorus dancer—Mili Joshi—was suddenly catapulted into the starring role of a film due to two acts of providence. One, the country's biggest star—Raj Kamal (Jackie Shroff)—saw her dance like a dream on a beach. And two, the original heroine of the film married her chauffeur and retired.

Walking the tightrope between reality and spoof, **Rangeela** was about the making of a film called **Rangeela**—directed by Steven Kapoor (Gulshan Grover), whose competition was not Chopra or Mehra but Coppola and Spielberg. The stray dialogues seemed to indicate a love triangle, though no other actor was seen and only the hassled producer called PC (Avtar Gill) popped up to provide comic relief.

There was also a tapori called Munna somewhere in the background who went about selling tickets to **Mr Bond** (also starring Raj Kamal) in 'black'.[7]

---

[7] *Blooper Alert*: In the poster of **Mr Bond**, the hero's name is written as Kishore ('In and As') though it is clearly referred to as Kamal's film. Incidentally, the producer's name is Jammu Patel—probably a play on Jhamu Sugandh, **Rangeela**'s producer.

Lamboo-ji Aur Tingoo-ji: 10 Movie Titles Of Extraordinary Length

*T*his could be the shortest list... or the longest. Or the most controversial.

With no definitive filmography of Hindi cinema, any list based on film titles is absolutely open to debate, dissent and bloodshed. But the subject of Bollywood is never too far from controversy and anybody who can't disagree shouldn't be discussing Bollywood, of all things.

Short Names a.k.a. film titles of two letters or less. There seems to be a wealth of three-letter names, so we will stop just short of that.

99 was the comic story of two collection agents (Kunal Khemu and Cyrus Broacha) working for a don in Mumbai, who came to Delhi chasing defaulters.

Why the name? The film was set in 1999, around the betting scandals that rocked Indian cricket. And the main characters all missed out on their goals—century—in life by a whisker.

Om was the handiwork of the redoubtable Ashok Honda (maker of Sunil Shetty classics like **Rakshak** and **Krodh**) and was about a young man avenging his sister's rape and murder, through blood, gore and long-handled swords.

Why the name? The aforementioned young man's name.

Ek was about a hitman who accidentally killed a rogue politician when he was hired just to injure him (and help him garner sympathy votes).
Why the name? Search me.

> *Cheat Alert*: The full name of the film is actually **Ek: The Power Of One**. Since Ram Gopal Verma never did make his terrorism saga, this two-letter film strictly doesn't exist.

D—the ultimate shortie—was the story of a constable's son who got into the underworld and eventually rose to the top with his hard work, intelligence and guts.
Why the name? Ostensibly from the initial of the lead character's name—Deshu. But when a guy with a name starting with D starts a company, we all know what that means—don't we?

Long Names a.k.a. film titles of thirty letters of more. All these whoppers have their stories almost completely embedded in their names.

Aamdani Atthanni Kharcha Rupaiya was allegedly a comedy about three couples whose coats were not cut according to their cloth and eventually the wives had to start working to augment the income. The MCP husbands took offence and devised elaborate schemes to keep them at home. The only thing longer than the title was the list of complaints against the film.

Albert Pinto Ko Gussa Kyoon Aata Hai was the story of motor mechanic Anthony Gonsalves finding his two long-lost brothers. OF COURSE NOT! Played by Naseeruddin Shah, Albert Pinto was a motor mechanic (that part was correct) in textile strike-infested Bombay and frustrated with everything around him.

> *Trivia Alert:* All of Saeed Mirza's films have titles longer than the films themselves. E.g. **Arvind Desai Ki Ajeeb Dastaan, Mohan Joshi Hazir Ho, Salim Langde Pe Mat Ro,** etc.

Main Madhuri Dixit Banna Chahti Hoon was the ambition of a million Indian girls exemplified by Chutki, who came to Mumbai to become a star. They don't come from filmi backgrounds. They don't have beauty queen titles. And still—despite a million hurdles—they soldier on.

Ab Tumhare Hawale Watan Sathiyo was supposedly a film to promote Indo-Pak friendship. It was made by Anil Sharma whose earlier credits include **Gadar: Ek Prem Katha**—which is about as chummy as he could have got with Pakistan. Akshay Kumar in a guest role, Bobby Deol in a double role and Amitabh Bachchan in a what-am-I-doing-here role did not help the cause too much.

Andheri Raat Mein Diya Tere Haath Mein was the title of a Dada Kondke film you don't want to hear too much about. You just have an inkling of the title's double meaning and you want to run away.

Netaji Subhas Chandra Bose: The Forgotten Hero is the forty-letter behemoth about one of the bravest names in India's freedom struggle. Based on the last five years of Bose's life, it traced his attempts to seek German and Japanese help to launch an attack on

British India. Even without a judgement on Netaji's controversial death, the film was rebuked for calling him a 'forgotten hero'.[8]

---

[8] Some people still believe that Netaji is alive because he disappeared after a mysterious plane crash and his body was never found.

Utterly Butterly Bollywood: 30 Amul Ads

*T*he Amul advertising campaign is one of the best barometers of society and culture in India. Anything that is in the news or touches our lives gets captured by Amul.

Bollywood has always been on Amul hoardings, with the frequency increasing sharply in the last decade or so. From the 1970s to the mid-1990s, very few Bollywood stars made it to the ads but the presence has been much more regular lately.

Part 1: New Releases

Pati Patni Aur Wah. One of the earliest films to be featured in the Amul creative, it was the extra-marital comedy twisted into a paean for the butter.

Khaike Pav Amul Wala, Khul Jaye Band Akal Ka Taala. This was probably Big B's first appearance on an Amul billboard with the superhit song from **Don**. He was to become the most regular film star to appear in Amul ads.

Rich taste se hum sabke baap lagte hai. Naam hai Amultabh Makkhan. Amitabh created mass-hysteria with **Shahenshah** and his signature line came up in all sorts of places.

Utterly Butterly De De. Humul. Again, Amitabh. This time, it was for his all-dancing-all-fighting avatar opposite Kimi Katkar in **Hum**. The *Jumma chumma de de* song became almost the national anthem at the time it released.

Little Bhatt-er goes well with Aamir Khan-a. Amul Butter: Dil hai ke mangta hai. Aamir Khan and Pooja Bhatt starred in one of the biggest hits of the day and Amul did a cute pun on the actress being the director's daughter.

Aati kya, Makhan dala! Amul: On everyone's lips. Aamir Khan's first foray into playback singing was *the* hit song of the day and Amul couldn't resist having a line with both of them being on everyone's lips.

Roti ke neeche kya hai? Amul: Asalnayak. Sanjay Dutt's controversial turn as the **Khalnayak** (while terror charges were being framed against him) was made doubly so by the double-meaning song from the same film.

Saif, for all Anaris and Khiladis. Akshay-ly Brat-erly Delicious. Akshay Kumar and Saif Ali Khan's jodi in **Main Khiladi Tu Anari** was a big box-office draw and Amul doffed a cap at the ad-line of the film, The Brave and The Brat.

Super Hit-ik Roshan. Amul: Kaho na bhookh hai. Hrithik Roshan burst into the industry with his monster-hit **Kaho Naa Pyaar Hai** and everybody was floored with this new sensation.

Dish Chahta Hai. Akhtarly Butterly Delicious. Farhan Akhtar's ultra-cool buddy flick, **Dil Chahta Hai**, gained a cult following across the country.

Amul Lagaana. Upon every slice in India. Once upon a time in India, there was a film which took on the British Empire, broke box-office records and went on to make an attempt at Oscar glory. **Lagaan**a on a slice of bread was an obvious line!

Lagate Raho Maska Bhai. Amul: Khole toh. The affable gangster's return was marked with new words (Gandhi-giri) being added to our vocabulary and older words gaining currency. *Bole toh*, the ideal setting for Amul to take out an ad.

Chakh Le India. Shah Rukh Khan's inspiring brand of patriotism in the backdrop of Women's World Cup Hockey had everything going for it, including a cute pun.

Savour-iya. Amul: Eat at Om. Two of India's biggest stars and biggest directors faced off at the Diwali box office and the entire country could not speak anything else but **Saawariya** and **Om Shanti Om**.

Himesha khao. Aap Kaa Ammuuul. People either hated Himesh Reshamaiyya, or they loved him. But sure as hell, they couldn't ignore him. Amul made a clever play on his debut film—**Aap Kaa Surroor**.

Kabhi Amulvida Naa Kehna. Amul: For Your Mitva. Karan Johar walked into 'serious' territory with his take on incompatible couples and infidelity. As the *Mitva* song played across the country, **KANK** was the subject of talk shows, magazine covers and advertising billboards.

Masake le. Amul: Belly Fix. Oscar-winner Rehman's best album in some time, **Delhi 6** had the hugely popular

Masakkali song both of which got a punny avatar in the Amul ad.

Bake up, **Sid. Amul: No Apologies**. Karan Johar's production, starring Ranbir Kapoor, ran afoul of Shiv Sena sentiments and the producer had to apologise to let his film run uninterrupted. The butter remained unapologetically good.

Khaa! Big A for small B. Big B's brilliant performance in R. Balki's **Paa** was a departure and a talking point.

Ibn-e-Butter-tha. Amul: Dishqiya. Vishal Bhardwaj's rustic romantic thriller, **Ishqiya**, had a quirky script and quirkier lyrics, both of which Amul used to great effect!

Part 2: Stars in the News

Khalnayak Nahin, Nayak Hoon Main. Amul: Utterly Dutterly Delicious. Sanjay Dutt was acquitted of terrorism charges by a court after years and Amul celebrated his return with a triumphant line from his most controversial film.

Heroine Addiction. Amul: Fida on you. M.F. Husain's obsession with Madhuri Dixit was not restricted to paintings and film viewings only. He made a film (**Gaja Gamini**) with the actress in the lead and Amul felt his was almost a drug addiction!

Soon after, when Madhuri tied the knot, Amul returned with another billboard which had the actress doing her saat pheras as the artist stood by morosely. The caption read **Madhuri's Fixed it! Amul: National dish**.

Aby to main jawaan hoon! Amul: The Big A. Amitabh Bachchan launched a company, went through an image makeover and launched a snazzy music video. The entire country thought he was much younger than he should be.

Tu hai meri Kiran. Amul: Super cop. Super taste. Kiran Bedi took over as the jailer of Tihar Jail and brought in widespread reforms, earning herself accolades from different quarters. Amul borrowed a line from **Darr** and gave a thumbs-up to her efforts.

Mallika Shararat. Amul: Chan Reaction. Sex-siren Mallika Sherawat grabbed eyeballs wherever she went and whatever she said. Her naughty pronouncements and her role in a Jackie Chan film was impossible to ignore.

Part 3: Obituaries

Amar Akbar Anthony & Amul. Bid You Farewell, Manji: Bollywood's biggest entertainer, Manmohan Desai, passed away and Amul's tribute went around his three most famous characters.

Hum tere tere tere chaahanewaale hai—Mehmood (1932–2004): Bollywood's most iconic funny man, Mehmood, was remembered with his superhit song from the film, **Gumnaam**.

Aye dil hai mushkil... Johnny bina yahan: Johnny Walker's passing away was remembered with a song he performed on-screen in the massive hit **CID**. The ad had a visual of his tel-maalish avatar from **Pyaasa**.

Zindagi badi honi chahiye, lambi nahin! Hrishida (1922–2006): Hrishikesh Mukherjee made a point in **Anand** and Amul returned the favour with the same line in this tribute.

Mogambo... dukh hua: Only one word from Amrish Puri's most famous line from **Mr India** was changed to make a very touching tribute.

An utterly heartfelt obituary

2

Manoranjan ka Baap

'Iss story mein emotion hai, drama hai, tragedy hai.'—
DHARMENDRA in **Sholay**.

There are some things in a movie that happen all the time but are just short of turning into a cliché.

The musical interlude composed entirely of covers and parodies of hit songs. Heroes fighting each other before they fight others together. A crisis that makes the lead character change—for better or for worse. Stars playing not just two—but many—roles. Known brands in the limelight. And unknown actors stealing the limelight.

◆ Face-Off: 11 Legendary Confrontations
◆ All together, now: 9 Musical Medleys
◆ Transformers: 10 Characters who Changed Beyond Recognition
◆ Three's a Crowd: 9 Actors who Played Three Roles or More
◆ Marketing in Bollywood: 10 Brand Placements
◆ Show-Stealers: 6 Roles that became Bigger than the Movie

Face-Off: 11 Legendary Confrontations

One beautiful thing from the good ole days of Hindi cinema was the Battle of the Middle Reels. In movies starring two leading characters (usually male), there used to be a fight to (almost) the finish after which the two leading characters discovered one of the following: (a) mutual respect, (b) blood relations or (c) change of heart.

Usually, this high-octane, crackerjack scene laid down the expectations for the climax. When you watched this scene, you got tense because two heroes would be at each other's throats but you also felt reassured that when these two would join forces, what an explosion it would be!

Johny Mera Naam, one of Dev Anand's biggest hits, was the quintessential Bollywood story of brothers growing up on two sides of the law—with Pran playing the brother gone wrong. The film kicked off with a school boxing match where the two brothers pummelled each other, much to their policeman father's exaggerated ecstasy and their mother's sobbing agony. And the opening sequence ended with the declaration that like every year, there had been two winners.

This boxing set-piece returned later in the movie as Dev Anand and Pran engaged in some solid knuckle-baazi, only to realise that they were both unbeatable. Given that the only unbeatable person each had met in his life was the other, a conclusion was drawn about their blood(y) relationship. Simple!⁹

Anil Kapoor and Sunny Deol starred in **Joshilaay**, a Western-style revenge film shot in the rugged terrain of Ladakh.

Originally supposed to be directed by Shekhar Kapur, this film had a laconic Anil and a garrulous Sunny fighting each other to catch an elusive bandit—Jogi Thakur (played gleefully by Rajesh Vivek). As they constantly clashed and the bandit escaped repeatedly, they made a pact. They would start fighting each other at nightfall and the man who would remain standing at daybreak would get to nab Jogi Thakur.

Needless to say, after the night of bare-knuckled daredevilry, both managed to stagger to their feet when the sun rose.

In **Khudgarz**—loosely based on Jeffrey Archer's *Kane and Abel*—Jeetendra and Shatrughan played foes turned friends turned foes turned friends.

The first time they met (as foes) was when they were both kids. Jeetu was being driven to school in his father's Mercedes which splashed mud on Shatru, who promptly shattered the windscreen with a stone. A very kiddish fight promptly broke out, post which Sushma Seth (Shatru's mother in the film) brokered a truce and they—even more promptly—became fast friends. Of course, they grew up to face the evil machinations of Kiran Kumar and became foes again. Only to kiss (not literally) and make up in the climax.

---

⁹ As an aside, it should be mentioned that the names of the two brothers were Mohan and Sohan. So, who was Johny?

Saudagar was again a film about two guys who oscillated between being friends and foes but concentrated on the enmity to keep the dialogue writers and action directors employed.

Dilip Kumar and Raaj Kumar's pairing as Veer Singh and Rajeshwar Singh was massively publicised. What was not publicised was Kamlesh Pandey's outing as a dialogue writer, who gave at least three Middle Scene Battles, without a single fist being thrown or a single bullet being fired.

For example, when Veer Singh offered Rajeshwar a gun to kill him, the reply was measured and regal. '*Hum tumhe marenge. Aur zaroor marenge. Lekin... woh bandook bhi hamari hogi, goli bhi hamari hogi. Aur waqt bhi hamara hoga.*' (I will definitely be killing you. But the gun will be mine, the bullets will be mine and the time chosen will be mine.)

In another scene, he explained the scale of his emotions by intoning, '*Rajeshwar jab dosti nibhaata hai, toh afsaane likkhe jaate hain. Aur jab dushmani karta hai, toh tareekh ban jaati hai.*' (When I make friends, legends are written. When I make enemies, history is re-written.)

Taaliyan!

Shah Rukh and Salman came together in **Karan Arjun**, a reincarnation drama. First, they were dhoti-clad brothers killed by Amrish Puri's goons and then, they were denim-clad city slickers.

Salman ended up becoming the henchman of SRK's lady-love's (Kajol) father and they engaged in a really bloody battle, which was stopped only by divine intervention (a clap of thunder, and lightning spread across the screen). Contrary to popular belief, the heavy punches they landed on each other were not enough to bring back memories of their previous birth simultaneously. That happened later—when they joined forces to fight the trans-generational crooks at the theatrical exhortations (*'Mere Karan Arjun aayenge...'*) of their mother (Rakhee, in the most irritating role of the century).

Not all confrontations were violent, though. Take the one between the dames of **Devdas**, for example.

This sequence was invented by Sanjay Leela Bhansali for the film as Saratchandra Chattopadhyay did not imagine that his characters would—one day—be played by Bollywood's Reigning Queen On Her Way Out and the Crown Princess On Her Way In. Madhuri Dixit and Aishwarya Rai pulled out all stops in this Saroj Khan-choreographed number, whirling like dervishes and sparkling like diamonds—satisfying all Bollywood lovers with a smooth passing of the baton.

Amitabh Bachchan is the acknowledged master of these Mid-film Mayhems as he has encountered countless villains, anti-heroes, side-heroes and brothers in breathless displays of dhishoom-dhishoom.

In **Zanjeer**, Amitabh Bachchan took on Pran—the leading character-actor of the times, who got almost equal billing in the posters because he was a bigger star when the film released. They met in a police station, where Police Inspector Vijay Verma kicked away the chair when Sher Khan tried to sit down. *'Jab tak baithne ko na kaha jaye, sharafat se khade raho. Yeh police station hai, tumhare baap ka ghar nahin.'*

Sher Khan taunted him back, saying it was the uniform speaking those angry words. In response, Vijay Verma landed up at Sher Khan's den in plain clothes and had a fight so amazing that when the Pathan gangster praised his adversary to be another *sher*, ('*Aaj zindagi mein pehli baar Sher Khan ki sher se takkar hui hai*') it seemed like almost an understatement.

Of the many legends, only one film—**Deewaar**—has the privilege of having two confrontations between its lead stars that have gone on to become Bollywood folklore.

The first confrontation of **Deewaar** was not a duopoly in the strictest sense since the mother (Nirupa Roy) weighed in towards the end. Placed perfectly at the stroke before the interval, the battle of the Good Son and the Bad Son was marked by Shashi's indignant demand— '*Bhai, tum sign karoge ya nahin?*' and Amitabh's poignant refusal to sign the confession unless his whole life was somehow rewound.

And the second—and even more famous face-off—happened when the Bad Son tried to save his brother from his own gang. To explain the futility of a police officer's battles, he pointed out his many riches. He had everything in the world. Except for the mother.

Probably Hindi cinema's most iconic line, '*Mere paas maa hai...*' has now been quoted at the Oscar ceremony by A.R. Rehman, no less.

In **Amar Akbar Anthony**, Amar Khanna was the dutiful inspector, looking for a smuggler who almost killed his foster-father. Anthony Gonsalves was the bootlegger in Bandra village, who helped the smuggler escape to make a quick buck. They met in front of Anthony's booze shop. They played a game of verbal one-upmanship. And then, they decided to go at each other with fists, headbutts, chickens and goats. And after an unseen explosion inside a poultry coop, Vinod Khanna carried Amitabh Bachchan out on his shoulders—unconscious.

As a seven-year-old Amitabh Bachchan fan, I remember being devastated by that scene as it was inconceivable for me to imagine my hero getting beaten. Even by his elder brother.

The scene from **Mard** was nearer to the climax but the situation was perfect.

The two people who could rub the British Empire's nose in the dust were not Mahatma Gandhi or Subhash Bose. They were Raja Azaad Singh (Dara Singh) and his long-lost son Raju (AB).

The devious British had imprisoned both of them and realised the only way they could be killed was by each other in a duel. But of course, the father and son would not fight each other. So, they convinced each of them that the other one in the arena would be a masked impostor. And that set up the two titans for an epic battle after which they realised their blood relationship and proceeded to polish off the British Empire.

Whose bright idea was it to let the real father and son in the same arena, so that they could find out about each other? Bob Christo's. As they say, blood is thicker than water but not as thick as Bob Christo.[10]

The under-rated Yash Chopra classic, **Kaala Patthar**, had three superstars of its times—Shashi Kapoor, Shatrughan Sinha and Amitabh Bachchan.

Amitabh played the silent and angry young man who was being constantly riled by escaped convict Shatru. After

---

[10] When I say Bob Christo, I obviously mean the character played by him. For Bob the person—God bless his soul—I have nothing but the deepest respect.

a super sequence at a chai stall where Shatru's verbosity and Amitabh's silence caused sparks to fly, came the lighting of the fuse. Shatru insulted Rakhee, who was Amitabh's love interest.

The simmering build-up was so fantastic that it was almost a relief when the fighting actually started. And the two nearly killed each other before Shashi came and separated them. And at the exact moment—Amitabh holding a spade, Shatru with a chain and Shashi pushing them apart—came the Interval slide.

Battles don't come any bigger or middler than this one.

All Together, Now:
9 Musical Medleys

*E*very once in a while, we have a film that gets together a million stars or a million tunes in one big spectacular sequence of songs. Medley songs—either covers or parodies of earlier hits—have been a regular feature in Bollywood. Sometimes they are competitive, sometimes funny. Sometimes they pass secret messages between the players and sometimes they are not so secretive. But they are *always* entertaining.

Ek Phool Do Mali Marriage Proposal Medley

One of the earliest parody-medleys was in the 1969 film **Ek Phool Do Mali** where a parallel comic-romance track was played out between Brahmachari and Shabnam. What would have been a passable item got a new dimension with the appearance of the indomitable Manorama as the girl's mother. To make matters even more interesting, David also popped in.

Using some of the most popular songs of the time—*Mere saamne wali khidki mein, Chal chal re naujawan, Dil ke jharoke mein, Jo vaada kiya*—the motley group played out a crazy argument about the boy wanting to marry the girl but being scared of her ferocious mom.

The film is known for its triangular romantic melodrama but this relatively obscure number still manages to evoke a few laughs.

Hum Kisise Kum Naheen Competition Medley

Nasir Husain never did teeny-bopper romances without at least one musical face-off between the two leads. And for that, he needed a rockstar composer.

With the Junior Burman composing, Manjeet (Rishi Kapoor) out-sang and out-danced several sissy competitors as his girlfriend (Kaajal Kiran) simpered coyly in the first row. Just when the judges gave only fifteen seconds for the next competitor to turn up, Tariq strummed his way on to the stage and sang *Chaand mera dil, chandni ho tum*. And what a contest it turned out to be!

An unknown lady in tight and sleeveless clothing ran on to the stage to give Tariq (musical) support. Kaajal Kiran commandeered her bevy of bimbette friends behind Rishi. Guitars, trumpets, white shoes, bandannas, R.D. Burman's voice were all called into action as the two maharathis sang to our heart's content and the whole thing stopped only because a heartbroken Tariq conceded the contest.

Why? See the sequence, no?

Chashme Buddoor Courtship Medley

How do you brag to your friends about how great a time you had with a babe? If you are a DU student? If your father is a small-time producer of Hindi films? And if you never really had a great time but only had to make things up?

Ravi Baswani showed you how.

Rather violently ejected from Deepti Naval's house by her karate-expert brother, he passed three hours in a cinema hall after getting bandaged at a clinic. And then, he went back home to tell his room-mates about the beautiful songs they sang from Dev Anand to Feroz Khan, from Meena Kumari to Asha Parekh. The hilarity got compounded manifold when we saw Ravi Baswani doing the Dev Anand swagger (*Chhod do aanchal zamana kya kahega*), the Dilip Kumar scowl (*Pyaar kiya to darna kya*) and the Feroz Khan shrug (*Aap jaisa koi*)!

Helpfully, the screens changed from colour to B&W to sepia as the songs merged from one to the other.

Oh—but how did he explain the bandages? Simple. He got injured fighting goons while his lady love sang *Logon, na maaron isse, yehi toh mera dildaar hai*!

Mr India Football Medley

What did you do as a kid when an irate neighbour confiscated your football? You pleaded with her. You asked your parents to buy you another. You and your friends pooled money together to get another. You played badminton instead. Right? Well, that's why movies were never made on you and you didn't have an uncle who went invisible. And—most importantly—your neighbour was not Sridevi.

Whenever you hear this sequence, you can almost imagine the twinkle in Javed Akhtar's eyes as he wrote *Na maangoo sona chandi, hum maange maafi didi* or *Topiwaale, ball dila*. Everybody—on-screen and off-screen—was clearly having a ball as Laxmikant-Pyarelal's old compositions were rummaged through to string together a sequence in which a gang of precocious kids, Anil Kapoor and Satish Kaushik pleaded with Sridevi to return their football. The southern siren—about to become Hawa Hawaii in the film—responded to their entreaties with an equally high dose of creativity and energy.

Maine Pyar Kiya Antakshari

One of the biggest problems of staying in a joint family and having a Satyanarayan pooja at home (attended by about 840 women in ghagra-cholis) is that you can't say 'I love you' to your boyfriend. However, that problem can be easily solved. All you need is a resourceful Manohar bhaiyya and an encyclopaedic knowledge of Hindi film songs.

This medley—designed to get Bhagyashree to say 'I love you'—was framed like a conversation for the most part. So, when Bhagyashree sang *Jahan main jaati hoon, wahin chale aate ho / yeh toh batao ke tum mere kaun ho?*, Salman replied by singing *Hum toh tere aashiq hain sadiyon purane...*

And it covered the whole gamut of Hindi music from **Jewel Thief** to **Himmatwala**, from **Dus Numbri** to **Sharaabi**, from **Rajkumar** to **Mr India**.

To my mind, this song was the biggest draw of the film and it was a very satisfying mix of nostalgia, topicality and Huma Khan (in what was her—probably—only non-B-grade role).

Lamhe Bollywood Medley

A medley must have a theme—be it an antakshari, introduction or entreaty (see above). And it must serve a purpose—be it saying 'I love you', getting diabetes or a football (see above). This medley did not have a theme but a vague motive.

Sridevi and Anupam Kher were trying to make the ultra-serious Anil Kapoor laugh and they did so by singing Hindi film songs because the NRI was apparently fond of them (as are half the world and their landlords).

So, you had Pamela Chopra doing a competent job while Sudesh Bhonsle brought the house down with his mimicry of Hemanta, Mukesh, Rafi and most notably— S.D. Burman. How could you not laugh your guts out when Sudesh Bhonsle sang *O majhi, mere saajan hain uss paar* and Anupam Kher floated around in a swimming pool.

Towards the end of the medley, the duo was joined by Waheeda Rehman doing a brilliant reprise of her **Guide** dance (*Kaanton se kheench ke yeh aanchal*) and it ended reasonably satisfactorily. If only Sridevi had danced to the *Ta thaiya ta thaiya* song.

Jo Jeeta Wohi Sikandar Competition Medley

When top colleges like Rajput and Queen's combine forces to participate in a college musical competition, can *pajama chhap* Model School ever hope to defeat them? Never, one would have thought. Not even if Model's star performer is one Sanjay Lal Sharma.

One of the best college films ever made, **JJWS** just rocked the scene with amazing music, brilliant acting performances and an achey-breaky love story borrowed from Archie Comics. And to build momentum for the climax, there was the inter-college music competition featuring three separate songs performed by the three main colleges.

Xavier's and Anne's performed a peppy youthy number, *Hum se hai saara jahaan*. Rajput and Queen's performed a hip, pseudo-Goan number—*Naam hai mera Fonseca*. And the underdog Model came up with *Jawaan ho yaaron, yeh tumko hua kya?* Naturally, the best song (though only just) was the last but was that enough to win?

Hum Saath-Saath Hain Family Intro Song

Buoyed by the tremendous success of **Maine Pyar Kiya** and the stupendous success of **Hum Aapke Hain Koun**, Sooraj Barjatya made **Hum Saath-Saath Hain**, which gave millions of viewers diabetes.

The only bright spot in this film was the point where Tabu (who—quite unbelievably—has also acted in **The Namesake**) entered Saccharine household and was introduced to the entire clan through a series of songlets performed by Saif and Karisma and compered by Ajit Vachani and Himani Shivpuri. And in an uncharacteristically immodest gesture, Sooraj Barjatya pushed in two songs from **MPK** and **HAHK** as well.

Mujhse Dosti Karoge Sangeet Song

The directorial debut of Kunal Kohli did not go down too well at the box office, despite the power-packed cast of Hrithik Roshan, Rani Mukherjee and Kareena Kapoor. And the love triangle predictably checked into heartbreak hotel, where Hrithik Roshan was about to get married to the woman he was *not* in love with. (Note the clever avoidance of spoiler!)

And the entire extended family of the three lead players as well as the immediate family of the producers (read: Uday Chopra) joined in singing hit songs across the ages. Some of them expressed undying romance and some were hidden hints to lost love. And some of them were plain and simple hilarious, especially when Satish Shah (as a Sikh) sang *Main nikla gaddi leke...* with his customary gusto.

Medleys are much more fun when they are illogical.

Transformers:
10 Characters Who Changed
Beyond Recognition

Very few film industries in the world run on adrenaline like Bollywood does. And one of the staple sources of that hormone is the 'emergence' of the hero(ine).

Wronged by humanity at large and Amrish Puri in specific, hero decides to take up arms. A montage of shots shows him pumping iron / practising dance steps / running as if the Devil was after him. Intercut by shots of heroine feeding him juice / mother feeding him *gajar ka halwa*) / coach feeding him hausla. Hallelujah—the He-man is born and the climax is precipitated.

A good-natured but socially inept person (a.k.a. geek) fell in love with an angel. For good measure, the person was old (I.S. Johar in **Shagird**), fat (Govinda in **Partner**) or not a Marathi manoos in Mumbai (Amol Palekar in **Chhoti Si Baat**). He sought the help of a dude (also known as 'date doctor') who appreciated the deepness of the geek's love and coached him to dating heaven (read: action on first date).

The coaches were radically different—from macho man (Salman Khan) to effeminate hero (Joy Mukherjee) to the indescribable Colonel Julius Nagendranath Wilfred Singh (Ashok Kumar). But the leading ladies were floored and romantic rivals were vanquished—except in **Shagird**, where the coach himself was the rival.

The world's most famous transformation story happened when a Cockney flower girl became a London socialite. **My Fair Lady** has been adapted a billion times, in a million languages. Basu Chatterjee directed **Manpasand**, the Hindi version where Dev Anand tried to make a lady out of Tina Munim—a loud-mouthed seller of *neem datuns* on Mumbai local trains.

The Rain in Spain transformed into *Charu Chandra ke chanchal chitwan* as the desi Dr Higgins ran the whole gamut of training for Kamli—from gait to giggle, from etiquette to petticoat (sorry, dress sense). Needless to say, many complications arose when the woman thought the whole exercise was for true love while the man was just trying to win a bet with his friend.

And do note how Tina Munim has transformed beyond the film as well.

A criminal wanted in eleven countries was killed. But the police officer in pursuit decided to keep that information a secret and infiltrated his gang with a look-alike. Thus was born the tale of **Don**.

The look-alike was a street singer from eastern UP—with a liking for paan and gaan. The criminal, on the other hand, was a suave and ruthless rake who went from one-night stands to gunfights without batting an eyelid. The change took all of three minutes of screen time and involved watching some random footage that the police had shot of the international smuggler. This lack of homework was explained by giving the 'Don' a bout of amnesia when he went back to the gang. That way, the gangsters themselves trained their nemesis.

In **Yaarana**, a villager with a golden voice was discovered and experts unanimously agreed on his potential to become India's biggest singing star with Polydor, then India's snazziest music label. But in the glitzy world of showbiz, a country bumpkin needed twinkle-toes and starry vibes to complement the golden voice.

To this end, Kishen the Villager was enrolled in language classes, etiquette classes and dance classes. Of course, mayhem ensued immediately afterwards. He gave the language teacher a tongue twister ('*kachcha paapad, pakka paapad*'), the etiquette guy a limb-twister and the fellow dancers a kick (literally) in the behind. Eventually, it took a beautiful instructor (Neetu Singh) and loads of senti speeches to kickstart the change.

What a transformation it was then! Nowadays, we see it every year on *Indian Idol.*

'*Veer bahadur ladke kaun? Rajput! Rajput!*'

This chant haunted Model School of Dehra Dun in general and the Sharma family in particular for many years. After Ramlal Sharma won the super-prestigious inter-school cycle race ages ago, nobody in Model was good enough to win it back. Till Mr Sharma's two sons came along.

When the elder one, Ratan, got into fisticuffs and was thrown off a cliff, it was the cue for the director's cousin, producer's nephew and Ratan's hitherto-good-for-nothing younger brother—Sanjaylal Sharma—to enter the race. And enter he did.

With a training regime involving push-ups, weights and power-cycling, he was up and running in a jiffy. Ably assisted by his girlfriend, Anjali, Sanju trained hard, raced harder and in the sharpest cycle race on this side of Tour de France, he pipped Rajput to win and, as they say, **Jo Jeeta Wohi Sikandar.**

In **Khoon Bhari Maang,** a gold-digger married a millionaire heiress—who was rather, ahem, plain-looking. He promptly pushed her off a boat into the jaws of a crocodile and returned happily to marry his moll. Except that Rekha had survived the sharks of Bollywood—and a crocodile was not going be the end of her.

With a hideously chewed-up face, Rekha sold her diamonds and flew abroad to a plastic surgeon. She returned to India with a new face, newer make-up and such an attitude that her husband resumed started wooing her in seven minutes!

Apparently, the good plastic surgeon managed to infuse some mutated genes during the operation because Rekha took over the climax of the film with leather jacket, stilettos and whips. Don't get naughty ideas. She used those to dump her hubby into the jaws of the aforementioned crocodile.

After a whole lot of solo transformations, it was the turn of an entire village. Thanks to the hot-headed Bhuvan, Champaner had no choice but to learn cricket and play a team of Englishmen in **Lagaan**. Not an easy task for people who had grown up on *gilli-danda*. Fortunately, a British coach was at hand and desperation made you do the strangest of things.

Very soon, the elderly Ishwar Vaid was keeping wickets. The chicken farmer, Bhura, was snapping up balls instead of cocks(!). The ironsmith, Arjan, was wielding a bat in the same way he handled a sledgehammer. A handicapped, scavenger Kachra, was turning the ball square. And the village madman, Guran, was behaving like, well, Sreesanth.

In probably the longest—but highly engaging— transformation shown in Hindi cinema, the rag-tag team of eleven cricketers came together like a symphony, played like a dream and ended on such a high that, 150 years later, we are still to fall out of love with the game.

Most transformations in Bollywood happen so fast that they *seem* like magic. But they *aren't*. Except in **Koi Mil Gaya**.

After his pregnant mother was caught in a freak road accident, Rohit had an abnormal birth and was a child with special needs. Having a slowly developing brain, he was the butt of all jokes—not least because of his sing-song voice. Basically, he was Hrithik Roshan As Never Seen Before.

Enter an alien who could convert solar power into supernatural power. Add to that the guilt trip of being partially responsible for Rohit's abnormality and you had the translucent blue alien transforming the scrawny Rohit into a muscle-bound Mr Universe lookalike (a.k.a. Hrithik Roshan, As We Know Him). Soon, he was slam-dunking basketballs, tearing shirts with his bulging biceps and singing songs with Preity Zinta.

Sequel Alert: He even went on to invent a Time Machine and father a super-hero. Here's one transformation too big for one film to contain.

Om Shanti Om was about a grand plan to recreate the '70s in the present day, and that needed the audacity of India's biggest superstar—Om Kapoor a.k.a. OK!

Looking for a girl who looked like yesteryear's star—Shantipriya—OK stumbled upon Sandy, a teenager from Bangalore with a predilection for blue hot pants and pink bubble gum. While the looks fitted to a tee, the dialogue delivery did not. Nor did she fit into the elaborate costumes from the Golden Age of Bollywood.

With the help of another yesteryear actress, Sandy went on to become Shanti with repeated costume changes, blessings of many well-wishers and parroting that one line about the value of a pinch of vermillion that had the potential of making a heroine's career in Bollywood—*Ek chutki sindoor ki keemat tum kya jaano, Ramesh Babu? Ishwar ka ashirwaad hota hai ek chutki sindoor. Suhagan ka sar ka taaj hota hai ek chutki sindoor...*

In a transformation, one is a changee. The other is a changer—or coach—who brings it all about. Except, in **Karthik Calling Karthik**, both were the same.

A hard-working, highly-intelligent doormat called Karthik changed into a smooth-talking, sharp-dressing rake called Karthik over one extended shopping session. All thanks to the counselling session provided by that confident dude on the phone with all the answers—who was also Karthik.

Karthik called Karthik every night and gave handy hints on wooing long-legged lasses away from their boyfriends, convincing the boss to give hefty raises and bullying nasty neighbours into submission. The hero Karthik followed the coaching of the on-phone Karthik blindly—and the world was at his feet.

He ignored only one teenie-weenie warning—don't tell anybody about this coaching. And you know what happens when people don't listen to coaches, don't you?

Three's A Crowd: 9 Actors Who Played Three Roles Or More

*E*ven before Bollywood discovered special effects for creating doubles, it had stumbled upon the brilliant plot device of long-lost twins. And double roles lived happily ever after. Literally, hundreds of actors and actresses have played twins, siblings, parent and child or simple look-alike strangers.

Triple roles have been fewer in coming. And triple+ roles, even more so.

Triplets—as plot device—are a little too fantastic even by Bollywood's standards. Amar, Akbar and Anthony are bad enough. Now if Nirupa Roy had to give birth to them all together, probably under a statue of Mahatma Gandhi while Jeevan was coming after them with a shotgun, it might have been a tad difficult for all concerned (not least of all, the screenwriter).

Therefore, whenever an actor or actress has played multi-roles, there has been an element of vanity around it. The story could have done without it but the box office probably wanted it.

12: Priyanka Chopra—What's Your Raashee?

As of now, the record for the highest number of roles played by a single actor in a single film is twelve, held by Piggy Chops—unfortunately—in the film which everyone refused to believe was by the director of **Lagaan**, **Swades** and **Jodhaa Akbar**.

NRI Gujju Harman Baweja zipped in from Chicago and went bride-hunting in Arranged-Marriage-Land, only to bump into twelve avatars of Priyanka Chopra—one for each sign of the zodiac. Keeping in mind Linda Goodman's sun sign traits as well as home-grown Indian astrology funda, the Priyankas turned out to be bubbly, balanced, bashful, brash, brazen, bizarre or behenji in turn.

A story, already unwieldy for a film, was not helped by the lead actor's rather wooden acting and the usually sensitive director's uninspired helming of the project. Priyanka tried valiantly to rescue the disaster but even twelve of her could not salvage it!

So, which sign did the guy eventually get married to? At last count, not too many more than twelve people cared.[11]

10: Kamal Haasan—Dashavatar

When Kamal Haasan is not getting intimate with heroines half his age, he is playing multiple roles in the same film including those of a woman, a leper, a dwarf, triplets and a gas cylinder. Okay, maybe not the last one. But Kamal did appear in ten roles in a film named after the ten incarnations of Lord Vishnu, no less.

George W. Bush, CIA agent, Punjabi pop singer and a giant were some of the zanier avatars Kamal Haasan appeared in, clearly having a ball in the process of creating the (then) world record of the maximum number of roles

---

[11] The same story was also made into an extremely popular 1980s TV serial—*Mr Yogi*—where, each holder of the zodiac sign was played by a different actress.

in a single film. A terribly convoluted story of a chemical weapon being delivered to Tamil Nadu around the time of the 2004 tsunami was only an excuse for creating ten roles for Kamal.

While at it, even lead actress Asin slipped in a double role of her own and the other actress Mallika Sherawat played a pole-dancer (where the pole looked suspiciously like Kamal in prosthetic make-up).

9: Sanjeev Kumar—Naya Din Nayi Raat

Sanjeev Kumar reprised a role made famous by the legendary Sivaji Ganesan in Tamil cinema and became something of a legend himself.

Modelled around the nine rasas (*shringar*—love, *hasya*—comedy, *raudra*—anger, *karun*—compassion, *bibhatsa*—disgust, *bhayanak*—horror, *veer*—heroism and *adbhut*—amazement), the nine roles popped up in the life of Jaya Bhaduri, who was on the run to escape getting married off by her father.

A leper, a dacoit, an effeminate actor, a macho hunter, a drunkard, an elderly widower, a doctor and a two-faced priest landed up with a life lesson each before the girl met the love of her life in yet another similar-faced symbol of shringar rasa. And of course, it all ended with the mandatory last scene of happy-ending Bollywood where all the nine rasas—with their trademark gaits, moustaches, guffaws and deformities—appeared for a group photo.

3: I.S. Johar—Johny Mera Naam

The perennial funny man, I.S. Johar, joined the already packed cast of **Johny Mera Naam** three times over and added to the mayhem. He was (were?) the simply named Pehla Ram, Duja Ram and Teeja Ram—three brothers who popped up in different uniforms in a film which already had the audience flummoxed about two brothers, Mohan and Sohan.

So Pehla Ram was a police constable (known for his shift-based honesty—'*Hum duty pe rishwat nahin lete*'), Duja Ram was an airline steward (known for his logic—'*Pehla duje ka judwa aur duja teeje ka judwa ho to...*') and Teeja Ram was a barman in Kathmandu (known for serving liquor in Coca-Cola bottles).

3: Mehmood—Humjoli

The first comic superstar of Bollywood was not Govinda, but Mehmood. In a film famous for Jeetendra playing badminton, not only in white shoes but white t-shirt and trousers as well, Mehmood stole the show with a triple role.

He did a killer mimicry of three generations of the Kapoor khandaan—Prithviraj, Raj and Randhir. In a song, he picked up a sitar, dafli and guitar to belt out a song in the trademark styles of the three Kapoors including even their voices. His spoofing of the Prithviraj baritone (made famous by the iconic 'Saleeeeem' as **Mughal-e-Azam**) laid down the blueprint that is used by comedians even today.

3: Amitabh Bachchan—Mahaan

Father and twin sons—finally, Bollywood of the 1980s cracked the code.

With Vinod Khanna taking sanyaas and Mithun Chakraborty not getting his disco shoes on yet, there was a serious dearth of action heroes that could have only been solved by having many Amitabh Bachchans in the same film. Add to that the standard mixture of the characters having varying shades of grey, different levels of silliness and the same baritone to create box-office gold.

Papa Bachchan was a lawyer, on the run from the law. Middle Bachchan was Inspector Shankar, looking to catch old lawyers on the run from the law. Junior was the all-singing, all-dancing comic relief.

The superstar—who started his reign in the 1970s—went through the 1980s on inertia. The box office was somewhat guaranteed and movies like these were horrible clangers. He was always accused of getting caught in his formulae though you've got to admit three formulae in the same film is not a formula any longer.

3: Rajnikanth—John Jani Janardhan

Non-believers (usually found on the northern side of the Vindhyas) would say that this film copied not only the premise (father plus twin sons in a triple role) of an Amitabh Bachchan film (see above) but even took its name from the hit Bachchan song from **Naseeb**. That's all rubbish. True believers know that Rajni had done an 'Inception' in the minds of **Mahaan**'s writers to see how the audience accepted this triple-role concept before he appeared in it himself.

Inspector John got killed. Wife delivered twins. One was adopted by childless Hindu couple. The other was brought up by Muslim maidservant. Spirit of father took over Hindu son, who then got framed with the help of Muslim son. I could go on and on about Rajnikanth's *apaar mahima* but then that needs a book of its own.[12]

3: Shah Rukh Khan—English Babu Desi Mem

What Amitabh Bachchan does, SRK can't be too far behind in doing.

In a film that came in the wake of **DDLJ** and was supposed to stamp SRK's stardom on the industry, Shah Rukh played three different roles and bombed spectacularly.

He was the NRI industrialist. He was the rebel son, who died after leaving a son of his own. And he was the youngest scion of the family out to look for his elder brother's son. He was also hamming it like he had done in no other film (and that's saying something). Add to that some bad wigs, worse moustaches and worst costumes and accessories (designed by Gauri Khan, no less), and here was a disaster you'd like to avoid at all cost.

Achha, in this inheritance saga, where did the Desi Mem fit in? Well, what else can you call Sonali Bendre?

3: Paresh Rawal—Oye Lucky! Lucky Oye!

As the father of India's biggest thief, he was a Sikh middle-aged man who had an edgy relationship with his son. As part-time wedding singer and part-time fence for stolen goods, he was the henna-haired Gogi Bhai. As a smooth-talking doctor not beyond fleecing even India's biggest thief, he was Dr Handa.

---

[12] *Issued in Public Interest*: The director of this movie was T. Rama Rao and NOT Trauma Rao, as often referred to by frivolous people.

Paresh Rawal's super-prolific career as comedian, villain and actor had an interesting confluence in **Oye Lucky! Lucky Oye!** in which he played three completely unconnected (no twin / triplet / look-alike funda) roles with aplomb. He was the perfect foil to the glib-talking handsome thief, Abhay Deol, playing the exasperated father figure, the slimy associate and trustworthy expert— sometimes all three in the same character.

Marketing In Bollywood: 10 Brand Placements

Brand placements in movies are common enough across the world though slightly less in India. But some really cool and some not-so-cool brands have made their mark in the movies. Some of the placements have been quite clumsy while some have been seamlessly merged. Some connection with the plot preferred, but not considered essential!

The most interesting brand placement was not about watches, cars or liquor. It was a brand placed on the name of the hero of the film.

In **English Babu Desi Mem**, Shah Rukh Khan's name was sponsored by the Bhilwara Group—owners of Mayur Suitings. As part of a very visible campaign kicked off at that time, the star was called 'Shah Rukh Mayur Khan' and this was extended to the movie where the lead character was called Vikram Mayur, the chairman of Mayur Industries.

The film's poor box-office collections did not do too much for the brand. But Mayur is still going strong and their latest campaign involves Virender Mayur Sehwag.

In one of the biggest hits of all times, **Dilwale Dulhania Le Jayenge**, we had a beer brand making an appearance— which is a rarity since alcohol brands are subject to strict advertising restrictions and there is always a chance that family audiences might baulk at the placement.

Nevertheless, Stroh's beer was consumed around a bonfire as Shah Rukh bonded with Parmeet Sethi. When asked why he had come to India, SRK gave a quizzical glance to the can in his hand and claimed his ambition was to put up a beer plant.

Stroh's beer cans and large posters were also displayed in Amrish Puri's departmental store, from where SRK hijacked a crate.

In **Baghban**, Amitabh Bachchan extended his celebrity endorser role for ICICI Bank right into the film. He played the loving husband, the dutiful father and a loyal employee of the bank. The bank's branch was the setting for some key scenes—including one where Amitabh withdrew his entire PF savings for his sons. Big B's boss behaved like a perfect banker and solemnly advised him not to.

It would have done the bank a world of good to have a handsome, credible gentleman manning their branch instead of, say, Emraan Hashmi who would have probably flirted with the customers at peak hour.[13]

Shah Rukh Khan has been one of the best marketed Bollywood stars. And he was one of the first people to get into product placement in a big way. His attic in **Dil To Pagal Hai**, for example, had a prominently branded Pepsi fridge (usually seen only in supermarkets).

For his first home-production **Phir Bhi Dil Hai Hindustani**, he managed to weave in a Hyundai Santro car

---

[13] *Trivia Alert*: In **Aankhen** too, Big B played a bank manager with Vilasrao Jefferson Bank. He was sacked from the bank but he returned to take revenge and rob the bank with the help of three blind men.

into the story—a brand he was endorsing then. SRK and Juhi Chawla escaped from a villainous gang in a Santro when we were nearing the climax in the film. In the chase sequence that ensued, the car's superior handling, brake efficiency, quick pickup and spacious interior were all aptly demonstrated.

However, considering that the film was supposed to be an attack on the commercialisation of media and how sponsorships have invaded every space, the product placements looked more than a little odd.

When Shashi Kapoor fell in love with a voice in the 1970s, it involved hiding behind bushes and listening to a scantily-clad Zeenat Aman on the sly. In **Lage Raho Munna Bhai** of the 2000s, all the lovable goon had to do was to switch on the radio.

Munna Bhai fell in love with RJ Jahnavi—who worked for WorldSpace Radio in the film. It was a small matter of detail that the satellite radio service did not have interactive programming in India, unlike the FM channels. But that did not stop the producers from putting up large branding all around the studio, where many of the film's pivotal scenes took place.

Vidya Balan, the effervescent jockey with a signature Good Morning, apparently trained with real-life RJ Malishka of the Red FM network to get the nuances right. But for all the efforts, WorldSpace did not continue in India and shut shop in 2009.[14]

---

[14] In **Radio**, Himesh Reshamaiyya played Vivan Shah, a RJ with Radio Mirchi. The film was promoted heavily by the network as the RJs kept aside their Himesh jokes for a while and said good things about the man who became their 'colleague' on-screen.

Weaving a brand into the story is never easy but it happened quite neatly in **Luck By Chance.**

Lovers Konkona Sen Sharma and Farhan Akhtar went shopping in a supermarket, discussed Konkona's erratic fridge and her lack of money to replace it. Almost casually, branded material of Godrej Eon Fridge appeared and at the checkout counter, Farhan wrote out a slogan for the brand (something about 'no frost, low cost') that could win them a new fridge. This small episode passed off almost unnoticed in the film until a brand-new fridge re-appeared—this time, in her house—as the promised prize.

Godrej followed up this brand placement with a 'Luck By Chance Contest' where all buyers of their products within a certain period were eligible for a lucky draw. Prizes included meeting the stars of the film, CDs of the film's music and even an all-expenses trip abroad to see the shooting of the producers' next film.

In **Gardish**, directed by Priyadarshan before his degeneration into Akshay Kumar, we had a relatively obscure but surprisingly blatant placement—of all things—of mosquito repellents.

Before the heroine ascended the stage for a song (a rousing medley, scored by R.D. Burman), the audience (in a hand-clapping style reminiscent of *Ek do teen*) chorused—'*We want hit song, we want hit song*'. This would have been quite innocuous if the heroine hadn't emerged from a dummy aerosol of Hit Cockroach Killer and large neon signs of Hit hadn't been revolving all around.

This was explicable because the producer, R. Mohan, was popularly known as Good Knight Mohan for creating the brands Good Knight and Hit (which were later sold to

Godrej). He was making an ad film free within the price of a feature.

In **Hero**, a reformed Jackie Shroff was released from prison and required to be rehabilitated. He was put up for a job at Rajdoot Motorcycle Company. And from then on, he popped up both inside and outside the factory to plug the Yamaha Rajdoot 350, then the flagship bike of the Escorts group. He called it the 'best bike in India' and even rode on it to participate—and obviously win—in a Mumbai-Panvel motorcycle race. And apart from the race and factory, logos of the company and advertisements of Escorts Shock Absorbers were strewn around liberally throughout the film.

The Hero-on-Rajdoot not only beat his romantic rival, Shakti Kapoor, who was riding a Honda bike in that same race, but even a trashing couplet was produced by Jackie's mentor (Madan Puri)—'*Honda ho ya Fonda, jeetega hamara munda...*'

From Rajdoot at the beginning of their careers, Subhash Ghai and Jackie Shroff moved on to Coca-Cola towards the end, and it was an almost unanimous decision that **Yaadein** was one of the most in-your-face examples of product placement.

Jackie sang soulful ballads holding a Coke can. His dying wife gave him a Coke keychain. Hrithik swigged Coke at parties, taking care to display the full logo. It was a triumph for Coca-Cola as the brand was not woven into the story but the story and situations seemed built around the brand.

And Ghai did not stop at Coke. Pass Pass mouth-freshener ('*Pass Pass khilakey pass pass aane ki koshish kar rahi hai'*) and Hero Cycles (*'Hero Cycles ki heroine Isha Puri...'*) made suitably cringe-worthy appearances in the film.

In **Koi Mil Gaya**, Hrithik Roshan played an adult with slow brain development, who had a fully mature body but with the mind of a twelve-year-old. And that quasi-kid, Rohit, was a walking-talking endorsement for Bournvita. He routinely asked for Bournvita when offered tea or coffee and did not desist from attributing his *'chusti aur phoorti'* to the health drink. Unfortunately, the subsequent beefing up of his muscles and the sharpening of his mental faculties were not credited to Bournvita but to an alien called Jadoo.

The association with the brand and the franchise did not end here.

In the sequel, **Krrish**, the focus shifted to Rohit's son Krrish who was born with supernatural abilities and thought nothing of running ahead of horses. Even he attributed his abilities to Bournvita and quite fittingly, a jar of the drink was a permanent fixture on his dining table.

Honourable Mention

The best unplanned product plug for any brand in a Hindi movie must be the one for Black Dog whiskey in **Shahenshah**. To explain the lusty feelings he had on seeing 'fair butterflies' like Meenakshi Sheshadri, Amrish Puri intoned *'Jis din main koi gori titli dekh leta hoon, mere khoon mein sainkro kaale kutte ek saath bhaunkne lagte hain. Uss din main Black Dog peeta hoon...'*

Wow—what articulation of brand benefits.

Show Stealers:
6 6 Roles That Became
Bigger Than The Movie

Quite a few characters have outshone the main characters of the movie.

This underlines the unpredictability of Hindi cinema, where people get together to make a movie in which the protagonist is so important that the film is named after him—and then comes a Lone Ranger, who steals not only the hero's thunder but all the memories associated with the film as well.

Imagine how difficult it is for a character to become bigger than the title role...

Loin—Kalicharan

Ajit's signature role was of the deadly smuggler, Lion a.k.a. Loin. The Punjabisation of Lion became a catch-phrase of the MTV generation as copywriters, VJs, screenwriters and magazine editors jumped on to the bandwagon of Ajit jokes.

In the movie, a bombastic Shatrughan Sinha was relegated to the sidelines as Ajit threw his lines around with aplomb in Subhas Ghai's earliest hit. It had a pretty interesting plot, with Loin killing off a police officer (Shatru 1) on his trail and the officer's superior replacing him with a look-alike criminal (Shatru 2).

For Spoiler, see below.[15]

Babumoshai—Anand

Raj Kapoor's term of endearment for buddy Hrishikesh Mukherjee was immortalised by the latter in a film dedicated to Raj Kapoor and the city of Bombay. Apparently, the characters of the two protagonists were modelled after their real-life parallels as well.

What was supposed to be an out-and-out Rajesh Khanna film turned out to be the first step to stardom for Amitabh Bachchan, with his understated yet intense portrayal of the Bengali doctor. Amitabh was more than a little unhappy with the script as he believed that the dying characters always got the audience's sympathy, but nevertheless, his character came out real like no other. Anand's lilting call of 'Babumoshai' added to the role—and the title became something of an epithet for *all* Bongs (till Sourav Ganguly became 'Dada' to the nation).

Bhiku Mhatre—Satya

The poker-faced Chakravarthy had the meaty title role of Satya—the rootless, amoral guy who rose to the top of the Bombay underworld. But Manoj Bajpai, after a string of obscure bit parts in Ram Gopal Verma films, hit pay dirt

---

[15] On his deathbed, Shatru 1 left behind a note for his boss which got misread as No. 17. Only at the climax, when a rotating disc with LION written on it was seen, did the not-so-bright boss realise that NO17 was nothing but LION written upside down. But he can be forgiven... after all, he was looking for Loin.

as the unkempt, unapologetic Bhiku Mhatre. His violence, his love, his grunting grin, his hysterical sobs, his domestic squabbles and his crazy gang went into cinematic lore as Ramu pulled off what he does best—gangster movies.

This one role was enough to get him into starring (**Shool**) as well as negative (**Aks**) roles but he was never able to repeat the manic energy he exuded with the '*Mumbai ka king kaun?*' line.

Even now, the character rules mindspace with a Wikipedia entry, nickames on Yahoo, Orkut and MSN, thousands of results on Google, and Isha Koppikar's role in **Shabri** (yet another gangster flick, produced by RGV) in which she wanted to be a 'female Bhiku Mhatre'.

Mogambo—Mr India

An obscure Clark Gable-Ava Gardner Hollywood starrer became the name of the second-most famous villain in the history of Hindi cinema. In one of the last films of Salim-Javed as duo, Anil Kapoor had the dubious distinction of being a hero where both the villain *and* the heroine (Miss Hawa Hawaii) completely overshadowed him.

An interesting story around the making is about when Shekhar Kapur asked Javed Akhtar to explain the character of Mogambo to him and Akhtar replied with '*Mogambo khush hua*'. The explanation was that it was the line of a megalomaniac who used verbal approval to reward his gang. To convince an incredulous Shekhar, Javed Akhtar told him, 'Shekhar sahib, when Kapil Dev hits a six over the grounds, people will shout *Mogambo khush hua*. When people play teen-patti and if they get three aces, they will say *Mogambo khush hua*. Trust me on that...'[16]

He was bang-on with this prediction as Mogambo became the newest icon as his signature line—performed by Amrish Puri with almost an orgiastic relish in the film—rivalled the best lines of Gabbar, with almost as much repeat value.

Genie / Genius—Aladin

Aladin Chatterjee was not the most nondescript of names. Khwaish was not the usual name of a city in a Bollywood film. And a resident genie at your beck and call was not your usual perk of college days. Riteish Deshmukh had all that in **Aladin** and he lost it all to—but of course—Amitabh Bachchan doing a comic turn as Genius.

The film did quite disastrously at the box office and all the interesting possibilities of modernising a well-loved fairy tale were squandered. Nor was it that Amitabh Bachchan earned kudos for the film. But it was one of those films where you never asked about Aladin and wanted to know who was playing Genie.

Auro—Paa

Amitabh Bachchan has made this into a bit of a habit—being the most important person in a film that is not named after him.

Abhishek Bachchan as the Paa of a progeria-afflicted teenager put in a sincere performance, but when a child

---

[16] Interesting details of the Mogambo character can be found on Shekhar Kapur's blog (shekharkapur.com).

dies in a Hindi film, the tears blot out everything around it. Add to that a powerhouse performance by Vidya Balan in the role of the mother and you have a clean sweep at the awards ceremonies. But to be fair to Abhishek, the film was never about the father.

Honourable Mentions

Ghajini Dharmatma is probably the first villain[17] in Bollywood to have a film named after him. But then, how do you remember him in a story which has Aamir Khan in six-pack abs and a crew cut? Of course, after the mind-numbing violence, very few people would remember the name of Aamir Khan's character[18] either. And it has been more than fifteen minutes since the movie got over.

No One Killed Jessica and almost no one noticed the actress playing the 'title role' either. Here you get featured in a film on one of the most controversial topics of recent times, with a solid star cast that gets very good reviews— and you get killed even before the first scene starts. Like Rani Mukherjee in the film, life can be a bitch too!

---

[17] He certainly wasn't the last since **Ra.One** burst out of a video-game soon afterwards and took on G.One.

[18] Aamir Khan's character in the film was called Sanjay Singhania.

3

THE SOURCE CODE

Genius is 1% inspiration and 99% perspiration—
THOMAS ALVA EDISON

*N*obody is inspired as often as Bollywood. Taking a winning idea and backing it with blood, sweat and tears is something that happens here on a daily basis. There are some favourite stories that inspire more than the others.

And some situations are so inspiring that they become clichés. Or might become.

- ◆ Inspiration + Perspiration: 7 'Lifted' Plots
- ◆ Hats Off: 7 Tributes by Filmmakers
- ◆ The Great Indian Movie: 7 Movies Inspired by Epics
- ◆ An Offer You Can't Refuse: 6 Remakes of **The Godfather** (or parts thereof)
- ◆ Coming Soon: 7 Clichés that are About to Happen

Inspiration + Perspiration: 7 'Lifted' Plots

O n one episode of *Koffee with Karan*, Javed Akhtar recounted a story from his salad days. He had gone to a producer to narrate a script and the man had listened to it without interruption. After finishing, a nervous Javed Akhtar asked, '*Sir, kaisa laga?*' The guy explained the risks of being original in Bollywood—'*Darling, story toh teri achhi hai. Lekin ek bada risk hai... Yeh kahani kisi bhi film mein aayi nahin hai ab tak!*'

'Inspiration' is a—well—inspired word in Bollywood. There are a million films to make but only a few tried and tested themes. And even fewer Hollywood movies.

Many directors have taken inspiration from films—some with credit and some without. Sometimes, the inspiration has taken the form of scene-by-scene replication and sometimes, the film has grown bigger than the original plot.

Plot: A spoiled heiress runs away to be with her lover and meets a reporter, who helps her, just to get an exclusive story, but ends up falling in love with her.

In 1934, **It Happened One Night** made a clean sweep of the box-office and the Oscars with a heartwarming tale, and it was only a matter of time before the Gods of Parental Opposition and Runaway Lovers made it into an Indian story.

Raj Kapoor and Nargis starred in **Chori Chori**, which added the only thing that was missing in the original—

superhit songs. Shankar-Jaikishan provided an eminently hummable score to make the film complete.

The charm of the story was not lost even six decades later as Aamir Khan and Pooja Bhatt got together in **Dil Hai Ke Manta Nahin**. And again, the plot was brought alive by crackling dialogue and great music.

Plot: Terrorised by bandits, a village enlists the help of mercenaries to protect themselves.

It started with Akira Kurosawa's **Seven Samurai**, which was followed by the Hollywood version (**The Magnificent Seven**). Again, the terror of dacoits, the visual delight of their rocky dwellings and the bravura of a small group taking on a large one were too much for Indian filmmakers to resist.

In India, two films—**Mera Gaon Mera Desh** and **Khote Sikkay** had very similar plots. And in recent times, it continued with Rajkumar Santoshi's **China Gate**.

The same simple tale was remade as the Greatest Story Ever Told, which is still considered to be the pinnacle of Indian cinematic success. The finesse with which the entire concoction was served differentiated this offering from any other mish-mash of borrowed plots and devices. **Sholay**, with its perfect orchestration of characters and emotions, rose above the ordinary and became an epic, which is many times the sum of its parts.

Sholay *borrowed not only its plot but a few catchy devices from other films as well. For example, the double-sided coin was borrowed from a film called* **One-Eyed Jack**. *And no, the title wasn't original either. B.R. Chopra had already made a film of that name, though he'd spelt it differently, as* **Shole**.

Plot: Villains kill a gentle soul but he is reincarnated and 'returns' to take revenge.

Subhash Ghai's **Karz** has borne the cross of being a copy of a Hollywood film, **The Reincarnation of Peter Proud**. While Peter Proud made quite a noise in its time, it is unlikely that Ghai turned to this for 'inspiration' because Bollywood had already produced several landmark films on the theme, like **Madhumati**. The cycle of death and rebirth is far more attuned to Indian philosophy, as is the theme of unrequited love. So, why the hell would Mr Ghai look Westward?

The allegation could be because Bollywood was seriously 'un-cool' in the 1980s and the English-speaking populace had to be totally derisive about it. So, here was a way to diss a big hit and demonstrate one's familiarity with Hollywood.

Plot: A geek falls in love with a beautiful girl and enlists the help of a date-coach to woo her.

This seemingly innocuous plot came under fire when Sony Pictures sued the makers of **Partner** for lifting the plot of their hit production—**Hitch**.

It was very embarrassing for the Indian film industry but if one stepped back a bit, one realised that the story had been in circulation long before **Hitch** hit the screens, in **Shagird** (starring Joy Mukherjee, Saira Banu and I.S. Johar).[19]

You only have to discount the details of whether the love guru trained one geek or many, whether the geek was a young man or old, whether there was a love triangle or quadrilateral etc., and you are looking at two more similar films—**Chhoti Si Baat** (starring Amol Palekar, Vidya Sinha and Ashok Kumar) and **Shreeman Aashique** (starring Rishi Kapoor, Urmila Matondkar and Anupam Kher).

---

[19] See chapter on Transformations (Page 51).

So, who copied whom?

Plot: A man goes on the hunt for his wife's killer, who had also injured him so badly that he now has short-term memory loss and forgets everything after every fifteen minutes.

This came first in **Memento**—the film which made a cult hero out of Christopher Nolan—and had all kinds of filmmaking stunts like going forward and backward in time as the hero hunted for clues and tattooed them on to his body to help him remember later.

A few years after **Memento**, posters of Tamil superstar Surya—with phone numbers and names tattooed on his muscular body—came up in Chennai for a film called **Ghajini**. This was subsequently up-starred to Hindi, when Aamir Khan got his six-pack to do the remake.

In response to allegations that the film was a copy of **Memento**, Aamir Khan said in his blog that apparently the scriptwriter (Murugadoss, who's also the director) heard about the story of **Memento** and wrote his own version of the script. When he saw the film later, he found that his version was very different from the original so he went ahead and made **Ghajini**. Aamir calls this a genuine instance of being inspired by something, and nothing beyond that. I guess we will have to take his word on that.

Plot: A man is imprisoned in an anonymous room for fifteen years and abruptly released. He assimilates the clues from those years to find out who was behind his fate.

Based on a *manga* comic, Korean film **Oldboy** took on a unique theme and fashioned a gruesome tale of violence, passion, forbidden emotions and heartbreaking loss. Critics across the world lauded director Chan-wook Park's achievement but none flattered him as much as Sanjay Gupta. Since imitation is the sincerest form of flattery, Mr Gupta ripped off the film—almost frame by frame, costume by costume.

Zinda was even set in supposedly familiar surroundings as the original, Bangkok, and Sanjay Dutt's character was fed Chinese dumplings—exactly as in **Oldboy**. One Indian hunting for another is far easier in Bangkok (and that was the exact opposite of the film's premise) but that didn't stop the director, who was also the scriptwriter (nudge, nudge, wink, wink).

Plot: Two people from warring families fall in love.

Mr William Shakespeare wrote the source code. Scions of the rival families of Verona—Montague and Capulet—fell in love and their story became the benchmark of doomed romance.

West Side Story transported this story to the gangs of New York in an exuberant musical. The Jets and Sharks fought in the streets as the siblings of the two gang-leaders fell in love.

Mansoor Khan is obviously fascinated with this story because he made two films around it. The first one starred his debutant cousin, and its freshness—despite a tragic end—gave romance a new life in Bollywood. **Qayamat Se Qayamat Tak** was *Romeo and Juliet* revisited and an all-time classic.

The second starred another superstar and was extremely similar to **West Side Story** in terms of the love interests, gang codes and structure. **Josh** did not too well—despite a stellar cast—but still manages to evoke a smile or two with its style and chutzpah. And for SRK singing his first song.

Hats Off: 7 Tributes
By Filmmakers

*B*ollywood is always reviled for imitating, and quietly lifting without telling. However, there have been several instances of filmmakers being genuinely impressed by people whom they consider idols and paying an affectionate tribute to them.

These tributes are always subtle and always original. And they are usually very clever—weaving a simple but telling detail into the narrative. It is a lot of fun to discover them, for it is very heartwarming to see open acknowledgment of an inspiration.

Main Hoon Na

Farah Khan is a self-confessed Bollywood addict, with a softer corner of her heart reserved for humour and the Hindi film 'formula'.

Her debut film was a tribute to both these things as she made a film on the much-loved, much-hated formula of long-lost brothers. And in a special tribute to one of her favourite films of all times, she named her two characters after the two brothers in Hrishikesh Mukherjee's **Golmaal**—Ramprasad Sharma and Lakshmanprasad Sharma.

Even the nickname was not spared. The anglicised Lakshman preferred to be called Lucky in both films.

Om Shanti Om

See above for Farah Khan's love for 'formula'.

In her second film, she took yet another formula—reincarnation. Projecting Bollywood stardom as 'a dream so big that one lifetime is not enough' to fulfil it, she had her hero coming back for more and built the entire film around the most famous reincarnation film—**Karz**.

The title was obviously from the biggest hit song of the film. Her film opened with a scene in which **Karz** is being shot, and in the shooting, two characters get into a fight over a jacket which Rishi Kapoor had thrown to the crowd. One of them was Om Prakash Makhija, played by Shah Rukh Khan. The other was a nameless woman, played by Farah Khan.

Kabhi Khushi Kabhie Gham

KJo's respect for the Yashraj banner is well known. Aditya Chopra is one of his best friends. Yash Chopra is a much-respected 'uncle'. And Johar's filmmaking style—especially his locales and sets—is unabashedly YRF-ish, sumptuous and larger-than-life.

His tribute to his gurus came through the title of his second film—**Kabhi Khushi Kabhie Gham**—which used a slightly unusual spelling in the second 'Kabhie'. This was taken from Yash Chopra's classic love story—**Kabhi Kabhie**.

Johnny Gaddaar

Sriram Raghavan is a fan of crime thrillers as a genre—both in books and films. In his second directorial venture, he doffed a cap to established masters of the genre in varying styles.

The title was an allusion to **Johny Mera Naam**, a taut crime caper directed by Vijay Anand. In fact, the film was 'dedicated to Thriller Maestros Vijay Anand and James Hadley Chase'. The thriller writer entered the film as Neil Nitin Mukesh read a book (*The Whiff of Money*) by him.

The other homage paid in the film was to **Parwana**, from which an important plot element was taken, but the director—instead of hiding the fact—actually showed the character getting the idea when he saw the film on TV.

Jaane Bhi Do Yaaro

The beginning of India's craziest comedy film (also, the most trenchant satire) was rooted in a classic film by Italian director, Michelangelo Antonioni—**Blow Up**. A photographer unknowingly shoots the scene of a murder and only realises it when he is back in his studio and enlarges—'blows up'—the negatives. This was exactly what the owners of Beauty Photo Studio also did when they were at the scene of Commissioner DeMello's murder.

Now the average Indian viewer wouldn't have heard of Antonioni—but the director had to acknowledge his debt. So, the murder and the photo shoot happened at Antonioni Park—prominently displayed on a signboard at the location.

Namastey London

The plot of the Akshay Kumar-Katrina Kaif starrer was a modern-day reprise of Manoj Kumar's **Purab Aur Pachhim**, where a son-of-the-soil married an anglicised girl in an effort to bring her to appreciate the wonders of Incredible India.

While the modern-day version did not have the bombastic patriotism of the first, it had to play the India Shining tune often enough.

And when Akshay Kumar had to lecture a group of posh Englishmen on Indian culture, he gave them an earful and concluded by saying to his interpreter (Katrina) that the rest of the lesson can be gleaned from a DVD of **Purab Aur Pachhim.**

Jhankaar Beats

Sujoy Ghosh's debut film was an affectionate tribute to 'Boss'—R.D. Burman—to the extent that the two heroes' names started with 'R' (Rishi) and 'D' (Deep). When a third member—Neel—joined their band, he made it R'N'D. In fact, they inducted this new member with a song about their hero ('*Boss kaun tha, maloom hai kya?*'). And in the climax, they played music by 'Boss' (*Humein tumse pyaar kitna...*) for **Jhankaar Beats**, a music contest they wanted to win very badly.

Apart from RD, the film paid homage to the Greatest Film Ever Made. The two heroes asked each other **Sholay** trivia ('*Gabbar ke baap ka naam kya tha?*'). They wondered about the characters ('*How did Thakur eat?*'). And they mouthed Sholay dialogue ('*Bahut yaarana lagta hai*').

If we start including all the films that have paid tributes to **Sholay**, *we will be here till eternity. Maybe there should be a separate book on that.*

A film-length tribute to the 'Boss'

The Great Indian Movie:
7 Movies Inspired By Epics

*T*o paraphrase a proverb—what isn't there in the *Mahabharat* isn't there in Bharat either.

Mahabharat and the *Ramayan* comprise a large part of the stories we listen to, the advice we heed and the dilemmas we face as individuals. Many people of India—business families as well as the political dynasties—are natural setups for tales of brotherly angst and violent power struggles. Needless to say, these dens of intrigue are fodder for movies as well. So, if epics are found in family feuds and family feuds are found in movies, it naturally follows that the epics will be found in movies.

Bollywood has drawn extensively from these two canons to devise interesting stories as well as life lessons for the masses.

Shyam Benegal's **Kalyug** had a stellar star cast from theatre and parallel cinema backgrounds, playing the Paandav and Kaurav brothers. The film did not go literal at any stage and did interesting, modern takes on the plot points of the *Mahabharat.*

There was secret help of technology from a foreign collaboration, which winched up enactments of the *Brahmastra* mantras. Instead of Draupadi's disrobement, there was an income-tax raid, with officers sifting through lingerie drawers as helpless husbands looked on. There were family gurus who came in when the couples remained childless for long periods. And there was a driver's son called Karan Singh, who was the differentiator between the feuding sides. And in the only literal scene that happened near the end, Karan Singh chose to travel through a deserted road—despite threats to his life—and had a flat tyre. He got down from the car to change it... And we all know what happens to tragic heroes when their chariot wheels get stuck, don't we?

Prakash Jha's **Rajneeti** saw one of the biggest assemblies of stars in recent times, and a story around the Greatest Indian Epic required no less of a cast. Played out in the divisive political landscape of present-day India, it had all the key elements of the *Mahabharat*. The reprisal in the modern context had to be easily identifiable and yet fresh, given the average Indian's familiarity with the epic.

The film started with a young girl's infatuation with a leader named Bhaskar and an illegitimate child was sired, who got adopted by a low-caste driver. Sons of two brothers fought for control of a political party and its attendant riches. A canny adviser named Brij Gopal guided the good guys, though, towards the end, we were never sure who the good guys were. In that respect, the film was closer to the present day Indian political scene than to the *Mahabharat*.

One of the least known but most faithful retelling of the *Ramayan* was a film called **Haisiyat**.

Lost in the mayhem of dancing among clay pots, nobody noticed this film in which Jeetendra played Ram, a union leader in the plant of a businesswoman Seeta, played by Jaya Prada. Ram sided with the labourers in a battle with the 'management' (thus abandoning the wife in response to complaints from the masses) and even went on a hunger-strike. Of course, the misunderstandings were amicably settled but the bad guy (Shakti Kapoor, who else?) kidnapped Seeta and held her hostage in a mansion that had—hold your breaths and your laughter—a minefield all around it. Our valiant hero crossed this metaphorical sea by tiptoeing between the mines, and razed the metaphorical Lanka to the ground.

The premise was very interesting—the exploration of Raavan's love for Seeta and the retelling of the epic from the villain's point of view. Add to that a legendary filmmaker like Mani Ratnam and an A-List Bollywood cast supplemented by the best of Tamil cinema, you are supposed to have one hell of a film— right? Wrong. **Raavan** managed to break every expectation and not one box-office record.

The eternal story of good triumphing over evil was given a modern and ambiguous twist. Mani Ratnam turned the war to rescue one's wife and honour into one in which the 'god' committed atrocities on innocent villagers to catch Robin Hood Raavan. The ambivalence of the director in taking sides would have been a great retelling if not for some childish dialogues and scenes.

Abhishek Bachchan played Beera Munda—a character supposedly based on the life of Naxalite Kobad Ghandy—and was the eponymous villain. But his mannerisms—instead of being fearsome—only ended up being a hindrance to understanding his complex character. A screeching, shrieking Seeta (Aishwarya Rai) and overly stoic Ram (Tamil superstar Vikram) did nothing to push the epic quotient.

We tend to lose ourselves between the songs and sacks of sugar of **Hum Saath-Saath Hain**. We completely overlook that it's a near-perfect rendition of the family compulsions of the *Ramayan*.

The ageing patriarch (Alok Nath) was coerced by his second wife (Reema Lagoo) to sideline her virtuous stepson (Mohnish Behl) and promote her son (Salman Khan) instead. When the oldest son accepted this decision, the youngest son (Saif Ali Khan) joined him in the back of beyond while the middle one—now the heir apparent—refused to accept the inheritance.

Seen from this prism, it is now easy to fit in every character into the *Ramayan* cast. True to the Barjatya tradition, there was no villain and Lanka was not part of the plot. Instead, there were elaborate feasts, gushing praise for all, traditional values and songs for *all* the characters.

Golmaal is arguably the funniest Hindi film ever. The extremely durable comic duo of Amol Palekar and Utpal Dutt made the film unforgettable with their zany capers.

But there is also a very strong *Ramayan* connection in this film. We, of course, had the two (?) sons of Dashrathprasad Sharma—Ramprasad and Lakshmanprasad (a.k.a. Lucky). Apart from that, we also had Urmila, who was wooed by *both* the brothers but fell in love with the clean-shaven Lucky. This was ordained since the times of the original epic since Lakshman's wife was indeed Urmila.

Any discussion on the influence of the epics on Bollywood has to, *has to*, HAS TO, talk about the climax of **Jaane Bhi Do Yaaro**. No amount of logic or analysis can succeed in understanding this iconic scene.

Draupadi leant on Duryodhan. Duryodhan—in turn—decided to 'drop the idea' of disrobing her. But the Paandavs tried to convince the Kauravs to go ahead with it. One bespectacled Duhshasan was chased by another in underwear. Bheem emerged in sunglasses and announced his 'shareholding' of Draupadi in a Punjabi accent. Drupad called Bheem *'durachari, atyachari, bhrashtachari'* and ended that diatribe with a *'Bol sorry'*. Eventually, Jalaluddin Mohammed Akbar entered and tried to pass judgement on the fate of Draupadi. All this while, Yudhishthir was trying to pacify his burly younger brother with the most cult dialogue of them all—*'Shaant gadadhari Bheem, shaant!'*

The inventiveness of the scene and its manic energy is something that never comes across in description. Even after being seen a million times (that's about the cumulative views of the scene on YouTube), it still manages to make you double up with laughter.

And when you do manage to stop laughing and get up from the floor, you share Dhritarashtra's plaintive query that is repeated throughout the scene, *'Yeh kya ho raha hai?'*

Yes, what *was* going on? And more importantly, what was the writer smoking when he wrote this scene?

Jaane Bhi Do Yaaro: An epic scene on the Epic

An Offer You Can't Refuse: 6 Remakes Of The Godfather (or parts thereof)

*E*ver since Francis Ford Coppola brought that Italian mob boss called Vito Corleone to the screen, it redefined gangster movies in specific and movies in general. The plot, the characterisation, the acting style, the mood—all of them became benchmarks for generations of filmmakers, working on gangster films or not.

The impact of **The Godfather** has spread far and wide, India not being an exception. In any case, Indian filmmakers are quite liberal with their sources of inspiration and this one was just too good to miss.

The rise of the small-time crook to the highest rungs of gangland. The benevolent anti-hero handing out jungle justice. The heir-apparent with a fatal flaw. The prodigal younger son. His love for a modern girl and marriage to a traditional one. All these themes have appeared in many films.

First off the block was **Dharmatma**.

Three years after the original, Feroz Khan directed the first Bollywood remake and played the Michael Corleone role himself. Grand locales in Afghanistan came to replace Sicily where Hema Malini sizzled as a gypsy dancer. The traitor in the family, the refusal to get into narcotics, the level-headed consigliore (played by the dependable Iftekhar), the beating up of rapists (by the voluminous Dara Singh)—were all there.

Feroz Khan reduced the number of Corleone brothers to one—himself—and made it into a tussle between the father's (played by Premnath) illegal ways of doing good and his own straighter intentions. He replaced the broody characterisations with dazzling dances, the sombre background score with a dhinchak one and had games of bouzkashi in Afghan plains instead of shootouts in seedy New York bars.

In the original, Michael Corleone came into the limelight only towards the end. But when that role is played by the über-stylish Feroz Khan, it would have been a crying shame to waste him like that—no?

After Part I's remake, it would be interesting to look at a remake of **The Godfather Part II**.

An immigrant in a big city excels in many ways and crime is probably the most interesting of those. Like the Sicilian Vito Corleone, Velu came from the southern part of India to Bombay and rose to become the messiah of the masses—**Dayavan** (literally, the benevolent one).

Feroz Khan's Godfather fetish was completely satiated when he remade Kamal Haasan's **Nayakan** in Hindi, with Vinod Khanna in the title role.

The desi Robin Hood, who becomes the champion of his people (immigrants in an alien land) on his way to the top of the underworld, is a theme no one tires of.

In **Aatank Hi Aatank**, Aamir Khan was the son who returned to take charge of his father's underworld empire after his elder brother (Rajnikanth in one of his last Hindi roles) was killed. Aamir Khan took a leaf out of the Italian mob boss's sartorial style with gelled-back hair, a moustache and waistcoats. Occasionally, he wore suits and wielded AK-47s to kill his father's enemies. In between, he romanced Juhi Chawla and Pooja Bedi (in yawn-and-miss and blink-and-miss parts respectively).

Before he decided to cut down on his assignments and concentrate on working in one film at a time, Aamir Khan did some unbelievably ruinous movies of which this is one.

Virasat was the story of Anil Kapoor returning to his native village for a holiday with his leggy, near-firangi girlfriend (Pooja Batra) and getting caught in inter-clan rivalry. The transformation of Anil Kapoor from a US-returned rake to a responsible chieftain was quite remarkable.[20] The film was about his growing emotional attachment to the village post his father's death and as that happened, his mannerisms started to resemble his father's.

If **The Godfather** is the story of an initial outsider who eventually sacrifices many of his ideas to discharge responsibilities expected of his family, **Virasat** was exactly that.

Complementing Anil Kapoor was Tabu who delivered a fantastic performance as the village belle who got married to the new Thakur. Overall, a beautiful film from the time when Priyadarshan actually put some thought into his films.

Dynastic politics—the subject of **Rajneeti**—is best exemplified by India's greatest epic. But in a story built around the *Mahabharat*, Prakash Jha incorporated distinct shades of **The Godfather**.

---

[20] **Virasat** was based on yet another Kamal Haasan film, **Thevar Magan**, leading one to wonder whether the south Indian thespian was also a Godfather devotee.

Arjun Rampal as the volatile elder brother, who had no respect for anything except his younger brother, was manic. On the other hand, Ranbir Kapoor put in a brilliant performance as the outsider who got reluctantly sucked into the cesspool of politics in an attempt to protect family honour.

The hospital scene—a father lying badly wounded and a boorish police inspector thrashing the son when he raised doubts about the security—was a direct replica of **The Godfather**. Even the severed horse-head scene returned in a modified avatar as a stubborn adversary was scared into submission.

The Godfather is the symbol of extra-constitutional power—a parallel justice system which offers remedies where governments fail to. We have many such power centres in India of varying degrees of influence. Irrespective of their power, the title accorded to these satraps is the Hindi word for government—**Sarkar**.

Ram Gopal Verma declared in the film's opening frame that this was his tribute to Francis Ford Coppola. Closer home, he previewed the film with Shiv Sena supremo Bal Thackeray and sought his 'blessings' as the lead character was said to be based on the life of the Maratha chieftain.

And he created a Godfather like no other.

Amitabh Bachchan's silences and stares spoke volumes as he dispensed justice through his durbar. He kept chief ministers on a tight leash and controlled trade—both legal and illegal—in the city. His power was challenged by a troika of gangsters, politicians and godmen—supported by his treacherous older son. His power was multiplied by the emergence of his younger son who gave up his US business plans to take on the Mumbai underworld. And as the second generation took over the reins of power, the man became weaker but the Sarkar became stronger.

As they said in the film, '*Subhash Nagre ek aadmi ka naam hai aur Sarkar ek soch. Aadmi ko marne se pehle uski soch ko marna zaroori hai.*'

The Godfather is, after all, not a person but an idea, an image, an inspiration.

Coming Soon: 7 Clichés That Are About To Happen

*I*t would be interesting to do a count of the number of times *'Main tumhare bachche ki maa banne wali hoon'* has been said on screen. Because this is probably the most clichéd use of a cliché. This phrase has been demonstrated as a cliché in real life more times than it has been actually said on screen.

The true-blue cliché is actually *'Sab kuchh theek ho jayega'*[21] as there was a time till the end-'90s before which I had not seen a single movie without this line being spoken.

One good thing about clichés is that you start missing them when they stop happening.

For example, one of the evergreen—but unsung—clichés is the hemming and hawing around a lip-to-lip kiss. It goes something like this...

The leading pair is in—what the newspapers call—a compromising position, more often than not after the hero has dispatched a few goons. They are murmuring sweet nothings as the hero is trying to get the heroine to do things that would allow the directors to show flowers touching.

Eventually, the hero points to a body part (say, shoulder) where he is hurt. The heroine demurely kisses him there. A bulb lights up somewhere. He points to another body part (say, wrist). The heroine kisses him there as well. Now

---

[21] This dialogue received a new-age non-literal translation in **3 Idiots**— *Aal izz well!*

(usually with a mischievous smile), he points to his lip and indicates pain. Bingo![22]

And since books and websites have already been devoted to listing the biggest clichés of Bollywood, we could turn the cliché around and do a bit of crystal-gazing to figure out which are the dialogues / scenes that are going to become clichés in a few years from now.

Exposing a gay relationship

Konkona Sen Sharma has become to this what Nirupa Roy was to motherhood. She has already done it twice (**Page 3**, **Life In A Metro**) and is looking good for more. With more and more films being made on realistic gay relationships, it is only natural that closet homosexuality will have to be depicted pretty regularly.

What will make it tiresome is the way it will be shown. In both the films mentioned above, the scene unfolds in exactly the same manner in which the hetero partner (cuckold?) arrives at the apartment of the closet-gay for a celebration (Konkona was even holding exactly the same things—a bottle of wine and flowers) and sees her lover in bed with another man.

How long before a man walks in on a lesbian couple? I can bet the expression would not be the aghast one the woman had.

Signs of suicide

More and more dysfunctional relationships on screen can mean only one thing: more and more suicide attempts. And,

---

[22] Note for directors: For best results, use at least two non-sexual body parts before the lips.

as in the socials of the 1960s, a close-up of the mangalsutra signified a married woman, we will keep getting close-ups of sutured wrists to show the harried woman.

The cliché will probably not be the fact that people try to end their lives but that these characters are always women. I guess men just choose a more leisurely way of ending their lives (ref: **Devdas**) but a slashed wrist is much more amenable to cinematic drama than an x-ray of a bloated liver.

Kangana Ranaut has tried both options (**Woh Lamhe, Gangster**) and she appears perennially poised on the edge of a parapet about to jump off.

Thirty-plus

Rajesh Khanna took almost fifteen years to get out of college. He started as a college student in one of his first hits—**Do Raaste** (late '60s)—and stayed on right till **Souten** (early '80s).

The scenario of a sixteen-year-old heroine falling in love with a nineteen-year-old hero continued till Rishi Kapoor just could NOT fit into the benches of the colleges that were hired for a film shoot. This cliché's last rites were performed when the only crib against **Rang De Basanti** was about the forty-year-old Aamir Khan hovering around the gates of Delhi University. Although we never raised an eyebrow when Mithun jumped around college campuses in his mid-forties.

Now, of course, the age combos have just multiplied with old-man-old-woman (**Baghban, Pyaar Mein Twist**), older-woman-young-man (**Leela, Oops**), young-woman-old-man (**Cheeni Kum**) all elbowing out the teeny-bopper romance.

The cliché around this is the forced ridiculing of the elderly member(s) of the family, which brings about a (temporary) realisation of the difference age makes. '*Aapko toh abhi bhagwaan ka naam lena chahiye...*' is usually the unsolicited advice for the couple to go to a temple instead of a disco. And it produces an equally stereotypical angry reaction, followed by doubts on the future of the relationship... and remorse.

Of course, sometimes the line is as funny as '*Uncle ko Durex chahiye*' (in **Cheeni Kum**) but the situation is a cliché (about an old man pursuing a physical relationship) and threatening to become bigger.

Old Man + Young Woman = Durex

For adultery only

Finally, Hindi cinema has managed to have people survive pre-marital or extra-marital sex. Till as late as the '90s, the lead players of Hindi cinema either died or got widowed or got tuberculosis or took to prostitution or had to smell an anaconda's fart even if their shadows touched during a song on a rainy night. And of course, they got pregnant.

Not any more! Mallika Sherawat (in **Murder**) neither died nor got pregnant for having an extra-marital affair (but she had to repeatedly kiss Emraan Hashmi, which is probably a fate worse than death).

Jokes apart, the cliché is the way in which a married woman and man approach a liaison.

The married woman is guilty and has pangs of conscience. She pulls away from the man and even exits the room. And then she comes back for a reason (or an excuse?) and is pulled into the whole 'mess'. She usually cries after the first time. The married man—on the other hand—is an unmitigated bastard who has no such qualms.

In an ironic way, this is the Sati-Savitri cliché and it will take some time to be junked.

The jehadi recruitment

Post 9/11, there is a new villain in cinema, and Bollywood adopts it as well—the Muslim terrorist. Sometimes he is a cardboard composition of villainy and bombast, sometimes he is the chocolate boy dealt with unjustly. Either way, he is about to do an awful lot of collateral damage. And he has recruited / is recruiting a group of jehadis for a suicide mission.

The cliché here is the recruiting process. You give the prospective jehadi a gun and ask him to shoot an innocent target. He pauses, he sweats, he trembles and eventually takes a shot. Entrance test passed!

What happens to the body of the innocent? You see, the shot was a blank one. The intention was to test whether the motivation of the recruit was strong enough to make him take a shot at an innocent unknown.

The flunked hero

What Rajesh Khanna and Shashi Kapoor were to *Maa-main-pass-ho-gaya-le-beta-mooh-meetha-kar-le-yeh-kya-tum-ro-rahi-ho-yeh-to-khushi-ke-aansoo-hain-beta-kaash-tere-pitaji-aaj-zinda-hote*,[23] Ranbir Kapoor is to the failed metrosexual. In two successive films—**Wake Up Sid!** and **Rocket Singh: Salesman Of The Year**—he either flunked or passed with grace marks, winning millions of hearts outside the campuses of IIT, AIIMS and SRCC.

He is the *number-kum-hain-dimaag-nahin* guy who's forced into academics (weren't we all?), while his true calling lies elsewhere. And of course, like all underdogs, he manages to score very satisfying victories for everybody including his distributors and producers.

Intel inside. Bollywood outside.

The first Hindi film to mention a computer was **Trishul**. When Shashi Kapoor returned from abroad, he called Raakhee (his father's super-efficient secretary) a 'computer' (*ek aisi machine jo har sawaal ka theek jawaab deti hai*)! Clearly, this 'computer is always right' notion was before GIGO (Garbage In Garbage Out) was coined.

---

[23] One of the most-repeated scenes in 1970s Bollywood, involving the emotions of a just-graduated son and his maudlin mother in front of the father's portrait, is now a rich source of spoofs.

We have come a long way from that to the point that it is probably becoming mandatory for Bollywood stars to have an active virtual life. First, it was supposed to be in their real life. But now—thanks to Himesh Reshamaiyya—even film characters must dodge in and out of Facebook and Twitter.

In **Radio**, RJ Vivaan Shah chatted on Facebook while his less-enlightened colleagues were still figuring it out ('*Yaar, yeh Phesbuk hota kya hai?*'). His relationship status was 'complicated'. His listeners complained about boyfriends on porn sites. All he didn't have was a Twitter handle.

I am inclined to believe this casual weaving of online stuff into filmi conversation is about to become a trend.

We have to wait only a little bit before the original cliché is turned on its head and the hero will be compelled to ask—'*Kya main iss bachche ka baap hoon?*'

Do you remember the first film that happened in?[24]

---

[24] KK's character in **Life In A Metro** is a gent suspicious of his own paternity, who asks his wife (Shilpa Shetty) this.

4

PEOPLE LIKE US

'Mere paas maa hai.'—SHASHI KAPOOR in **Deewaar**

'Mera baap chor hai.'—Tattoo on Amitabh Bachchan's arm in the same film

*T*here are a million people around us—friends, relatives, professionals. And they became so much larger than life when they are on the silver screen. They are more emotional. They are more humorous. They are more pure. They are more dishonest.

And some of them are deadlier...

- ◆ Cine-Maa: 15 Mothers
- ◆ The Baap of all Lists: 12 Fathers
- ◆ Phoolon ka, Taaron ka: 12 Brother-Sister Pairs
- ◆ Salaamat Rahe: 15 Friends
- ◆ Class Acts: 10 Star Teachers
- ◆ Author, Author!: 7 Men of Letters
- ◆ Canvas on Celluloid: 8 Artists
- ◆ Jab Tak Suraj Chand Rahega: 10 Politicians
- ◆ Killer Kaun?: 13 Clues to Identify Killers

Cine-Maa: 15 Mothers

*I*f one character distinguishes Hindi cinema from the rest of the world, it is the Mother. No other country in the world has so many different variations on the mother-son relationship (almost never mother-daughter) as in Bollywood. And thanks to the predominance of 'formula' in Bollywood, one can even categorise the mothers of Bollywood and list the 'top moms'.

Mother India

Starting with Nargis in the role of the heroic mom, this is the self-righteous mother who puts nation, honour and duty before son. So, the son may have killed a guy double his size for her and may have brought her an apartment block in south Bombay but she would still give him up for the greater good of society. Or better, shoot him. Nargis showed the way as she gunned down her dacoit son to save the honour of her village.

The mother's dilemma between love and duty was brilliantly articulated when Nirupa Roy (in **Deewaar**) handed over the gun to her police officer son and 'prayed' for his weapon to remain steady—'*Bhagwaan kare goli chalate waqt tere haath na kaanpe...*' Having done her duty as a woman, she left to wait for her errant son immediately afterwards. '*Aurat apna farz nibha chuki. Ab maa apne bete ka intezaar karne jaa rahi hai.*'

Agneepath's mother (Rohini Hattangadi) was a watered-down version of this character as she berated her son for his gangster ways, and promptly forgave him when he promised 'to return to the village'. Eventually, the son died on the mother's lap—having cleansed himself of all sin by passing through the path of fire.

One of the recent avatars of this mother has been in **Vaastav**, where an obviously doting mother (Reema Lagoo) shot her gangster son (Sanjay Dutt) partly for his wrong-doings and partly to end his sufferings as a fugitive and a drug-addict.

This character received a 180-degree makeover in **Aatish** in which the mother (Tanuja) defended her smuggler son's (Sanjay Dutt) actions to her police officer son (a wimpy Atul Agnihotri) by pointing out that his elder brother's criminal takings had funded his education and career.

Hip Mom

Reema Lagoo broke off her B-grade shackles and emerged as the nation's coolest mother as **Maine Pyar Kiya** became the first movie to have a 'mom' instead of a 'mother'. Here was a really cool lady who threw darts, was okay with a bob-cut (though not for her own daughter-in-law), actually mouthed the word 'mini skirt' and even dyed her hair. She was such a relief from the grey-haired, saintly souls that she had millions of similar roles to do after that one.

Farida Jalal of **DDLJ** was the other iconic representation of the Hip Mom—when she asked her daughter about her dream man and even egged her to elope. Her son-in-law was, of course, a chauvinistic wet blanket and refused to run away without the dad's permission... Somebody slap him!

After these two, almost each of the Yash Chopra genre movies has had a variation of this kind of mom.

An extreme variation on this kind of hip mom is the smoking and promiscuous kind—made famous by Mita Vasisht in **Oops**. The lady thought nothing of having an affair with her son's friend and went about in slinky clothes, with a sultry look and a lighted cigarette for most of the film.

Monster-in-Law / Step Mom

Now, there are the moms who are after blood. It is usually the rebellious daughters-in-law's blood—though property, villainous uncles and children from the husband's earlier marriages bring about similar levels of dementia. Of course, in all such 'social' films, the mother never dies. She just reforms.

Bindu and Lalita Pawar are the most famous practitioners of this genre.

Bindu's role in **Biwi Ho To Aisi** was one of the greatest examples of unintended hilarity in Hindi cinema. Her refrain of '*Secretary, follow me*' and constant harangue against her bahu Rekha were stuff legends are made of. All this while her wimpy son (Farooq Shaikh) looked on balefully.

Aruna Irani in **Beta** had one such epic battle with her daughter-in-law (Madhuri Dixit) as the step-son (Anil

Kapoor in the most undeserved title role of all times) looked on, smiled foolishly, was torn between the two super-heroines and finally got poisoned before rising from the dead to save his mother.

Tragedy Queens

These are the Single Moms—women who are punished for having sex before getting married. Actually, they did get married in the eyes of God but that does not count in the real world. So, the object of their affection either dies on them or deserts them after impregnating them during a night of passion. They are left to a life of sacrifice and determination to bring up their sons (always *sons*) so that they can roshan family names or take badla.

It was the former in the case of **Aradhana** as Sharmila's son grew up to be yet another dashing air force pilot with the same drop-dead good looks as his father. The mother survived unwed motherhood, a jail sentence and very bad make-up to bring up a son as her would-have-been husband would have wanted.

Badla was the objective in **Trishul** as Waheeda's son grew up to take on top industrialist R.K. Gupta for his mother's humiliation. He did not fear death or destruction because he was used to his mother's slow descent into death, and he articulated that with an explosive line like '*Jisne pachchees baras apni maa ko har roz thoda thoda marte dekha ho, usse maut se kya dar lagega?*' And as her dutiful son, he repaid his illegitimate father by going all around Delhi putting up boards of Shanti Constructions, which were taller than RK Group's.

Mandakini in **Ram Teri Ganga Maili** probably falls in this same category but nobody remembers anything from that film except the waterfall song.

Heartless Moms

These are the terrible mothers who abandon their families either on the provocation of evil relatives or—even worse—to pursue a career. But the Bollywood mom NEVER leaves her children. So each one of them comes right back, sacrificing wealth and career to be with their brats.

The desi version of **Kramer Vs Kramer—Akele Hum Akele Tum**—had Manisha Koirala leaving super-chauvinistic-really-atrocious hubby (Aamir Khan) to put up a fight for a career in films. Then, horror of horrors—she got into an ugly custody battle for which the now-martyred Aamir had to sell off his precious musical compositions.

Karisma Kapoor, the rich kid, had a whirlwind romance, quick marriage and quicker son with taxi-driver **Raja Hindustani** before she left him at the behest of her 'evil' mamaji.[25] Though she came back just in time for the climax in which her laadla son was tossed around like a football in the Super Bowl—by the aforementioned mamaji.

Honourable Mentions

Aruna Irani had a classic 'mom'-ent in **Doodh Ka Karz**, when she breast-fed a snake (yes, a 100-per-cent authentic, ISO-certified serpent and not an ichhadhari one) along with

---

[25] What's with Aamir? Even his real-life wife left him.

her son (who grew up to be Jackie Shroff). Of course, her milky ways earned her the eternal gratitude of the snake, who returned time and again to help her (human) son.

Saawan Kumar Tak (of **Souten** fame) made a film initially called 'Mother 98' (because it was supposed to release in that year) but it was released as **Mother** three years later. It had Rekha in the title role and the object of the game was to find out which of her three lovers was the father of her daughter. The contestants were Rakesh Roshan, Jeetendra and Randhir Kapoor.

The Baap Of All Lists: 12 Fathers

*T*he Father Figure is there in many movies in different ways. Sometimes they create an impact with their presence and sometimes with their absence. A taskmaster, a darling, a hero, a villain—he's been all of those characters and more.

And just like the iconic mothers, you can segregate them in buckets and identify the most iconic fathers in each.

The Photographic Father

An alarmingly large number of fathers in Hindi movies have been two-dimensional. They have existed only in photographs for their widows to stand in front of and declare tearfully to the son, 'Kaash tere Babuji aaj zinda hote...'

The most striking example of this was **Jaane Tu Ya Jaane Na**—in which Naseeruddin Shah showed just how good great actors can be, even when they are confined within a frame. As a *Ranjhaur ke Rathore*, he was quite sick of the pacifist bull his wife was feeding his son and from his perch, he made his displeasure clear. And in the end, he had a victory of his own.

The Missing Father

In **Deewaar**, the father—for most part—was missing. He was only seen on the tattoo of his elder son which was not just a mark on his left forearm but on his soul, his existence, his entire being. The son didn't understand why he ran away. He didn't know that his father had made a huge sacrifice for him and the family. He was just plain angry with him.

When his turn came, he didn't run away because he was not about to let his unborn son face the same accusation he did—'*Mera baap chor hai*'.

In **Masoom**, the son was thrust upon the father suddenly—when he wasn't even aware of his existence. The illegitimate son entered the happy family of his father, without knowing it and yet enjoying the experience. The son's affection for the father and the father's restrained emotions were gut-wrenchingly real.

In a poignant scene, Jugal Hansraj drew a bespectacled figure and introduced it to Naseer as his father. Naseer asked, '*Aap ke papa chashma pehnte hain?*' When the boy said yes, he paused and slowly took off his glasses.[26]

The Hitler

With more films on the education system that go beyond '*Maa, main pass ho gaya...*' it is only natural that the over-ambitious (but well-meaning) parent would be depicted in some form or the other. The name of this category is taken from **3 Idiots**, where Farhan's father was referred to as Hitler Qureishi. Here was a man who thought ninety-one per-cent was a disastrous performance but at the same time, installed

---

[26] Naseeruddin Shah seems to have made a career out of playing illegitimate fathers. He was last seen in such a role as artist Salman Habib who abandoned his pregnant girlfriend and went off to Spain in **Zindagi Na Milegi Dobara** (only to be tracked down by his son).

an AC in his son's room so that he could sleep well. He thought photography was a dumb career choice but gave in when he realised that it made his son really happy.

You could say Ishaan's father in **Taare Zameen Par** would have gone on to become Mr Qureishi if he hadn't met Ram Shankar Nikumbh.

One hideous character—falling under the same heading—whose writ ran farther than academics was Bhairav Singh of **Udaan**. Imperious in nature, impervious to others' wishes and often violent, here was a man who made one want to wring his neck. Ronit Roy put in the performance of a lifetime to portray a man whom everyone hated from the bottom of their hearts.

The Romance Killer

For decades, this gentleman of regal countenance has stormed down the ornate stairs of his haveli to stop his daughter (or son) from marrying a person unworthy of his khandaan. And obviously, the suitor never did anything to help his cause.

Look at the best example. In **Dilwale Dulhania Le Jayenge**, Shah Rukh vandalised Amrish Puri's store, ran away with beer and then tried to run away with his daughter as well. Amrish Puri—on his part—wagged his never-ending finger, upped the volume of his baritone and made his eyes so big, you could play ice hockey on them.

But then for all their fury, these dads are dads after all. When he realised how much the upstart from London loved his daughter (and maybe, what his net worth was), he let her go and garnered the maximum applause for that.

(Repeat after me in Amrish Puri style, '*Jaa Simran jaa...*')

The Friend

DDLJ had a counterpoint too.

Shah Rukh was brought up by a father who spoilt his son silly. He raised a toast to his son's great achievement of failing in England ('*Hum toh sab Hindustan mein fail huye. Tu ne London mein fail hoke dikha diya...*') and urged him to live life to the fullest.

First of all, he was not Dad. He was Pops. He was a friend who shared a beer. He was a confidant who conspired to get his son the girl he loved. And under the friendly banter, there was the doubled love of a single parent. ('*Main sirf tera baap nahin, teri maa bhi hoon.*')

The Fighter

After the father dies, the son grows up and takes revenge for his death. But sometimes, it is the son who dies, and the father who takes up arms.

And in the most famous example of this, the father did not take up arms in a literal sense. But in a metaphorical way, ex-headmaster B.V. Pradhan found a new meaning of his life after his son passed away. In **Saaransh**, Anupam Kher played the role of a lifetime as he took on the recalcitrant state, first in a bid to get his son's ashes home and then to seek justice for a helpless young woman.

The Priest

All fathers are not biological. Some of them are theological too.

The familiar, benevolent figure in the white gown uttering words of solace is someone we have grown used to. After all, he's the go-to man for confessing our sins and getting sane advice that we eventually ignore.

Naseeruddin Shah in **Kabhi Haan Kabhi Naa** is one such lovable Father—who was constantly ticking off his wayward parishioners and commandeering vehicles to hitch rides in opposite directions. When met with protests, he inevitably said that all roads led to God. So there.

The Odd Ones

And finally, we have two oddball fathers who were way out of the ordinary and, quite coincidentally, they were both played on-screen by two actors related to each other.

In **Paa**, Abhishek Bachchan was the father of Amitabh Bachchan, a patient of progeria (an advanced aging disease)—a very unusual casting choice. Writer-director R. Balki said that he got the idea in a meeting where Amitabh was fooling around while Abhishek was all serious. So, he researched and dug out a disease that could make this happen. Simple.

Amitabh's make-up and acting, however, were not that simple.

The father who became the son

And finally, the last word must belong to the 'father of them all'—**Shahenshah**. You know, the guy who said '*Rishtey mein toh hum tumhare baap hote hain...*'

Phoolon Ka, Taaron Ka:
12 *Brother-Sister Pairs*

*B*rothers and sisters in Hindi cinema should be the easiest to write about since they appear in every second film, and a sister's rape and brutal murder is always the chief reason for docile village bumpkins to become AK-47 toting vigilantes. Either that scenario, or maudlin weddings in which the sisters tearfully sit in the doli for which brothers have worked night-and-day to accumulate the necessary dowry.[27]

Interestingly, **3 Idiots** injected a vial of wicked humour into the usual despondency of unmarried sisters. All the clichés of *bimaar baap, lachaar maa* and *kunwari behen* were brought together in a *triveni sangam* of spoofs as Raju Rastogi's unwed sister popped up every now and then, as a potential bride for Farhan Qureishi. And a potentially insignificant track in the film became a laugh riot.

However, it is not merely about all the brothers-and-sisters in the world. It is about star pairs in the sibling domain.

The most high-powered brother-sister duo in Bollywood has to be the Aishwarya Rai-Shah Rukh Khan pairing in **Josh**. As Max and Shelley leading the Eagle gang in Goa,

---

[27] Incidentally, it is always *bhai ki padhaai* and *behen ki shaadi* for which a man works. It is never the other way round.

Ash and SRK were twins in the film. Despite putting up a decent show as siblings with typical over-protectiveness, rivalry and affection in equal measure, they could not save the film from sinking and thus, nearly putting an end to the casting of top stars as siblings.

Aishwarya has played sister to two of Bollywood's biggest stars—SRK and Big B.

She was the sister of her real-life father-in-law in **Hum Kisise Kum Nahin**, where he played a shrink and she was being wooed simultaneously by Ajay Devgn and Sanjay Dutt (who was also a mafia don and AB's patient). Shades of **Analyse This** (starring Robert De Niro and Billy Crystal) crept into this intended-to-be comic caper by David Dhawan but nothing seemed to click.

Talking of top stars as siblings, **Andhaa Kaanoon** paired Hema Malini as Rajnikanth's elder sister—putting a distaff twist to the usual Bollywood formula of a righteous outlaw and his dutiful blood-relative.

Hema Malini did everything to stop her brother from killing their father's killer (including wearing a havaldar's cap at a jaunty angle) but the now-red-eyed-now-white-eyed Rajni escaped to the accompaniment of tossed cigarettes and flaring nostrils.

No sibling discussion can be complete without a mention of Sooraj Barjatya and his films. The poster-child of Great Indian Family Values gave half of India and their bhabhis diabetes with his saccharine-sweet brothers and sisters living under one huge roof.

In **Hum Saath-Saath Hain**, we had two reigning stars (Salman and Saif Ali Khan) and one major character artiste

(Mohnish Behl) playing brother to Neelam—one of the top heroines in her time. They all ate together, prayed together, pulled legs together, smiled together, simpered together and even whimpered together before getting one big group hug... Bhaiyya!

All people remember of **Trishul** are the Three Faces of Man—Sanjeev Kumar, Amitabh Bachchan and Shashi Kapoor—and all they speculate on is if the rivalry between two construction tycoons is inspired by real life. What they forget is that Poonam Dhillon—fresh from the success of **Noorie**—was Shashi Kapoor's sister (and Amitabh's step-sister). She was the archetypal spoilt kid sister—who sang inane songs (*Gapoochi gapoochi gum gum*), drove Merc convertibles recklessly and fell in love with short men in yellow pullovers. Her wedding—or whatever was left of it—ultimately formed the climax of the film.

Smita Patil was the reigning deity of art cinema. Mithun Chakraborty was the god of pelvic thrusts. Nobody really expected them to come together but they did.

In **Dance Dance**, Smita was the elder sister who brought up her snotty kid brother to make him the country's biggest all-singing-all-dancing star. And she was not merely the backroom manager but the lead vocalist in the band as well. She eventually married the drummer, Shakti Kapoor (inexplicably called Resham) and settled down in happy domesticity. And if you know good ol' Shakti, you wouldn't dare think that was the end of it.

In **Fiza**, we had two huge stars as siblings. Hrithik Roshan was on his way up and Karisma Kapoor was on her way out.

Written and directed by noted film critic Khalid Mohamed, the film was a sister's quest for her missing brother, an unusual enough storyline. Add to that the complexities of a Muslim youth's alienation post the Bombay riots of 1993, his allegiance to terror networks, and Sushmita Sen's item song while his sister was looking for him—and you have **Fiza**. The film did not do too well—as movies featuring top stars in sibling roles never seem to do.

There is a general custom in India of tying a rakhi to neighbourhood goons, to ward off their clumsy (and potentially dangerous) romantic advances. Conversely, brothers of bombshells have thankless jobs as they are entrusted with the aforementioned task... of protecting the sisters. Leading the list are Anil Kapoor and Nana Patekar, who had the unenviable task of shepherding Katrina Kaif in **Welcome**. On one hand, they had a bespectacled sissy like Akshay Kumar whom their sister was hopelessly in love with. On the other, they had international dons called RDX (Feroz Khan, quite naturally) to ward off.

In recent times, one of the funniest—and most natural—sibling relationships has been portrayed by Genelia D'Souza and Prateik Babbar in **Jaane Tu Ya Jaane Na**. There were no maudlin moments, no promises to protect honours and no rakhis either. Instead, there was the beautiful wistfulness of a brother who saw his sister make other friends and a sister's quiet pride at her brother's talent. And several kick-ass sibling banter moments. One of which stands out for its deadpan humour:

Genelia: *Do minute baith jaoon?*
Prateik: *Tera ghar, tera bum—baith.*

My Brother Nikhil had Juhi Chawla and Sanjay Suri playing the siblings in a tragic tale. Built around the theme of homosexuality, AIDS and our intolerance of both, debutant director Onir put together a fantastic depiction of sisterly love and helplessness. Sanjay Suri—not an A-list star then—created a niche for himself as an actor of sensitivity and a producer of distinction as he went on to do several off-beat films of value.

There have been many real-life brothers and sisters in Bollywood too, all wildly successful and at least one big enough to become a spoof.

In **Golmaal Returns**, Tusshar Kapoor's character had a sister called Ekta—who watched soaps, got totally immersed in them and made important life decisions based on what she learnt from the serials. Played by Kareena Kapoor, Ekta was not beyond using the names of popular soaps in her daily conversation and the rest of the gang was not beyond thrashing Tusshar just for being his sister's brother.

As the last word, it has to be *that* film. The one with *the* Brother-Sister Song, even though the filmi brother was old enough to be the sister's father in real life.

And the story was the mirror image of **Fiza** as the brother went looking for his sister, Jasbir, in the dope dens of hippie-infested Kathmandu. In between, there were at least four more hit songs (including the grown-up version of *Phoolon ka taaron ka*), estranged parents, a stolen deity, Mumtaz, and a girl called Janice who urged us to take a puff... **Hare Rama Hare Krishna**.

Salaamat Rahe: 15 Friends

*E*ver since one blind boy latched on to the elbow of a disabled boy, singing plaintive songs on the empty streets of 1950's Mumbai, Bollywood latched on to the formula that would not be given up EVER! Friends have gone on bikes with sidecars, on horseback, in Mercedes convertibles and even on hearses... basically, from here to eternity. Though some pretence of variety is made, there are essentially three genres of 'friendship' in Hindi cinema.

The Sidekick: Oye pappe!

This is applicable when the solo hero is either too intense (wooden?) to carry off comic scenes or too big a star for the producer to afford a second hero. The sidekick anchors the comic sub-plot, without getting involved in any philosophical discussions and is restricted to buffoonery and assistance during eloping.

To start off, we have to rewind to the 1960s and get Rajendra Nath into view as Shammi Kapoor's ubiquitous henchman. The most abiding memory of this comic genius is probably **An Evening in Paris**, where he played Sardar Makkhan Singh and romanced the heroine's sidekick with a brilliant invitation to a secluded spot—'*Aaja* Honey / *Mausam hai* funny / *Charon taraf sannata* / *Itthe koi na marega mainu chaanta*'. Slapstick was never this poetic.

Coming to the 1990s, we had Deepak Tijori as the leading 'friend' of the industry, playing second fiddle to most of the leading stars of his time. Films with him as the solo hero bombed spectacularly.

He started with a not-so-big star in **Aashiqui**. As Rahul Roy's resourceful friend in the film, he had a funny hand-gesture that became quite the rage in college campuses at that time.

The most famous female exponent of this character is Guddi Maruti.

Despite the predominance of male friendships in Bollywood, this is one glass ceiling that was completely shattered. In her many—almost identical—roles, she overshadowed pretty much everybody else with her girth and glee.

And finally, we have the Ultimate Sidekick whose character has got completely welded to the name of the hero, helped in creating a multi-film franchise and been responsible for a large part of the series' popularity—Munna Bhai and Circuit.

In Arshad Warsi, we had the Don's henchman who was the right mix of menace and masti, reality and fantasy, humour and emotion. Without exaggeration, we can happily borrow a line from their film and say, '*Jab tak sooraj chand rahega, Munna-Circuit ka naam rahega.*'

The Sacrificer: Dost dost na raha...[28]

And then there is the most popular geometrical figure in Bollywood—the triangle.

Employed by producers without the budget for two leading pairs (and thus calling the film a multi-starrer), this

---

[28] In an attempt to steer clear of the obvious, two films about great sacrifices by friends—**Dostana** and **Yaarana**—are not listed.

Friends who pee together, stay together

is how you have three stars, get the 'extra' one to sacrifice so that the 'pair' can live happily ever after.

And since it is always about the friend and never about the girl, the reason for sacrifice isn't always the girl.

One of the biggest hits of the genre with three major stars—Raj Kapoor, Rajendra Kumar and Vyjayanthimala—was **Sangam**. Poor-boy fell in love with rich-girl who fell in love with rich-boy after poor-boy supposedly died, but married poor-boy when he came back from the dead. Don't even bother to keep track of this three-line plot since it took the director the better of four hours to narrate it on screen.[29]

Shot extensively in Europe, the strangest bit of the triangle was the fact that Raj Kapoor got the girl in the end but still sang the Anthem of the Betrayed—*Dost dost na raha...*

---

[29] **Sangam** had two intervals when it first released in the theatres.

He apparently apologised to Rajendra Kumar later, saying it was too good a song to give up.

Feroz Khan's crime caper was named after the philosophy of sacrifice and had an energetic title-song on the many therapeutic effects of **Qurbani** (among other things, *Allah ko pyaari hai qurbani...*). Feroz Khan and Vinod Khanna were both head over heels in love with Zeenat Aman. With Zeenie Baby slinking around in green bikinis and sheer thigh-slit gowns, you could hardly blame them. She divided her screen-time and songs equally between the two heroes and remained blissfully unaware of their feelings—till the last scene. And after the usual drama of misunderstandings and accusations, Feroz Khan exercised the Director's Prerogative (see above) and got Vinod Khanna to take a bullet.

Not all films have to end with a death, though.

In **Saajan**, the heroine fell in love with a poet whose identity was assumed by a handsome rake and she had a perfect boyfriend—uniting a poet's mind and a hunk's body. Of course, the poet and the hunk were the best of friends and they both relinquished their love for the other's sake without asking the lady in question whom she would prefer. Eventually, she did come up with a point of view. This was the 1990s, after all. And soon, one of the two gentlemen handed over the lady to the other and walked off with a smile.

Shah Rukh Khan made his name as a tragic hero—who never got the girl but died trying.

In **Deewana**, he was a spoilt brat in love with a widow but before he could move from singing-in-the-valleys to consummating-a-marriage, the lady's husband returned from the dead. **Deewana** deserves a mention in this list not because one of the two male leads died, but that the usual Rule of Bollywood Triangles was violated and the first person in love with the girl did not get her. If you think about it, all films till now had the second lead as an interloper who always died/left. This film broke that rule.

The Greatest Film Ever Made with The Greatest Star Cast Ever Assembled also had The Greatest Friendship Anthem Ever Composed.

Yeh dosti hum nahin todenge was—and remains—one of the most hummed songs as two fast friends did unbelievable things with a motorcycle, a sidecar and a two-sided coin. Their friendship remained tongue-in-cheek as Jai tried to marry off his friend in a manner you reserve for your worst enemies while Veeru had no stated use of his friend except to babysit his children. Except in the final showdown, when Jai pitched in with a non-romantic sacrifice.

When initial box-office reports of **Sholay** came in as lukewarm, the team debated whether to re-shoot the end to make Jai live on. Thank God they didn't because Bollywood's most perfect film is so much better because of the slight heartbreak at the end.

The Eventual Lover:
Ladka ladki kabhi dost nahin ban sakte...

This is the To-Become-Sexual Friendship. Bollywood has never been able to keep heroes and heroines from pawing each other—eventually. The progression from friends to lovers happens only when the heroine (initially a tomboy) starts to develop femininity. Basically, a guy finds a girl (sexually) unattractive when she is playing basketball or getting into fisticuffs. The moment she puts on false eyelashes, Tarun Tahiliani lehengas and Saroj Khan-induced coquettishness, he gets a hard-on from here to Ludhiana and rides off into the sunset with her.

Maine Pyar Kiya was the first time the lead players of a romantic film did not get into mock-quarrels or a battle of one-upmanship. They became friends. And they did not say 'sorry' or 'thank you' either—by some strange code of their friendship. Prem and Suman remained the best of friends (for all of one song and three scenes) till some one pointed out 'ladka ladki kabhi dost nahin ban sakte'—and nobody explained the concept better.

Incidentally, **MPK** managed to incorporate two kinds of Bollywood friendship—Sidekick (Salman and Laxmikant Berde) and Sexual (Salman and Bhagyashree)—in the same film.

Rahul thought love started with friendship (*Pyaar dosti hai*) and that lovers should be friends first. In **Kuch Kuch Hota Hai**, he happily made friends—and then tied the knot—with college-belle Tina while his best friend Anjali was left bouncing a basketball. Of course, his pronouncement came back to him via his dead wife's letters and a precocious daughter. And he had to meet Anjali once again. Except this time, she had a hunk by her side, whom she was engaged to.

Again, two kinds of friendship: Sacrifice (Salman and Shah Rukh) and Sexual (Shah Rukh and Kajol). Again, a record-breaking hit. Is there a formula here?

Jaane Tu Ya Jaane Na had all the ingredients of this genre of buddy films. Tomboy heroine—check. Friendship mistaken as love—check. Promises to find mates for each other—check. Boorish boyfriend of heroine—check. Incompatible girlfriend of hero—check. Late realisation of love—check. Déjà vu—check.

In fact, the director very cleverly channelised the déjà vu into a plot device by turning the story around and narrating it in flashback. You always knew the boy and girl would marry, right? You only wanted to know *how*.

Khubsoorat is a slightly sly entry into the ladka-ladki friendship list because the two friends were Ashok Kumar and his would-be daughter-in-law, Rekha.

Rekha started a game to point out to her sister's conservative in-laws that a girlfriend-boyfriend thing can't be all that bad. She deduced that since Ashok Kumar was neither a female nor her enemy, he could only be her boyfriend—thus embarrassing him ceaselessly. And in the end, Ashok Kumar returned the compliment by calling Rekha his girlfriend. Keeping the family audience in mind, Rekha turned suitably coy and insisted on being called bahu. As I said, '*Ladka ladki kabhi...*'

The Final Two

The two best buddy films—**Dil Chahta Hai** and **3 Idiots**—are the most difficult to slot into any of the above types. Despite one of the friends in both being a huge star (Aamir Khan), the other two had well-developed characters and backstories. There was an air of sacrifice in both though no sexual tension between the friends. They were both as real as friendship got in real life, and friendship sometimes means nothing more than having cake, getting drunk and pulling legs. And of course, believing you when love affairs with teachers were confided.

Class Acts: 10 Star Teachers

*T*he college is a common setting for—well—college romances. Heroes on the wrong side of forty have often been seen wooing heroines on the right side of forty (but only just) on the corridors and lawns of H.S. College of Arts & Commerce. The dashing leading men and women of Bollywood have almost always been the students, leaving the act of teaching to the supporting cast. Scratching at the blackboard while love notes are being passed around elsewhere is *so* not fun.

But there have been a few occasions when the stars have gone on to teach as well—sometimes as the strict disciplinarian, sometimes as the friendly guide. Admittedly, the actual act of teaching has been relatively less portrayed in films.

Dharmendra was supposed to be the professor in **Chupke Chupke**. As Parimal Tripathi, he was the star botany professor (a.k.a. *ghaas-phoos ke daktar*), whose books were read by students far and wide. He played the watchman, the driver, the husband, the friend and occasionally even the fool—but he completely, totally, entirely forgot to play the teacher.

But that's not why this film is in this list. His friend—professor of English, Sukumar Sinha (played brilliantly by Amitabh Bachchan)—came in with a twist. He was co-opted to impersonate Parimal Tripathi, as part of an elaborate practical joke. And the English professor had to teach botany to a beautiful girl. Despite his heroic attempts to plug *Julius Caesar* as a 'sublime tragedy', he had no option but to memorise the functions of 'corolla' late in the night to conduct tuitions in the morning.

From being a reluctant teacher, Amitabh was pitched into the role of a full-time college professor in the first of his two roles in **Kasme Vaade**. Though, like most Bollywood professors, he was more gainfully engaged in keeping his spoilt brat of a brother (Randhir Kapoor) out of trouble, singing songs on his birthday and wooing his artist girlfriend (Rakhee). Not much screen time was wasted in class, where he was seen teaching Hindi poetry and throwing rogue students out of class for aiming paper planes at him! The lines that he discussed in class were from the poetry of Harivanshrai Bachchan and talked about 'the rush of life' (*jeevan ke aapadhapi mein...*).

> *Bonus Movie:* In **Mohabbatein**, though, there is no ambiguity. We knew exactly what he taught. He taught *Anushaasan*—which he said with as much passion as Baba Ramdev reserves for his breathing exercises. As the headmaster of Gurukul, he seemed to be only the administrative head as music classes were better left to frivolous people.

Spectacles are the easiest props in Bollywood to signify erudition. Anil Kapoor appeared as a schoolteacher in **Andaz** with over-sized ones, just in case everyone thought our favourite neighbourhood tapori was not intellectual enough to be associated with academics. But then, academics were strictly avoided as a love triangle between the teacher, his wife (Juhi Chawla) and a student (Karisma Kapoor—in the mandatory minis of a girl student) developed. In any case, Anil Kapoor's erudition would have been terribly misplaced in a school—hilariously named Nalanda—which counted Shakti Kapoor among its students.

Oh—Anil did teach the students. How to eliminate terrorists who attack schools—a very useful life lesson, as you have seen.

In the title role of **Sir**, Naseeruddin Shah entered with a rain song. Err, not the usual kind. He walked into a classroom on a rainy day and immediately escorted his entire class to a glasshouse (presumably, on the college roof) for a session of music. He good-naturedly told his students that they would anyway copy and pass their exams but such a wonderful day was not to be wasted in class.

WHERE IS NASEERUDDIN SHAH AND WHY WASN'T HE MY TEACHER IN COLLEGE?

He was soon employed by mafia don Velji-bhai (Paresh Rawal) to coach his stammering daughter (Pooja Bhatt) into confidence and that was the end of any classes in college. Dialogue-training Pooja, stopping gang-wars in Mumbai, keeping Paresh Rawal from killing his daughter's suitor AND going on college picnics constitute a full-time job, you see.

True to his lover-boy image, Shah Rukh Khan has never indulged in any serious teaching. He has once been seen as the games teacher in **Chamatkar**—where his chief contribution to a cricket victory was to negotiate the participation of a ghost (Naseeruddin Shah) to assist his losing team. Before anyone screams blue murder, let me quickly assure them that the opponents were cheating very badly.

On the other occasion, he walked into the Cradle of Educational Discipline (see earlier) handing out flowers and playing the violin, offering to teach music to students. The headmaster thought it was a waste of time but indulged him anyway. As is normal for Yash Raj heroes with violins and smart pullovers, SRK floored the entire school with his music and held open-air classes with many students till... Till, he gave the heroes the bright idea of eloping with their lady-loves.

From being a reluctant teacher, SRK went on to become an even more reluctant student when he—as Major Ram—went undercover to guard the general's daughter in **Main Hoon Na**. Part of his reluctance vanished as he landed in picturesque Darjeeling to attend school. The remaining parts vanished when the chemistry teacher, Chandni Chopra, walked in through the school gates. Sushmita Sen turned out to be *that* teacher we all have crushes on—multiplied by Avogadro's number. She was seen in the posters of the film with the formula of benzoic acid written on the board behind her but in the film, she did no teaching and was only seen in shimmering chiffons giving grooming tips to Amrita Rao.

Taare Zameen Par is probably the only film where the teacher spent substantial screen-time doing what he was supposed to do. As the stand-in art teacher Ram Shankar Nikumbh, Aamir Khan directed himself and Darsheel Safary to deliver one of the best adult-child combinations in the history of Bollywood. Appearing only after the interval, the teacher's character was the catalyst in the blooming of the talented, dyslexic kid. From letting the child express his talent to coaching him to overcome his disability and from convincing headmasters to counselling parents, Aamir was the teacher-from-heaven.

In **Paathshaala**, Shahid Kapoor was an English teacher at Saraswati Vidya Mandir, seen scrawling William Wordsworth's name (if not his poems) on blackboards. But Wordsworth's poetry was no match for Bollywood lyrics and Shahid was soon doubling as the music teacher and wooing the school nutritionist (Ayesha Takia).[30] Needless to say, music teachers (even part-time ones) are cannon fodder for stern headmasters—in this case, Nana Patekar—and a confrontation suitably brought the climax.

> *Bonus Movie:* While on the topic of Shahid Kapoor, we might as well point out his ex-girlfriend's one teaching assignment. After eloping (and being dumped) in **Jab We Met**, Kareena Kapoor was taken under the wing of a nun and started teaching in a convent. For brief bits within a song, Kareena was shown writing desultorily on the blackboard—before she was rescued by Shahid.

After spending many years as a college student romancing Neetu Singh, Rishi Kapoor returned as maths teacher Santosh Duggal in **Do Dooni Chaar**. The film zipped through the manadatory elements of a middle-class teacher's life—confiscating video games in school, rushing

---

[30] Ayesha Takia is an inspired choice for playing a nutritionist because she started her career—as a child actor—in a TV commercial for Complan. And while she was the 'Complan Girl', Shahid Kapoor was the 'Complan Boy'.

to tuition class, disciplining naughty students, soaking in the adulation of loyal ex-students and maintaining idealism amid the heartbreaks—on his trusted scooter, fondly called Duggal Express. With wife Neetu Singh in an anti-glam but marvellous role, Rishi Kapoor brought a heart-warming dignity to the teacher's character as he constantly balanced his books to make $2 + 2 = 4$ (and not 5, as his uncle famously did about two decades earlier).

When education gets contaminated by commerce and politics, only the most idealistic and charismatic of teachers can rescue it. In Prakash Jha's **Aarakshan**, Amitabh Bachchan was Dr Prabhakar Anand, the principal of Shakuntala Thukral Mahavidyalay. He was a teacher who could walk out of a job for his principles as well as make Bernoulli's Theorem look really simple to everybody.

Partly based on a person who started Super 30 (where meritorious students from disadvantaged backgrounds were given free tuition for IIT entrance), Amitabh's character was really the ideal teacher—strict yet kind, serious yet approachable, solid yet fun. As he kept saying in the film—QED (Quite Easily Done).

Author, Author!
7 Men Of Letters

*B*ollywood was never about high literature. Sure, Bimal Roy made the odd Saratchandra novel into a social film but that was that. The overwhelming majority of filmi fodder has come from the made-to-order familiarity of Bollywood screenwriters. Till recently, even bound scripts were a rarity in tinsel town—leave aside bound novels.

That hasn't stopped Bollywood from having poets and novelists infesting their films. Dreamy-eyed men of letters have spewed poetic lines and ornate words, enthralling—or pissing off—millions.

In **Pyaasa**, Vijay (Guru Dutt) was the archetypal impoverished poet. He was unemployed, misunderstood and radical. And like the true-blue unsung artiste (think Van Gogh, but with both ears), he managed to remain unsold in his lifetime. Only when the false news of his death spread and his girlfriend got his poetry published (as a collection titled *Parchhaiyan*), he became hugely popular though other people duly took credit and the royalties. Vijay made a proper filmi (re-)entry with his trademark poetry renouncing the world, the world of mansions, thrones and crowns (gasp, a Communist!). And promptly went back into oblivion. Did he write again? Who knows?

Anand opened with an awards ceremony, where Dr Bhaskar Banerjee was the recipient of the Saraswati Puraskar (instituted by one Rustomjee Trust) for his autobiographical book—*Anand*. He was a part-time author, the material for which was fed by his day job as a cancer specialist. His story was one about having a big life, not a long one. It was about realising that we are all puppets on a string and it could be curtains any moment now. The subject was a terminally ill patient, Anand Sehgal—who won a million hearts on his way out.

But even after his death, Anand lived on in the 'pages' and on the celluloid of the immortal film. As the author said in the last line of his story—Anand did not die. *Anand* does not die.

In **Kabhi Kabhie**, Amit Malhotra was not an impoverished poet. We had moved on from **Pyaasa** by now. In fact, Amit was one of the most impeccably turned out poets in history.

His poetry (ghost-written by Sahir Ludhianvi) and his voice (provided by Amitabh Bachchan) were magical enough to reduce women to putty though he didn't get to marry his beloved and sent his book of poems as a wedding gift instead. She and her husband spend their *suhaag raat* singing the title poem. He was *that* good.

Like so many other things, Big B is one hell of an award-winning novelist.

In **Baghban**, he was Raj Malhotra, a bank manager who used his entire life's savings to prop up his sons' careers and lives—only to be dumped in his old age (along with his beautiful wife, Hema Malini). His philosophy of a man being a gardener who raises his children like flowering plants and his pain at being ill-treated resulted in *Baghban*—a novel that was written partly in a youth hangout called Archies Music Café and partly at night, disturbing his son with the clacking of typewriter keys. All of that got sweet redemption as his novel went on to win the Booker Prize (!) and he hammered his entire family in the acceptance speech.

In **Shabd**, a much-tattooed Sanjay Dutt was Shaukat Vashisht, an author who bagged a Booker Prize with his very first novel, *Mindscape*. Snippets of various reviews and profiles showed that the novel had a 'deeply human core' while its author was 'a (literary) supernova'. He walked past quick cuts of applauding hands and impressed foreigners, going on to release his second novel, *And Time Stood Still*. This time, the reviews were as unanimous as the first ones, but in the opposite direction. 'Can we have a real story?' asked one while 'lack of experience leading to unreal characters' proclaimed another. Shaukat's indignation led him to create a real-life experiment where he pushed his wife (Aishwarya Rai) into an affair with a younger colleague (Zayed Khan) to get the emotions evoked by marital infidelity realistically. Not short of imagination, surely.

Thoughts and inspiration in a messy room = Booker Prize

Fans driven to the point of hallucination is not something one usually associates with Bobby Deol. But that did not stop the makers of **Nanhe Jaisalmer** from featuring a camel-riding kid tourist guide in Jaisalmer, who was such a big fan of the youngest Deol that he had imaginary conversations with the star. Before you scream 'Calvin and Hobbes', let me quickly add that Bobby did indeed land up in Jaisalmer at least once in the film.

The kid's education, his sister's wedding and his experiences as a tourist guide eventually ended up becoming a book that wins the adult Nanhe (Vatsal Seth) the Booker Prize (yet again).

And guess who lands up at the awards ceremony? Offoh, not Big B—you idiot!

The stuff that gets read in millions of train rides and during lazy afternoons is not high-falutin literature—but pulp fiction.

In **Manorama Six Feet Under**, junior engineer Satyadev wrote exactly that, but he soon found out that writing popular shit was just as difficult as writing critically acclaimed shit. His first—and last—novel, *Manorama*, sold some 200 copies and he was relegated to being a frustrated and corrupt public servant in a desert town.

But his reputation as a crime novelist was enough to get him a client who claimed to be the irrigation minister's wife and wanted him to do some snooping on her husband's purported extra-marital affairs. Satyadev soon found out the minister had a nasty bunch of goons on his payroll and a slinky woman on his arm. And his own irate wife wasn't liking his detective-giri. And after all that, his client was not in a position to pay him for his troubles. Surely, fodder for another novel...

Canvas On Celluloid: 9 Artists

*E*ver since it was revealed that M.F. Husain had painted film posters, poster-art gained respectability. Coffee-table books emerged on the subject, shopkeepers in Chor Bazaar increased poster prices and this kitschy art found newer followers. Over time, the hand-drawn Bollywood poster gradually made way for digital art.

As the poster art changed, so did the artist in the Bollywood film. In olden days, the artist lived—if not in abject penury, at least—in tight financial conditions. In fact, the poor artist was always rejected by many a heroine's father in the olden times.

The new Bollywood artist is not poor by any stretch of imagination. His art may not be selling like hot cakes (yet) but he is firmly in Page 3 territory, holding a champagne flute and looking handsome.

In **Mr & Mrs 55**, a wealthy dowager wanted somebody poor and malleable enough for a shotgun marriage to her niece. And who better fits the bill than a newspaper cartoonist? All he had to do was to stay married for a few months, collect his money and run. Except the cartoonist was Guru Dutt. He not only had a point of view but dialogues by Abrar Alvi as well. Add to that the drawing skills of R.K. Laxman (who did the cartoons in the film) and you had Preetam Kumar— a struggling cartoonist, an artist with a twist.

And a killer introduction. After his speech on the plight of the poor, the aunt taunted him, *'Kya tum Communist ho?'* He smirked and said, *'Jee nahin, cartoonist hoon!'*

An artist and a charmer make for a deadly combination. **Mere Jeevan Saathi** was that, and added were Rajesh Khanna's looks. Also add blindness, a cruel princess, a Good Samaritan, a mindblowing soundtrack and filmi dilemmas. Rajesh Khanna did not waste too much time wielding a brush. The paintings on display in his house and studio were—quite inexplicably—of hungry beggars, or abstract art. He went around singing songs in shiny velvet waistcoats, and the paintings just paled into insignificance.

But really, Rajesh Khanna's artistic style could well have been his looks and gift of the gab. He presented his 'most beautiful work' to his heroine and whipped off the cover with a flourish—only to reveal a mirror. And if that was not enough, he sang '*O mere dil ke chain...*'

Women artists are few and far between. Rakhee as Miss Suman in **Kasme Vaade** was one of this rare breed. As an artist, she painted a mother-son piece called The Heart's Smile which was adjudged the best painting and immediately went under the hammer. Her own brother-in-law (Randhir Kapoor) tried to buy it but was outbid by his filthy-rich rival (Vijayendra Ghatge). The painting was finally sold for ₹ 20,000. If we adjust for inflation, that translates into quite a pretty packet! After her boyfriend's death, she spent the rest of her life painting his pictures. (Sales reports of these are not available.)

Two debuts marked the standard Love in the Times of Choleric Parents film—**Painter Babu**. The hero was Rajiv Goswami, son of Harekrishna Goswami a.k.a. Manoj Kumar. The heroine was Meenakshi Sheshadri, whose claim to fame was still one film away. A childhood romance got nipped in the bud when the hero's father fixed an economically motivated match for him, in order to save the family business. Son indignantly walked out, got framed (not for his painting but for murder) and shuttled in and out of jail. When he was finally released, he found out that the heroine was already married...

Hello? One second—where is the artist? Why is this film in the list?

Arre yaar, the hero was supposed to be interested enough in painting to make it into a profession. On top of that, look at the title. How can it not be included?

Confess, you never realised Aamir Khan was an artist in **Mann**. Confess, you never realised that **Mann** existed in the first place. Well, it did exist and Aamir was a rocking filmi painter at that.

He started off as a gold-digging playboy—with an artistic bent—till he met the first woman he couldn't seduce (Manisha Koirala). Almost immediately, he broke off his engagement to a rich heiress and became a pauper. And just when you thought it couldn't get any more filmi, he decided to make a fortune for himself by painting.

And like all famous painters (see the M.F. Husain story earlier), he kicked off his career by painting film posters and, before you could say 'Raja Ravi Varma', people were buying his art in droves and women were throwing themselves at him.

If you can withstand the high drama of Inder Kumar films, and Aamir's high art, which was about as artistic as crockery design, you can attempt to watch this movie (and figure out the similarities to **An Affair to Remember**, of which this is supposed to be a copy).

Dil Chahta Hai is—what you could call—a buddy film. Three south Mumbai dudes went about life, Goa and everything in style. And their professions were far less interesting than their girlfriends, even though one of them chose a more colourful vocation.

The film opened with a manic dash by Aamir and Saif to reach Akshaye's studio to see his latest painting. Whether the pencil sketch of the Rubenesque nude actually looked like their economics teacher, Mrs Kashyap, was debatable but it set the tone of the film. Akshaye found a muse in Dimple Kapadia, who looked as radiant as ever and totally deserving of the luscious portraits Akshaye drew of her. And as the portrait session went on, we had probably the most 'artistic' of Bollywood songs in which Akshaye Khanna inhabited a painter's visual landscape of unsaturated dabs of colour.

And not only the visual feel, Akshaye Khanna's career as an artist seemed to go through a steady progression from sketching at parties to recommendations from a critic at the exhibition to inclusion in an artist's retreat at a hill-station to painting in solitude at an uncle's farmhouse.

So did he sell any of those paintings? Your guess is good as mine.

Ishaan Awasthi was the boy with an incorrigible attitude, impossible teeth and incredible talent. Except, everybody was so busy turning him into an engineer that they did not notice. And the poor fellow—already handicapped with dyslexia—moped about for half the film and got sent to a boarding school. Enter Ram Shankar Nikumbh, maverick art teacher by day and all was well.

In Aamir Khan's directorial debut, **Taare Zameen Par**, art was the centre of it all. A talented boy's journey towards public recognition and self-belief was brought alive by an amazing performance from Darsheel Safary and some evocative art by Sameer Mondal—who did the kiddie art as well.

Starting from Ishaan's hyper-creative images of the solar system to his bright portrait by the art-teacher, the paintings added an extra dimension to this film. Even the album and disc covers of this film were full of doodles and scrawls that wonderfully added to the mood.

If the universe conspired to let more sisters into their brothers' rooms, we would have discovered many more talented artists than we have currently. This was a hypothesis put forward by **Jaane Tu Ya Jaane Na**, which had a sub-plot of sibling rivalry between heroine Genelia D'Souza and her artist brother, Prateik Babbar.

That Prateik was an artist was not revealed till quite late in the film when his sister's suitor walked into his room. His room turned out to be a mix of Dali, Munch and maybe even Abbas Tyrewala, with surreal subjects and bold colours. There was art on every wall, window and piece of furniture—so dense that it was difficult to distinguish between painting and sculpture. Eye-catching, for sure.

But for all his talent, Prateik made no pretence of trying to sell or even exhibit his work in the film. He seemed quite content in his stinking-rich father's bungalow, playing with his pet rat when not spewing pithy epigrams at his sister.

There is something about the brooding, loner image of Aamir Khan that draws artist roles to him like a magnet. His wife, Kiran Rao, cannot but agree.

In **Dhobi Ghat**, he was the reclusive, eccentric artist who shifted from house to house in Mumbai and hated the exhibitions where his art got sold. He was obviously affluent (big flats in Mumbai) and successful (exhibitions in Australia).

His art was about the city he lived in and loved. He dedicated his exhibition to Mumbai—'my muse, my whore, my beloved'. It was as much about the geography of the city as it was about the politics, because the exhibition he introduced was about the migrant labourer population of Mumbai and there was a statement in that.

According to the director, some aspects of Aamir's character were modelled on artist Sudhir Patwardhan, and Aamir worked with Ravi Mallick for the art.

Honourable Mention

It would be a shame to not mention the contributions of the filmi artist mentioned in the beginning. M.F. Husain was the ultimate Bollywood fan, not beyond watching favourite films hundreds of times and deriving inspiration from heroines.

One of his earlier contributions was in Raj Kapoor's **Henna**—for which he did the paintings for the title cards.

Some time after that, he grew inspired by Madhuri Dixit and promptly knocked off a series of paintings—all of which were sold for figures with countless zeroes in them. He did not stop there and made a full-fledged feature film, **Gaja Gamini**, with Madhuri Dixit in the title role and multiple roles thereafter, including that of the *Mona Lisa*.

Jab Tak Suraj Chand Rahega: 10 Politicians

*B*ollywood rarely goes beyond fisticuffs to solve problems. Televised debate is just not their thing. Two maharathis are more adept at picking up swords than a megaphone. Though occasionally, there has been the appearance of the khadi and the Gandhi topi—uniform of the favourite whipping-boy of Indian cinema.

But while politicians have been all over the place, they have essentially been effete or villainous caricatures, always at the receiving end of bombastic speeches or severe beatings by the hero or heroine. The nitty-gritties of political strategy and the real hurly-burly of political action have been in the limelight fewer times.

Aandhi still remains an iconic film depicting Indian elections in partly realistic, partly air-brushed glory. With the streak of white in her black hair, Suchitra Sen will always be the on-screen Indira Gandhi despite hectic clarifications that the character was based on nobody in particular.[31]

An initially Bohemian daughter of an established and overbearing politician fell in love and married an hotelier. Unable to take the twin pressures of her father's political

---

[31] It has sometimes been reported that the character was based on Nandini Satpathy, ex-chief minister of Orissa.

ambitions and being a wife, she walked out of the marriage and the town. She came back several years later to fight an election (under the symbol of a bird) and rediscovered her love for the estranged husband. All hell broke loose as her rivals started to dig up skeletons and scandals around this 'affair'.

People tend to remember this film only for the absolutely stupendous soundtrack (probably the greatest of Gulzar-RD collaborations) but the entire electoral process was reasonably well-sketched—including a satirical song on politicians returning to constituencies every five years. What a pity it was the weakest song in the album.

You cannot talk about elections in films without **Coolie** and **Inquilaab**—and they are obviously connected.

Needless to say, they were the most unrealistic films of them all. But then, if you want realism, you may as well go and watch *Bigg Boss*. Also, the elections were only a small part of the overall package of the two films, in the true tradition of all Amitabh films of the early-'80s (where everything, except Amitabh himself, was a small part of the overall package).

Given the topicality of Amitabh's entry into politics around that time and that the political sub-plots in both films were so unconnected to the initial storylines, they might well have been written halfway through the shooting. Or maybe, on the morning of the shoot.

In **Coolie**, Iqbal went from a porter to a trade unionist (for other porters) to organiser of strikes to an election candidate—who then got blackmailed into almost withdrawing by villains (who had kidnapped his mother).

In **Inquilaab**, the transformation was even more dramatic. Amarnath started off as a blackmarketeer of tickets. He became a police officer. He was promoted to ACP. He killed a dreaded smuggler—Khoya Khoya Attachi—after which he was made the leader of 'Garibon Ka Party'. He won the elections in a landslide and became chief minister. What he did at his first Cabinet meeting is something I dare not repeat, lest some young turks get ideas.

Aaj Ka MLA Ram Avtar proved anybody—absolutely anybody—could become an elected political representative. Even your friendly neighbourhood barber called—you guessed it—Ram Avtar.

Rajesh Khanna played barber to the minister who got pole-vaulted into politics when his minister's party ran out of candidates. The genial shaver entered the fray with the good wishes and votes of his many supporters, who expected the simple do-gooder to push their case. But Ram Avtar transformed into one slimy politician once he got the MLA stamp after his name. To paraphrase a famous line, since he did not die a hero, he lived long enough to become a villain.

But the good thing about Bollywood is that redemption is just a climax away.

It may have been the elections for only a village cooperative, but Shyam Benegal infused it with all the emotion that is normally associated with elections in India.

Manthan saw the sarpanch (Kulbhushan Kharbanda) being pitted against lower-caste Naseeruddin Shah in an election to manage their milk cooperative, an unequal battle catalysed by the modern-thinking Dr Rao (Girish Karnad, playing Dr Verghese Kurien's role). Given the social churning that was brought about, the sarpanch, who was used to winning elections unopposed, lost this first election he contested.

In recent times, one of the most politically charged films has been **Yuva**.

Set against the volatile politics of Bengal, the countryside, the rural elections, the strong-arm tactics of the ruling party and the idealism of college politics were brought out vividly. After a maze of machinations by the villains and some depressing violence, the three young men—led by Ajay Devgn—managed to win their first elections and walked into the Assembly to become three spots of blue denim in a sea of white dhoti-kurtas. You couldn't help but feel a frisson of happiness at even this obviously unrealistic situation.

When you see the film, you wonder, why was it set in Calcutta? But then, where else?

In Anurag Kashyap's edgy **Gulaal**, a college election took on epic importance. Hanging in the balance was not just the lakhs that could be siphoned off from the college festival fund but how the winner would impact the separatist movement for Rajputana.

Pitting the volatile Ransa (Abhimanyu Singh in a short but brilliant role) against the steely Kiran (Ayesha Mohan), the entire build-up to and conduct of the election was played at a hurtling pace. The campaigning, the abrupt and brutal murder of a candidate, emergence of a replacement and the subtle rigging to swing the results were paced breathtakingly and filmed in a jagged, realistic style.

Political satires are few and far between in Bollywood. After all the intensity and unrealism of the previous films, we have **Chintuji**—with Rishi Kapoor in the title role.

Ostensibly playing himself, the film star landed up in his (semi-manufactured) village of birth—with a PR manager in tow—to contest an election, and promptly got embroiled in many complications. The film took a caustic look at two of India's most visible careerists—film stars and politicians—borrowing extensively from real-life characters and creating a hilarious mockumentary at the end of it.

Ram Gopal Verma's **Rann** viewed election and politics through a different prism. It examined how the media looks at politics, how it becomes part of it even without wanting to. Or, how it wants to.

With Paresh Rawal as the unscrupulous PM-in-waiting, Mohan Pandey, the films followed the fortunes and dilemmas of idealistic media baron Harshvardhan Malik (played with his usual aplomb by Amitabh Bachchan). The two were supported by a very talented ensemble cast as the film did a reasonable recce of politics in the times of 24×7 news cameras. Sting operations, orchestrated riots, moles in media, the business of politics and the politics of business made for a realistic film that was an almost unceasingly cynical view of our times. And that was probably best brought out by an acidic reprise of our national anthem that was considered too explosive for public consumption and not passed for cinematic release.

Sigh—ban on a film on media.

Probably the most definitive film on contemporary politics is Prakash Jha's **Rajneeti**.

Here, we got to see the whole gamut of dirty politics that included but was not restricted to sex, money and power. The plot was a condensed version of the

Mahabharat[32]—the go-to manual for politics, anyway—packed during the campaigning for a state's election.

Brothers of all kinds—full, half, step-, illegitimate—lived and died as dynastic politics kicked in at its ugliest. The film climaxed with the entry of Katrina Kaif on the political arena, playing the young widow of the scion of a political family. She went hoarse trying to explain that the role was not based on the life of Sonia Gandhi but her point would have been a little easier to believe if she hadn't worn those cotton sarees and styled her hair a little differently. And yes—her accent wasn't similar. Wait, why did she have an accent in the film? Well, she has an accent in every film.

---

[32] See chapter on Epics in Bollywood (Page 85).

Killer Kaun? 13 Clues To Identify Killers

*T*here have been very few true-blue murder mysteries in Bollywood to start with. Some of them got lost in the million other sub-plots that are almost habitually present in every Bollywood film and the identity of the murderer (or the murdered) is never as important as the next song.

A list of murderers can be most intriguing—and even funny—in the Bollywood context but there is the problem of spoilers. So, this list is constructed as a quiz with two parts. The first part is a hint about the identity of the killer and the second part (should you choose to read it) reveals the film from which the killer is taken.

1　The killer wore different-size shoes (8 and 9).
2　The killer had a bracelet, with a horse emblem dangling from it. The kid hero saw it (only it and nothing but it) peeping from inside a cupboard.
3　The killer has an overgrown toe.
4　The killer was a tiger. No, wait—he was a man. Nope—he was a tiger.
5　The killer got on the train at VT. He got off at Dadar, commited the crime and took a flight to Nagpur, from where he got back on to the train. A perfect alibi of being on the train all the time.
6　The killer had a bandhgala with a button missing. Each button of that bandhgala was a precious stone in an exquisitely crafted setting, worth about a million bucks each.

7 The evil killer had a twin good brother. The evil one killed his brother and set it up as if he had been killed himself. And prepared for a lifetime of respectability.

8 The killer had a slow twin.

9 The killer was the one who was the victim all this while.

10 The killer was the heroine's uncle.

11 The killer was not a killer. Because the victim was not dead.

12 The killer murdered his wife and went to the police to report a case of a missing person. But a woman turned up, claiming to be his wife.

13 The killer had a cigar. And a hat. And an overcoat in peak summer. And dark glasses in a dimly lit nightclub. Oh wait—he was not the killer. He was 'the CID'.

---

* * SPOILER ALERT * * SPOILER ALERT * * SPOILER ALERT * *

---

1 Ajit's different-sized feet (and therefore, shoes) were probably the most celebrated physical deformity in Bollywood (apart from Shah Rukh Khan's stammer).

   In **Yaadon Ki Baaraat**, Ajit played Shaakaal—the goggled super-villain who thought nothing of killing painters who could paint his likeness for the police. But he never bargained for the painter's three sons who would see his different-sized shoes and one of whom would grow up to be the He-est Man in Bollywood. Great music, super dialogue and a breathtaking pace... we almost forgot that there was a murderer.

2 It's Ajit again, underlining how pervasive the Loin was as a villain in the 1970s.

   In **Zanjeer**, he played Teja—the mobster who went to become the don and had to contend with honest police officers with a bad temper and great lines (written by the hottest scriptwriters of the country). The father who got killed was totally inconsequential in the greater scheme of things while the killer's distinctive bracelet assumed a bigger role by haunting the son throughout his life.

3 Paresh Rawal's gigantic toe gave him away.

   In **Baazi**, he was the slimy Deputy CM Chaubey who was not beyond harbouring terrorists in his own home and molesting dancers he took a fancy to. He got chopped up by a Special Branch officer, who realised in the climax that Chaubey's big toe was the same size as his father's killer's (who also made lewd propositions to his mother, for good measure). To know how that little boy saw the killer's toe but not his face, you have to see the film.

4 It was Rahul Roy, who looked dangerously close to being naked in some scenes.

In **Junoon**, he was the ichhadhari tiger (which was such a welcome change after years of icchadhari nagins). As every little child with a very basic knowledge of biology knows, a human turns into a tiger every full-moon night if he is bitten by a cursed tiger. This was exactly what happened to him. The mild-mannered Rahul turned into a Big Cat, only to devour all those he did not like in his human avatar.

5 It was the Big B, in one of his earlier roles as a crazed lover.

In **Parwana**, he was an artist, Kumar Sen, who faced the double whammy of being rejected as suitor by his supposed girlfriend's uncle while the girl fell in love with Navin Nischol. But he solved both these problems in one fell swoop when he murdered the uncle and framed his girlfriend's lover for the crime. And he did this with extensive help from Indian Railways and Indian Airlines.

6 Premnath was the über-cool Good Samaritan who turned out nothing like he pretended to be.

In **Teesri Manzil**, he was Kunwar Sahab, the millionaire with a heart of gold who went all out to help the hero clear his name as a murder suspect. Not only that, he was the ever-smiling elder statesman who supported his romantic pursuits as well. Except that he had had a relationship with the dead woman whom he pushed from the eponymous floor. And in the scuffle, the victim wrenched a button off his coat.

7 Anupam Kher was the one zipping between saints and sinners.

In **Roop Ki Rani Choron Ka Raja**, he played Jugran—the mastermind of jewel heists who assumed the persona of noted industrialist and do-gooder, Manmohan Lal. He had fooled everybody because they had given up the villain for dead. Along came a Beauty Queen and the King of Thieves, who realised that the bruises on Jugran's wrists were exactly the same as those on Manmohan Lal's.

8 Keith Stevenson played the two roles of the retarded and the cruel brothers.

In **Akayla**, he was Tony Braganza who was regularly arrested at crime scenes by an alcoholic cop in a yellow Beetle. And every single time, his lawyer managed to get him off the hook by showing irrefutable proof of his presence at a different place at the same time. It was working like a dream till the cop's girlfriend took him to see a film called **Seeta aur Geeta** (incidentally, directed by the same director).

9 Urmila Matondkar played the girl all alone in a mansion, terrorised by strangers.

In **Kaun**, she was forever shivering and giggling as she went traipsing all alone in her house having heard the news of a serial killer being on the prowl. A garrulous door-to-door salesman landed up as did a gun-toting silent type. They were soon fighting to save the helpless girl from each other. And when one of them reached the attic to pacify the girl, there was a body there. Soon, there were two.

10 Anant Mahadevan, known for his studious looks and mild demeanour, was the man out to get his niece's inheritance.

In **Khiladi**, he was the insignificant brick in the even-more-insignificant background wall as a group of college kids played a kidnapping prank that went wrong and one of them ended up with a knife in the back. There was a brother who was a police officer. A dancer who tried to run down people with her car. A comedian who was hard of hearing. And a 'player' who bet on everything.

11 Well, there was no killer but it was Surendra Kumar who orchestrated his own death.

In **Do Gaz Zameen Ke Neeche**, one of the earlier Ramsay Brother spooks, he was a part-time scientist and full-time millionaire who was 'murdered' by his gold-digger wife and her shady uncle. Burying him in a grave two yards deep (how did you ever guess?), the duo started robbing his mansion and strange things happened. Money and jewels vanished, their plans were thwarted and finally, the grave turned out to be empty.

12 Rishi Kapoor was the very unlikely wife-killer.

In **Khoj**, he was initially the hassled husband—Ravi Kapoor—who reported his wife to be missing. A woman emerged soon after, claiming to be his wife. Ravi went blue in the face telling everybody that she wasn't his wife but she seemed to have every proof including wedding photos and marriage certificates. Very soon, a priest emerged to support the story and there was only one way left for the husband to convince the world that this wasn't his wife—by confessing where he had hidden her body after killing her.

13 Iftekhar—he of slim build and slimmer moustache—has been playing these laconic roles since eternity.

In **Khel Khel Mein**, he appeared on the sidelines of a college prank gone wrong. A group of students had written a letter to blackmail a jeweller, who was killed immediately afterwards. Threatened with a possibility of being seen as murderers, they embarked on an elaborate cover-up mission as the mysterious man landed up at every place they tried to hide in.

So, if he wasn't the killer, who *was* the killer? Well, that's one spoiler less then.

5

OBSESSIONS

'Sau saal pehle mujhe tumse pyaar tha, aaj bhi hai aur kal bhi rahega.'—DEV ANAND in **Jab Pyar Kisise Hota Hai**

We, the people, are obsessed with a whole lot of things. Some of them are oh-so-happy things like music, travel and sports. Some of them are morbid thoughts of disease and death. Some of them stem from our curiosity to know all about the world around us. And some of them are about wanting to talk to the entire world.

- ◆ Dawaa Ya Dua: 8 Kinds of Diseases
- ◆ Howzzat: 15 Cricketing Moments
- ◆ Beyond the Boundary: 10 Sports
- ◆ Here and There: 7 Filmi Places
- ◆ Lifeline of the Nation: 10 Trains you Shouldn't Miss
- ◆ The Truth about Cats and Dogs: 10 Filmi Pets
- ◆ Stop Press: 8 Filmi Newspapers
- ◆ Waak Engliss, Taak Engliss: 15 Lessons in English

Dawaa Ya Dua: 8 Kinds Of Diseases

A doctor comes out of the OT (a red bulb switches off), takes off his glasses and morosely pronounces, '*Inhe ab dawaon ki nahin, duaon ki zaroorat hai...*'

This is the cue for the kin to break for a kirtan (Asha Parekh) or a diatribe against God (Amitabh Bachchan). But what are the diseases being fought? Apart from accidents, and pregnancy (which IS treated as a disease), what are the other afflictions? In short, what ails Bollywood?

Cancer

The Big C is undoubtedly the most popular disease for the absolute surety it brings to the death of the protagonist. Rajesh Khanna would have to be the brand ambassador of the disease, with deadly performances in two landmark films—**Anand** and **Safar**. They had everything an ideal cancer patient should exhibit—stoicism, joie de vivre and an ability to sacrifice everything on his way out. Anand even had a name for the illness—lymphocarcoma of the intestine. And was very proud of the regal sound of it: '*Jaise kisi viceroy ki naam ho...*'

Jaya Bhaduri had it in **Mili** as AB played a reformed alcoholic, watching the love of his life wither away in front of his eyes. Probably the most touching film on the subject, it was made priceless by the song about the emptiness of life in Kishore Kumar's voice ('*Badi sooni sooni hai...*').

Amitabh Bachchan—tired of seeing people die around him—got the disease (lung cancer) himself in **Waqt: The Race Against Time**. And he had nine months to make his son stand on his own two feet before he died. In those nine months, his son fell in love, went on a honeymoon and became an action star who did his own stunts. Wow.

Brain Tumour

The other 'fatal' disease in Bollywood is brain tumour.

In two movies—**Kaash** (directed by Mahesh Bhatt) and **Anjali** (directed by Mani Ratnam)—it is a child that has the tumour, making things all the more tragic. While the former had a star couple trying to patch up a marriage for the sake of their son, the latter had a group of siblings starting to accept their terminally ill sister back into their household. Both gut-wrenching.

Big B had a brain tumour with a bizarre twist in **Majboor**. When diagnosed with the disease, AB was faced with an operation with limited chance of success and potential paralysis. Instead, he chose to confess to a millionaire's murder and redirect the informer's reward to make his mother's and siblings' lives secure. On death row, he had a seizure, was operated upon and had his tumour successfully removed. Now, he was in jail wrongly accused of murder (which he had confessed to himself) and a healthy life ahead of him. *Kya hua next?*

Heart Diseases

Usually, the extreme form of this is used to dispatch Daddy when the baaraat goes back for want of dowry or when the daughter runs away to marry out of caste. Nazir Hussain specialises in rolling his eyes, stopping mid-sentence, clutching the left side of his chest and collapsing in a heap. There are way too many scenes like that to keep count.

The long-drawn-out heart disease is used to keep the viewer in suspense over the fate of the patient. This disease is also a money-sink for which the patient's relatives have to adopt desperate measures.

Shah Rukh Khan's tragic act in **Kal Ho Naa Ho** remains the beacon of all cardiac plotlines of all times. He cracked jokes with Saif, wooed Preity and generally acted like the Good Samaritan, but when your cardiologist Dr Sonali Bendre leaves you for Sanjay Kapoor, you should commit suicide if not die of a terminal illness.

Sometimes kids get afflicted with these as well. Ajay Devgn's nephew in **Pyaar To Hona Hi Tha** had a hole in his heart, for which Ajay went around stealing stuff. Like the adult patients of this disease, this kid also turned out to be good-natured and led to a greater number of wet hankies.

Amnesia

The signature line of this disease is *'Main kahan hoon? Main kaun hoon?'* accompanied by a take on the first question and a double take on the second.

Sadma had selective amnesia, where Sridevi forgot everything between age five and her current age. (Evil reviewers commented that there was not too much of a gap between her mental age and that of a five-year-old, anyway.)

But her act as a little girl in a twenty-one-year-old body was quite good, although all people remember from that film were Yesudas' songs.

Another movie to star Amnesia—actually Retrograde Amnesia (whatever THAT means)—was **Salaam-e-Ishq** (which has also been referred as Salaam-E-Eeks). Vidya Balan remembered everything in her life except John Abraham. Our dude had to do what he never did before... he tried to remind a girl of himself. Maybe Vidya had a secret affair with Hrithik and wanted to forget John. Either that, or women forget their husbands two years after marriage.

The most hilarious amnesiac of them all was Aamir Khan in **Andaz Apna Apna**. He pretended to lose his memory after Raveena Tandon hit him on the head with a stick, and thus became her house-guest. Since he did not even remember his own name, he was christened Teelu (because he was found on a teela) and had to be treated by Dr Prem Khurana (who was '*Iss dhande mein bahut purana!*').

Blindness

It started off with **Dosti** and has carried on beyond **Fanaa**.

Most of the biggies of Hindi cinema—Rajesh Khanna (**Mere Jeevan Saathi**), Sanjeev Kumar (**Qatl**), Amitabh Bachchan (the unreleased **Zamaanat**), Mumtaz (**Jheel Ke Us Paar**), Kajol (**Fanaa**), Naseeruddin Shah (**Sparsh**), Rani Mukherjee (**Black**), Akshay Kumar (**Aankhen**), Deepika Padukone (**Lafangey Parindey**)—have played blind people.

And some of them have pretended to be blind as well (Amitabh Bachchan in **Parvarish** and Mehmood in **Johar Mehmood in Hong Kong**).

Nirupa Roy has turned blind on-screen—when a tree descended on her—and then regained her eyesight after she fervently prayed to Shirdi waale Sai Baba. In **Amar Akbar Anthony**, twin flames emerged out of the eyes of the Baba, travelled all the way to the back of the prayer hall and inserted themselves in her eyes. And she saw again! *Zor se bolo jai Baba ki! Phir se bolo jai Baba ki!!*

AIDS

One reason why AIDS is yet to catch on as a life-ending disease in Bollywood is because of the doubt it brings about the patient's character. Imagine Bhaskar Banerjee thinking about Anand, 'Hmmm, the bugger was getting it on the sly... that's how he got the virus...' Poof! All the poignancy and sympathy would fly out of the window. Hence, it has been seen only in serious movies dealing specifically with the problems associated with the disease.

Phir Milenge (directed by Revathy) had Salman Khan infecting Shilpa Shetty with the virus after a one-night stand, but the movie was so sparsely watched, nobody thought of burning their effigies for promiscuity and moral turpitude.

Onir's **My Brother Nikhil** was probably the first Indian movie to show a gay relationship realistically, without either of the partners being a pansy, or cracking any jokes about homosexuality. Sanjay Suri delivered a first-rate performance as the award-winning sportsman who got ostracised because of his disease.

Others

Devdas is the poster-boy of liver disease (presumably cirrhosis) since he was the pioneer of drinking-to-death.

Chhoti Bahu of **Saheb Bibi Ghulam** is, of course, the poster-girl.

Sanjay Leela Bhansali was not happy with Rani's triple handicap in **Black** so he gave Amitabh Alzheimer's (probably the only time in Hindi cinema that the disease has featured).

Amitabh Bachchan made Progeria famous with his glorious performance in **Paa**, complete with a young boy's shuffle, prosthetic make-up and 'shitty' dialogue.

Not to be left behind on uncommon diseases, Shah Rukh Khan became the Asperger's Syndrome-afflicted Rizvan Khan in **My Name Is Khan** and gave this version of autism a visibility that only he can bring.

Filmi Diseases

And, of course, there are diseases that could not have happened anywhere in the world except in Bollywood. Hyperactive imaginations have come up with some really crazy afflictions.

Like Loveria, for example. In **Raju Ban Gaya Gentleman**, SRK and Juhi Chawla had this disease characterised by deep sighs, insomnia and general unease. An elaborate song-and-dance routine was created around it, which soon topped every music chart in town and nobody wanted to get well too soon.

In **Bol Radha Bol**—a maniacal comedy by David Dhawan—Kader Khan turned blind at 6 pm every evening. And you thought that was funny? Well, at the climax, his eyesight was restored to 24×7 but his hearing vanished at the same time of day.

Beat that! Or better still, find a cure for that.

Howzzat: 15 Cricketing Moments

*I*n a country that is so obsessed with cricket, it is quite strange that not too many films have been made on the sport. Of course, making cricketing action look authentic is one big challenge but lack of authenticity has never deterred our filmmakers from attempting anything. The number of films that have a passing mention of cricket is quite high, though.

Guest Appearances of Cricket

Amitabh did a fantastic monologue in **Namak Halaal** on the partnerships of Vijay Hazare and Vijay Merchant, Wasim Bari and Wasim Raja... which was elevated to a different level of nonsense by his accent.

Latching on to an India-Australia match in Melbourne 1929, he explained the exploits of Vijay Hazare and Vijay Merchant in elaborate detail.[33] When rudely interrupted, he shifted to Wankhede 1979 where Wasim Raja and Wasim Bari were playing against India.[34]

---

[33] Vijay Merchant and Vijay Hazare batted together probably just once—in Delhi 1951 and *not* Melbourne 1929 (when neither of them had even started playing cricket).

[34] The second pairing is more accurate—though not completely—as Wasim Raja and Wasim Bari *did* play together in Wankhede 1979 but they never batted together.

Anupam Kher in **Darr** was Juhi Chawla's cricket-crazy brother who watched matches with full cricket gear on because, given the state of the Indian team, he expected to get a call from the team at any moment. And as cricket fans in our country know, this is a very clear and present danger.

In the film **Chamatkar**, SRK—assisted by Naseeruddin Shah's ghost—played a college cricket match (which had bookies betting on it) against a nasty opposing team, which was captained by Ashutosh Gowariker. Maybe the **Lagaan** idea originated then?

The first scene of **Kabhi Khushi Kabhie Gham** showed the last ball of a cricket match in an idyllic English field, where Hrithik Roshan invoked the spirit of his parents and family to hit the ball for a towering six as Karan Johar's sweeping camera covered the lush fields, palatial mansions and Hrithik's dimples in a magnificent sweep.

And no description of cricket in Hindi cinema can be complete without **Hum Aapke Hain Koun** which has the distinction of being the only time a cricket match has been played with a non-human umpire. Salman Khan's entire family gleefully appealed to the Pomeranian as it dutifully displayed 'Out' and 'Not Out' cards.

Guest Appearances of Cricketers

There have been several such appearances in Hindi films—including some extended ones.

Sandeep Patil, thoroughly misguided about his looks and sex appeal, acted opposite Debashree Roy in a movie called

Kabhie Ajnabi The. The movie also starred Syed Kirmani as a villain.

The '70s cricketer Salim Durrani's celluloid debut opposite Parveen Babi in an obscure film called **Charitra** has been much discussed in many forums though the film itself remains elusive on VCD lists and YouTube.

Sunil Gavaskar acted in a Marathi movie (**Savli Premachi**) before he was called upon for an extended guest appearance in the film **Maalamaal**. Naseeruddin Shah played a cricket-crazy tapori in the film who was asked to spend ₹ 30 crore in thirty days as part of a bizarre inheritance challenge. And in one of the ploys to blow it all up, he invited Gavaskar to play against his Chawl XI in the Wankhede Stadium.

In **Mujhse Shaadi Karogi**, the battle for Priyanka Chopra's attentions that raged between Akshay Kumar and Salman Khan throughout the film found its climax in a cricket stadium. And a full team of Indian cricket stars popped up. Navjyot Singh Sidhu was in the commentary box and Kapil Dev delivered sage advice while the likes of Harbhajan Singh, Irfan Pathan, Mohammed Kaif and Ashish Nehra pretended not to be excited by Salman.

Starring Roles of Cricket

Lagaan is the certified cricket epic of Bollywood—which took our love for the game to the biggest cinematic stage of the world and came back without the trophy, thus keeping the 'choker' reputation of Indians alive.

Foreign coaches, coloured clothing, match-fixing, team politics, captaincy tussles, even the doosra from the current cricketing world went back a couple of centuries to give us one of the most satisfying films about sport in any language.

Of the few films that have been made around cricket or cricketers, one of the first was **All Rounder**. This had Kumar Gaurav playing a talented cricketer, egged on by his rustic villager brother (Vinod Mehra in one of his many sugary-sweet do-gooder roles). Gaurav's character broke into the national team, only to be framed on some trumped-up charges of ayyaashi (this is an all-encompassing term for drinking, boozing and womanising) by Shakti Kapoor and thrown out. All of it came to a happy end when the charges were cleared and Kumar Gaurav made a triumphant return to the team—but not before beating Shakti Kapoor to a pulp with a cricket bat. This was a cricket film, you see.

In recent times, **Hattrick** was about the stories of three cricket-crazy fans. In one of the tracks, cricket-ignoramus Rimi Sen started watching the game at her husband's (Kunal Kapoor) insistence and fell in love with M.S. Dhoni. In a slightly misguided tribute to MSD, one scene had the couple making love and Rimi screaming out the Indian captain's name in ecstasy.[35]

A young cricketer's journey towards the Holy Grail of the Indian national side is fraught with many heartbreaks. And if the cricketer is hearing- and speech-impaired, the journey could well be impossible. A film on this subject

---

[35] In **Meerabai Not Out**, Mandira Bedi played Meera Achrekar—a cricket-obsessed maths teacher with a crush on Anil Kumble.

could descend into melodrama very easily but Nagesh Kukunoor helmed the project really well and Shreyas Talpade excelled as **Iqbal**, the fast bowler whose actions literally spoke louder than words. The realistic atmosphere of the state cricket matches, with Girish Karnad as the deal-brokering coach, Shweta Prasad as the affectionate sister and Naseeruddin Shah as the alcoholic coach, made the film an under-rated gem. Super-feel-good—just the way cricket matches should be.

And as a direct counterpoint to the many films where Indians took on the world in cricket, we had **Patiala House**.

Pargat Singh Kahlon's—a Southall Sikh—teen exploits included getting Nasser Hussain (the former English captain) out in three successive matches. Kept away from playing for England by his jingoistic dad (Rishi Kapoor), he ran a grocery store till he was given a chance to make a comeback at the age of thirty-four. Playing for England, he had a showdown with Andrew Symonds (playing himself) and in true filmi style, got his redemption at Lord's in front of his cheering family and approving dad.

What—did you say 'spoiler'? Arre bhai, what do you expect when Akshay Kumar plays a cricketer? That he will give away sixteen runs in the last over and be dropped never to be picked again? Then you should also ask why Nikhil Chopra is giving Hindi commentary in an England-Australia match in London—no?[36]

And the last word in cricket films can only be Dev Anand's magnum opus **Awwal Number**.

---

[36] *Trivia Alert*: Balwinder Singh Sandhu, medium pacer in India's 1983 World Cup squad, is credited as 'Bowling Coach' in this film.

Dev Anand's character in the film was an absolute rarity—a Police Commissioner of Bombay who was also the Chairman of the selectors. And if that was not enough, his brother (Aditya Panscholi) was the top batsman of the Indian team. Dev dropped his brother from the team because he was doing ayyaashi (see definition given earlier) and took a baby-faced boy called Sunny (Aamir Khan in his pre-one-film-a-decade days) in his place. Aditya took grievous offence to this and teamed up with a terrorist outfit to bomb the stadium from a helicopter above it. In a double-barreled climax, Dev killed Aditya before he could kill anybody. And Aamir killed the Aussies by hitting a six off the last ball. This was slightly disappointing because one expected Aamir would take out the helicopter with the same shot which would eventually be the winning six.

Beyond The Boundary: 10 Sports

*I*s there life beyond cricket? Of course. At least, Bollywood seems to think so. Various sports have dribbled and feinted in and out of the silver screen— sometimes with a full film devoted to them and sometimes with a fleeting glimpse. The charm of an underdog winning against all odds goes beyond India's richest sport.

Football

One of Anil Kapoor's earlier hits—**Saaheb**—was a remake of a Bengali film of the same name. The maudlin plot was about a good-for-one-thing youth who played football and had it in him to make it big. He blew it all away when he sold off a kidney to pay for his sister's wedding.

In Prakash Jha's debut feature film, **Hip Hip Hurray**, Raj Kiran was the newly appointed portly sports teacher of a rag-tag school with a talented bully in the football team. With his sincere efforts, he managed to regroup the team to eventually beat a rival school in football while he found love in the form of Deepti Naval.

Dhan Dhana Dhan Goal, starring the super-fit John Abraham, was the story of an Asian team (Southall United) in the English league which made it to the top despite their paunches, John's shaky nose and Arshad Warsi's flowing hair. The film was loaded with solid desi jingoism and decent sporting action, supported by super-fit Bipasha Basu as the team physio in spandex.

Karan Johar put his SRK-obsession on a giant screen in a New York soccer stadium when he showed a close-up of Shah Rukh's eyes as he was about to take a penalty shot. Filling up a soccer stadium in USA is something only Dharma Productions can do. SRK, of course, did not become famous, and ended up being a frustrated coach in the film (**Kabhi Alvida Naa Kehna**) though no football stadium was ever shown again.

Aamir Khan played football without touching the ball in one hilarious sequence in **Andaz Apna Apna**, where he described his sporting exploits to demonstrate the return of his truant memory. As a star forward for Mohan Bagan, he claimed to have scored six goals in a match and he recreated the magic in a jiffy by rearranging mocktail glasses on a coffee table.

Hockey

India's pride was completely sidelined in Hindi cinema, except for that one shining mass of patriotism, inspiration and girls in sleeveless vests and mini-skirts—**Chak De India**. The film addresses important issues of women's careers, politicking in sporting bodies and marginalisation of Muslims, but when India defeats Australia in a World Cup final led by Shah Rukh Khan in jeans and aviators, everything else pales in comparison. Finely choreographed sports sequences blended effortlessly with the story and in one stroke, SRK launched the careers of sixteen heroines.

The Indian sports fan's ultimate fantasy—defeating Australia in a World Cup Final.

Apart from this, there have been very few instances of hockey appearing on the silver screen. It happened once when Rishi Kapoor and Rakesh Roshan (many kilos and lots of hair ago) came in from behind to win their college hockey match in **Khel Khel Mein**. The match was all of five minutes in screen time.

In two comedies by Hrishikesh Mukherjee and Basu Chatterjee respectively, hockey matches kicked off the films' comic plot.

In **Golmaal**, Amol Palekar got caught at an India-Pakistan hockey match by his boss and had to invent a clean-shaven twin.

In **Lakhon Ki Baat**, Farooq Shaikh played a sports reporter knocked out by a hockey ball, which led to a lawsuit by his lawyer brother-in-law, Sanjeev Kumar.

Basketball

Kuch Kuch Hota Hai started with Kajol and SRK fighting it out in the coolest college in India and they followed up their on-court rivalry with a game played by Kajol in a saree, which had her demonstrating some sexy moves instead of smart dribbles.

Aishwarya and Hrithik tried to be hip and cool in **Dhoom 2,** as they bandied a basketball around while keeping a banter going but the dialogue was way too flat for the scene to be interesting.

Table Tennis

In **Chhoti Si Baat**, the introverted Amol Palekar was coached by Wilfred Julius Nagendranath Singh on how to gain the upper hand in life, which included a table-tennis session won by upsetting the opponent's rhythm.

In one song sequence in **Maine Pyar Kiya**, Bhagyashree and Salman appeared in full sporting attire to tap a few ping-pong balls here and there. You can count that if you like.

Billiards

Raaj Kumar played it with great style because this is the only game which permits heavy-duty dialogue-baazi while moving around slowly between shots (ref: **Tirangaa**).

Or, flirtatious heroes tried to teach heroines the game by embracing them from behind and trying to steal a kiss or two (ref: **Janbaaz**).

Rugby / American Football[37]

Whenever Bollywood needs to show the hero as a global hunk, he is thrown onto a rugby field, after which he dodges past millions of burly blonds to score facile touchdowns.

Dilwale Dulhania Le Jayenge had SRK as the ultimate British jock (but who respected *bharatiya sanskriti*) racing across a rugby field as the foreigners licked the mud left in his wake.

John Abraham in **New York** was the all-American rockstar who introduced Neil Nitin Mukesh to the game in a wonderfully leafy New York park, as the World Trade Centres and Katrina Kaif vied for attention in the background.

Cycling

Veer bahadur ladke kaun? Rajput! Rajput!

Sanjay Lal Sharma—the perennial last-bencher—rose against this slogan of the elite Rajput College to participate in a cycling race that was last won by his school when his father raced. His brother—who looked set to win it—was put out of commission by the same Rajputs. In **Jo Jeeta Wohi Sikandar**, Aamir Khan played a cyclist who won the race of his life after just two weeks of practice. Did anybody say 'spoiler alert'? Well, did anybody expect Aamir to lose the race?

---

[37] Rahul Bose was a member of the Indian rugby team, where his short height earned him the nickname of Pygmy. He is yet to appear in a scrimmage on screen.

Kickboxing

The India-Pakistan rivalry is riveting stuff, even without the cricket. And after hockey, it was the turn of kickboxing to renew the passion. In **Lahore**, an Indian kickboxing team reached the city of the same name to play a match that would settle a championship as well as the Indo-Pak peace initiatives. Estranged brothers, simmering political tensions and the uneasy calm between the two nations formed the backdrop for some literally kick-ass boxing action.

Boxing

Many years ago, Mithun Chakraborty took a break from his disco-dancing to appear in a film called **Boxer**, which was about swimming across the English Channel in the month of December. Uffoh—joke, joke! It was about boxing, in which a son went back to the ring as redemption for his father, with many bloody noses and teary eyes thrown in.

The boxing plot cupboard in Bollywood seems to be pretty bare, roughly the same as **Apne**—the Deol family enterprise—in which two sons (Sunny and Bobby) enter the ring to prove their father's coaching abilities.

Badminton

Of course, no mention of sports is complete without the mention of the epic badminton match played by Jeetendra and Leena Chandraverkar in **Humjoli**.

It is momentous for several reasons: it gave Jeetu a valid reason—if he ever wanted one—for wearing white pants and shoes. The game was choreographed to the tune of a song. And most importantly, the sounds of the game (the shuttle cork hitting the racquet with a 'tuk') were incorporated into the soundtrack. And we have this absolute gem of a song...

*Dhal gaya din *TUK* Ho gayi shaam *TUK**
*Jaane do *TUK* Jaana hai *TUK**
*Abhi abhi toh aayi ho *TUK**
*Abhi abhi jaana hai? *TUK **

Maybe, I overdid the TUK a few more times than actual... but then, great sporting achievements are meant to be exaggerated.

Here And There: 7 Filmi Places

$\mathcal{B}$ollywood filmmakers seldom bother with geographical accuracy. Usually, they end up choosing locations for their scenic beauty and not for their connection to the screenplay. Occasionally, very occasionally, we have films that name fictional places as a part of the script and even more rarely, they get a life of their own.

One of the infinitesimally few examples of punning in Hindi cinema, **Dongri-La** was the antithesis of idyllic Shangri-La since it was ruled by always-cruel, always-correct Dong ('*Jo kabhi wrong nahin ho sakta*'), played with great relish by Amrish Puri in **Tahalka**.

Dong had a Chinese get-up (complete with pigtail) while the opening voice-over intoned that the country was located on the snowy boundaries of India as the camera focused on a crudely drawn map showing Pakistan and China. Since much of the action in the film was on snowclad peaks and mountain slopes, one can conclude with a shiver that Dongri-La was probably perched on the outer reaches of Siachen glacier.

Rampur was where Lakshman hailed from, in the eponymous film.

Lakshman, played by Kareena and Karisma's father, sang a wonderful song of losing oneself in another '*Gum hai kisike pyaar mein...*' which was about his only claim to fame.

Mr Kapoor sang energetically about how he was a *Rampur ka baasi*, for those amoeboid organisms who came to see the film but did not catch on where the hero hailed from. Unfortunately, there was no information of the location of Rampur. Presumably, there was no connection between this Rampur and the one of long-handled knives. After all, Lakshman hung around with only a long staff. No, not that kind—you perverts—I meant a lathi.

Dhanakpur was where it all started.

Thakur Dhanraj Singh killed Ratan Singh to avenge an injustice to his sister. And then, a couple of decades later, his son Raj came back to this place and fell in love with his arch-enemy's daughter, Rashmi.

This was a place close to Delhi, possible to travel to on a day-trip by bike. That was how Raj went there. It also had a sessions court where Ajit Vachchani was a paan-spitting lawyer. And if you were lucky, you could see Rashmi Singh—in a yellow dress—riding a horse. But then, the guy who saw her like that died in her arms at the stroke of sunset. Lucky?

Rakesh, son of T.C. Trivedi-ji, stayed in Fursatganj. Vimmi Saluja, whose parents wanted her to marry a head clerk, stayed in Pankhinagar. Their nicknames were **Bunty aur Babli**.

Pankhinagar was in the Lucknow district (as a Miss India organiser of Kanpur said) and Vimmi got off at Lucknow from the Jhansi Mail.[38] So, Pankhinagar was probably somewhere around where real-life Sultanpur exists. Fursatganj remained steadfastly coordinate-less.

From the pictures of the towns, the mindscapes of its residents and their trajectory after they leave, these could

---

[38] Incidentally, there is no Jhansi Mail which stops at Lucknow. Maybe it was Gwalior Mail.

be Anytown in Uttar Pradesh—where walls do not constrain dreams, where Bombay is the Holy Grail and where Himesh Reshammaiya is God.

Champaner was the village[39] where a rag-tag band of eleven Indians defeated the British in a game of cricket to escape **Lagaan**. In 1893, a guy called Bhuvan went up to one Captain Andrew Russell and challenged him to him a game of '*firangi gilli-danda*' and, to borrow a Ravi Shastri cliché, set a cat among the pigeons.

The drought and the landscape seemed to indicate a mid-western location for the village. There was an English cantonment posted nearby. The Raja of the princely state had his palace very close to the English barracks. The forest outside the village did not have game, only tame animals.

The crew shot near Bhuj and the language was a happy mix of central Indian dialects of Hindi.

Kashiram. Dhaulia. Imam Sahab. Ahmed. Basanti. Mausi. Radha. Ramlal. Even without the main players, the village of **Ramgarh** was well populated and had a life of its own.

The ironsmith's shop. The village well, where the dead body of Ahmed arrives. The thakur's house on a hillock. The famous water tank. The mango orchard. The talao. The Shiv mandir. The Holi maidan. We have been subjected to these set pieces so many times that if we were dropped off in the village, we could easily find our way around. And since the entire village was actually mapped and constructed, there is not a false step and no geographical inconsistencies either.

---

[39] A real Champaner exists in Gujarat, about fifty km from Vadodara.

When the Imam's son Ahmed was offered a job in a beedi factory in Jabalpur, Basanti mentioned the two 'large cities' close by—Meerut and Moradabad. So, the badlands of central UP was where Ramgarh has to be located.[40]

---

[40] Wikipedia lists ten real-life Ramgarhs in India and there could well be more.

Lifeline Of The Nation: 10 Trains You Shouldn't Miss

*C*hugging along across the length and breadth of the country, the humble train is a great unifier as everybody seems to have only happy memories associated with rail journeys. Add those happy memories to the beautiful memories of Bollywood and that's the most good you've felt in some time. Hindi cinema and trains have crossed paths many times though trains have been in a 'character' role for most.

One train we cannot miss is the most famous human one.

In **Ashirwad**, Ashok Kumar—an accomplished singer in his time—returned to playback singing with what is called the first rap song of Hindi cinema. As a train of little children went around him in a park, he sung to the beat of a moving train. Rhyming stations from all over India came alive as he breezed through Mangalore-Bangalore, Malegaon-Talegaon, Sholapur-Kolhapur, Jaipur-Raipur, Khandwa-Mandwa, Nellore-Vellore as part of some very crazy lyrics written by Harindranath Chattopadhyay. The joys of those childhood train journeys came alive as scenes zipping past the windows were brought to life once again.

One of the earliest train movies was called, well, **The Train**.

Rajesh Khanna was the CID officer who had to crack a series of crimes that seemed have a rail connection (pun not intended). Soon, he was climbing on top of train roofs in three-piece suits after taking a break from singing songs with a train beat. People kept getting murdered in first-class compartments as the good officer ran helter skelter before guiding the film to a suspenseful climax.

> *Never-Forget Alert:* The song that effectively ensured Rajesh Khanna's ascendancy to the Superstar throne was one involving a train too. Rajesh sang '*Mere sapnon ki rani*' in a jeep running abreast the Himalayan 'toy' train in which the comely Sharmila Tagore simpered and pretended to read an Alistair Maclean novel.[41]

Disaster movies have never been popular in Bollywood. This is strange because a dysfunctional group of underdogs rising to the occasion—a key aspect of disaster movies—is a very popular theme in Bollywood.

One of the very few disaster movies made in India—and probably ahead of its time—was **The Burning Train**. It was about a skyscraper hotel in which terrorists stormed a mahurat and took film stars hostage. (*Bwahahahaha... what foolishness, I say!*)

It was about a Super Express that was supposed to go from Delhi to Mumbai in fourteen hours. Vinod Khanna was the chief engineer of the project ('brain behind the train', you could say) but a jealous colleague bombed the damned thing on its inaugural run and we had a runaway

---

[41] *Can't-Avoid Alert*: Emraan Hashmi got embroiled in his usual extra-marital affair and a false murder rap-yet again-in a film known as **The Train: Some Lines Should Never Be Crossed**. There seemed to be no rail connection in the film except that he met his mistress on the Bangkok Metro.

train on the loose and burning with thousands of passengers from every corner of India on board. To the passenger list, add the chief engineer's wife and son, his best friend's ex-fiancée, another star couple who were falling in love and you have Mayhem on Metre Gauge!

The film was packed with more stars than sardines in a tin. Needless to say, three of them—Vinod Khanna, Dharmendra and Jeetendra—got together and brought the train to a screeching halt, though not before a few songs in flashback, reunions of estranged couples and general patriotic bonhomie.

Sholay opened with a train chugging in and it ended with another one going out.

Seven minutes into **Sholay**, there was a train action sequence so spectacular—and so advanced for that time— that it blew (and continues to blow) people's minds.

Shot on the outskirts of then-uninhabited Panvel, the producer employed international action directors, desi fight-masters and a visionary director to make a scene that set the tone for the rest of the movie.

Police Inspector Baldev Singh was returning to his post with two petty criminals in a goods train when a band of dacoits attacked them. The dacoits hadn't bargained for Bollywood's three most iconic daredevils to be on the same train and after a massive gunfight involving dynamite, guns and country liquor, they were well and truly beaten.

The trio went on to fight bigger battles.

Basu Chatterjee put Tony Braganza and Nancy Perreira on a Mumbai local from Bandra to Churchgate and showed a romance that must have happened to thousands of Mumbaikars.

In **Baton Baton Mein**, Amol Palekar and Tina Munim *became* those people as they passed notes, cast some furtive glances, exchanged shy smiles before falling head over heels in love. The helpful 'localite' passed on their notes from one end of the compartment to the other as Tony sketched Nancy and made polite conversation with her uncle at stations.

Of course, those were less hurried and less crowded times. But when you get on to a local even today, you still come across a young couple or two smiling at each other. And even with iPod headphones on, they can still talk, listen and fall in love—*Kahiye, suniye, baton baton mein pyaar ho gaya.*

The life-blood of India's fastest city—the Mumbai local— has been like a character in several films. Except the one in which it is supposed to have a title role.

Abhay Deol missed **Ek Chalis Ki Last Local** (that plied between Kalyan and Kurla). The two-and-a-half hours that he had to spend before the 4:10 ki first local was the subject of a gripping movie. Among the events that played out in real time, Abhay Deol met a beautiful woman, went into a beer bar, met a mafia don, played some high-stakes *teen-patti*, got into serious trouble and nearly had his ass taken—not your usual whiling-away-time-at-the-station stuff.

It started on Eurail.

Simran Singh was about to leave on a holiday with her friends... and she was late. As she ran through the station towards the only open door of the train, a dimpled smile and a friendly hand pulled her in. That was Raj Malhotra and Simran hated the flirt at first sight... but we all know how these things turn out, don't we?

A few months later, Raj was in Punjab—trying to get Simran back from an impending marriage. And all his efforts finally boiled down to a showdown on a railway platform. Raj was on the footboard of the train about to leave and Simran was being held back by her father. And at the last possible moment, her father released her and she ran toward the extended hand in the train once again... in one of the most whistle-inducing scenes of Bollywood. Whether it is by Eurail or Indian Railways, **Dilwale Dulhania Le Jayenge**.

Jaa Simran, Jaa... gaadi bula rahi hai

Coming on the back of the monster success of **Mr India**, **Roop Ki Rani Choron Ka Raja**—with the same producer-actor-actress team—was supposed to be India's answer to Hollywood's technical wizardry and break all box-office records. In reality, it was a disaster and the world's greatest train-robbery scene was lost in the debris.

Master-thief Romeo struck a deal with criminal mastermind Jugran to steal a trainload of diamonds. Romeo's separated-in-childhood elder brother, police inspector Ravi Verma, got a tip and also arrived at the scene. And thus began the spectacularly choreographed sequence, where Romeo landed on the train and completed the heist in the three minutes it took to pass through a wilderness.

At the time of release, it was one of the most eye-popping displays of action and technical wizardry in Bollywood. It still compares favourably with the best action from anywhere in the world.[42]

In **Ghulam**, Siddharth Marathe was the local Mumbai tough, who didn't think twice before getting into a scrap. When he picked a fight with Charlie and his—no, not chocolate factory—biker gang, he was challenged to a different game. Called the '*Dus dus ka daur*', it was a deadly race towards an approaching fast local train (of 10:10 PM that gave the race its name) near Saanpada station. Starting from a pre-determined point, it tested how fast one could run towards death before developing cold feet and jumping out of its way.

Shot with multiple cameras, the scene put to test Aamir Khan's fabled perfectionism because he did the scene without a double and waited till the very last minute before jumping off the track.

The final mention is a film where the train has no connection to the story. But when Malaika Arora's slim

---

[42] Train heists are surprisingly common—or many, at any rate—in Bollywood. In recent times, two major films—**Dhoom 2** and **Tees Maar Khan**—had a train robbery as an important plot point.

midriff fills up the entire screen and our collective senses, you can do nothing but go '*Chhaiyya chhaiyya*' to the tune of A.R. Rehman's rocking music.

In **Dil Se**, Farah Khan choreographed this every unusual—but unforgettable—sequence with Shah Rukh Khan and Malaika, using multiple cameras, a massive crane and a toy train chugging through north-east India. It was a terribly complicated shoot as the train passed through tunnels and an assistant was placed at the front to scream a warning whenever a tunnel approached (so that the crew could duck in time).

Her effort ensured that Farah Khan picked up the Filmfare Award for Best Choreography and she called it 'the happy ending everybody wanted from **Dil Se...**'.

Dil Se had the most magnificent train and passenger combination in history

The Truth About Cats & Dogs: 10 Filmi Pets

*I*n Bollywood, friends turn foes and foes turn friends at the drop of a hat. However, it would be apt to introduce a different kind of friend who won't turn foe for anything.

These friends are the four-legged stars of Bollywood, the valiant and honourable pets who have fought villains, shed tears (crocodiles not included), taken bullets for their masters, danced to Bappi Lahiri's tunes and even umpired cricket matches.

The logic was impeccable. If Dhanno—a mare—could pull a tonga, why couldn't a woman drive one? And thus was born probably the most famous human-best friend combo in the history of Bollywood—Basanti and Dhanno. Thanks to **Sholay**'s iconic status, Dhanno has become a full-fledged character that has stayed on and on (going on to become the name of a rickshaw in **Main Hoon Na**).

But for all her loyalty, she was treated rather cavalierly by her malkin. We didn't get to see her at the end of the film. Veeru and Basanti rode off in a train and not on her tonga...

Bonus Joke: Why did Dhanno run so fast to save Basanti? Well, there were four horses after her as well!

Try jumping off the roof of a train. With a gun in one hand. And a falcon perched on the other. Whenever you are unconvinced of the divinity of Amitabh Bachchan, visualise any scene from **Coolie** and your atheism will vanish faster than the falcon flutters its wings.

The falcon—named Allah Rakha—featured in the super-charged 'entry dialogue' by Amitabh in which he pegged his identity to the protection of Allah and the assistance of his faithful feathered friend—'*Bachpan se hai sar pe Allah ka haath, aur Allah Rakha hai apne saath...*'

The falcon appeared in key sequences—snatching guns off villains, dropping garlands during courting songs—and his presence reached a climax when Amitabh ascended an election podium with a huge falcon on the backdrop and the real one perched on his forearm. What did I say about *Allah Rakha hai apne saath*?

How many films can you remember that were named after an animal? Well, **Haathi Mere Saathi** was one for sure.

Rajesh Khanna shared equal screen time and less-than-equal screen space with the four tusk-eteers—whom he called his 'brothers'. And their roles in the film were no different from that of the standard-issue 'good brother' in Hindi cinema. They helped Rajesh Khanna grow up, earn money, woo Tanuja and scare away villains. The only thing they did not assist the hero in was—presumably—fathering the child.

Most dog-lovers have asked—how much can a dog do? The question the maker of **Teri Meherbaniyan** (the legendary K.C. Bokadia) asked was different—what do you *want* a dog to do?

Moti, the ubiquitous black Labrador of Bollywood (who always got separate billing as 'Wonder Dog') was literally the hero of the film as he did matchmaking, shed copious tears, performed the last rites of his master (Jackie Shroff) and took revenge.

Rub your eyes and read those last ten words again. Yes, Moti carried the water-filled kalash ahead of the funeral procession, went around the pyre with a burning log and finally lit the fire.

When it went on to kill Amrish Puri after that, it seemed like an anti-climax.

Only one question: How much was Jackie paid for this film? And how much Moti?

A dynamic horse-dog duo was the main supporting cast behind **Mard** Tangewala's crusade against the British Raaj. Moti returned (as Moti) as did Badal, the white steed that has been the preferred mode of transport for a million characters in historical—or even not-so-historical—films.

Badal got his separate comic sub-plot where he fell in love with Lord Curzon's mare (which was part of a statue) and even eloped with his lady-love at the very end. Moti got his action sub-plot where he stormed a Britishers Only club—assisted by one Mr Amitabh Bachchan—and managed to uproot that insulting notice once seen at the entrances of British-owned establishments: Dogs and Indians Not Allowed.

Imagine two animals getting star billing and separate sub-plots in an Amitabh Bachchan movie. That probably makes them bigger stars than Deepak Parashar.[43]

---

[43] Moti has got separate sub-plots in several films. For example, he single-handedly cared for an infant in **Maa** when the baby's mother passed away.

Bollywood's favourite black Labrador returned in **Bol Radha Bol**, a David Dhawan thriller in which an industrialist (Rishi Kapoor) was being swindled out of his inheritance. As the industrialist returned from a romantic sojourn in a village, he came face to face with a lookalike who had taken his place. The industrialist called for his trusted dog to prove his identity but the dog turned out be an impostor, thus making it a very rare animal double role. Of course, the heroic duo overcame the evil machinations of the villainous clique to chase the impostors—human and canine—out.

Salman Khan and Sooraj Barjatya's debut—**Maine Pyar Kiya**—was a history-altering hit and also had the biggest pet hit song in *Kabootar ja ja ja...* The pigeon of the song delivered love letters—ping-ponging between Bhagyashree and Salman. The pigeon was no ordinary bird—as it got star-billing in the credits as Handsome.

But if we delve into the history of the pigeon (in the film, not real life!), we realise that he actually belonged to Seema (the vamp, played by Pervin Dastur) whose cruel brother (Mohnish Behl) planned to used the bird for target practice. On being saved by the simpering Bhagyashree, Handsome pledged undying allegiance to her and even returned in the climax to take revenge on Mohnish Behl, thus rendering PETA largely redundant.

Whenever Indian cricketers get out to dubious umpiring decisions, we miss cute little Tuffy (the cuteness quotient debatable, though) who wore an umpire's hat, sat on a high chair and put up notices to give umpiring decisions in **Hum Aapke Hain Koun**. And that was just the first scene.

Sooraj Barjatya maintained his tradition of a 'complete' happy family by showcasing the only Pomeranian in the world which didn't snap at strangers. During the film, Tuffy assisted wedding rituals by couriering shoes, did matchmaking (a basic minimum requirement of Bolly pets), acted cute, and finally brokered a happy ending by delivering a letter to the wrong person. Overall, Tuffy upstaged Handsome, the pigeon of **Maine Pyar Kiya** and—some dog-lovers claim—even Laxmikant Berde.

Bonus Pet: In a bid to upstage the pigeon and the dog, Sooraj Barjatya introduced an animated parrot in **Main Prem Ki Diwani Hoon**, which spoke only in film titles.

A monkey—called Bajrangi—formed a seamless trio with Govinda and Chunky Pandey in **Aankhen**, and all of them did a lot of monkeying around, with the real one being the most serious of the lot. The monkey's place in the sun was assured when the trio had to perform in front of the Gateway of India to earn their daily bread (after Kader Khan kicked them out of their house). The monkey was the top dog in the song as he was compared to fighting-dancing stars ('*Nache to Jeetender, Maare to Dharmender...*')—which may have melted Maneka Gandhi's heart but the reactions of the aforementioned stars remain unavailable.

The crocodile in **Shaan** was a pet with a difference. You couldn't have possibly petted it. Neither did it have a name. But the efficiency with which it discharged its carnivorous duties was very commendable. Swimming in an enclosed pool under rotating chairs (which had traitors shackled to it) was a dirty job but Mr Croc did that too. The moment the traitor was upturned into the pool by his master—bald-headed villain Shaakaal—he came charging in and promptly dug in. Except when he met his match in Amitabh Bachchan at the climax who drove a stake through his jaws and—to quote Arnold Schwarzenegger—'he was luggage'.

Honourable Mention

You could say that the cat called Radha had a guest appearance in **Jaane Tu Ya Jaane Na**. Actually, not even a guest appearance since the film opened with the announcement of her death by a solemn doctor and Ms Aditi (Genelia D'Souza) grieving at her funeral. But the cat's contribution has to be seen in the greater context as the heroine's depression and a first-class A.R. Rehman song ('*Kabhi kabhi Aditi...*') were the clear by-products of her untimely death.

The length of a role is never a measure of importance to a movie. Remember, even Naseeruddin Shah never came out of the photo frame in the same movie.

STATUTORY DECLARATION:

NO ANIMALS WERE HARMED DURING THE MAKING OF THIS CHAPTER.

Stop Press: 8 Filmi Newspapers

*J*ournalists have been beacons of hope in many films. Over many years, we had newspaper reporters and photographers chasing crooked politicians and evil businessmen. Now—in the last decade or so—we have TV journalists coming into the fray as well.

A journalist in a Bollywood has always been clearly typified—wearing a kurta-pajama (for the Hindi press) or jeans with a photographer's jacket (English)—but their newspapers less so. Which newspapers did they work for? What were their editors like? Their owners? Their editorial policies? Do they ever show anything about the making of the newspaper except the mandatory shot of the printed papers pouring off the press?

Daily Toofan

When you had an editor who climbed on tables while talking to his star reporter, who paid extra money to get a scoop on an absconding heiress and who popped pills while trying to tear out his hair, the newspaper he ran was bound to be super-interesting.

In **Dil Hai Ke Manta Nahin**, Tiku Talsania ran the aptly named *Daily Toofan* and had explosive tiffs with his smart alec crime reporter Raghu Jaitley. But he was not beyond consoling the guy when he had a breakup and resembling the Bollywood father figure: a heart of gold inside a tough exterior.

The Crimes Of India

Do we have so many crimes and misdemeanours going on around us that we have a full newspaper dedicated to it? Of course, we do. In fact, the crime situation can be so bad that we would need an invisible hero—**Mr India**—to solve it.

The Crimes of India had Mr Gaitonde as editor, who continuously got wrongly connected calls (from international smugglers and housewives seeking dry-cleaners) and a vivacious journalist called Seema Soni—who hated kids.

Annu Kapoor did a superb comic turn as the hassled editor of the newspaper which loved doing interviews with criminals just released from prison. Apparently, the newspaper also carried ads for houses on rent and you had simple people like Arun Verma (played by the one-costumed Anil Kapoor) walking in for that. The mistaken identity was only one of the many states of confusion that the newspaper endured but Mr India solved it all. Except the mystery of Mr Gaitonde's telephone, that is.

The Independent / Swatantra Bharat

The meteoric rise of **Guru**—Gurukant Desai—was precipitated by the strong support he got from upright newspaper editor and owner, Manik Dasgupta, of *The Independent*. Right from the pre-Independence days, this editor had championed causes that were right. So, when Guru turned truant, it was Manik Dasgupta (a.k.a. Nanaji) who let loose his best journalist (Shyam Saxena, played by Madhavan) to expose him.

The film's story was believed to have been loosely based on Dhirubhai Ambani's life and his run-ins with Ramnath

Goenka of *The Indian Express* and Madhavan's character was apparently based on that of Arun Shourie.

Mithun Chakraborty delivered a brilliant performance as the honest and eccentric Bengali editor of the principled daily and Mani Ratnam's eye for detail ensured that the look of the newspaper was very real—right from the masthead down to the columns.

Manik Dasgupta—Editor-in-Chief, *The Independent* and *Swatantra Bharat*

New Delhi Diary

Jeetendra's few offbeat roles—in between his white-shoe-pencil-moustache-energetic-dance routine—tend to get lost.

In **New Delhi**—a songless thriller—he played a journalist who got beaten to paralysis and was then jailed by an evil politician duo. After coming out of prison, he—along with his girlfriend—started a newspaper called *New Delhi Diary* which seemed to have a knack for getting exclusives ahead of everybody else from its mysterious reporter, Vishwanath.

In a plot lifted partially from Irving Wallace's *The Almighty*, Jeetendra delivered a restrained performance as the newspaper editor who plotted brilliantly to bring his powerful enemies to their knees.

Incidentally, there was a scene in this film where Jeetendra singlehandedly made the entire front page of the paper's launch edition. Real-life editors have confirmed that this is a task probably even beyond Superman. But not the Bollywood hero.

New Delhi Times

Written by Gulzar and set in modern New Delhi, the film of the same name traced the experiences of editor Vikas Pande (Shashi Kapoor in a National Award-winning role) as he unravelled the sinister connection between a hooch tragedy and the murder of an MLA against a backdrop of political unrest.

The political pressures on a leading daily's editor, the editor-owner relationship, the ambitious and ruthless politician, the perils of idealism and even the work-life balance of a journalist were brought out brilliantly in the film. The film had a wealth of acting talent—the characters of Om Puri as a politician, Sharmila Tagore as the editor's wife, Manohar Singh as the newspaper-owner and A.K. Hangal as the editor's idealist father were all wonderfully etched.

Samaadhan

What kind of newspaper sends reporters to jail to track convicts who may actually be innocent? That too, lady reporters in bright yellow dresses. But then, the reporter was the jailer's daughter and when she (Raveena Tandon) was attacked by burly goons, there was a burlier hero (Sunil Shetty) to save her.

This was **Mohra**. Raveena Tandon worked for a newspaper called *Samaadhan* under the able editorial guidance of Yunus Parvez and she was ever-ready to assist Inspector Amar (Akshay Kumar) on undercover missions, as a cabaret dancer.

But except for the first few minutes of the film—in which she embarked upon a crusade to free the wrongfully convicted Sunil Shetty—Raveena did nothing even remotely resembling a journalist's normal work. But then, you did not go to watch her pen an op-ed piece. You went to see her dance in the rain, wearing a clingy yellow saree.

Khabardaar

Two struggling photographers trying to run a studio got commissioned to take pictures by a newspaper out to expose the high and mighty. The sting was to be done on a well-known builder, who had a finger in a Commissioner's murder and they all ended up in a live play with a corpse, which had become something like a proof of the murder. Those who have seen **Jaane Bhi Do Yaaro** would realise what an inadequate description of the story this is and how every single element added exponentially to the mayhem.

Bhakti Bharve played the no-nonsense editor of *Khabardaar*, a newspaper which stayed true to its name by being a whistle-blower. The editor was not beyond flirting with her freelance minion (Naseeruddin Shah) to get him to swear undying loyalty to her. Nor was she beyond a few behind-the-scenes deal-making to get a good price for the pictures.

Was she a typical sting editor? Was **Jaane Bhi Do Yaaro** a typical comedy?

Nation Today

Page 3 became the first newspaper section to be made into a film and Konkona Sen Sharma played the journalist zipping around high-society parties in Mumbai as she faced taunts from colleagues about whether her beat was news or entertainment. Madhur Bhandarkar is known for the meticulous research he puts into his films and this one was no exception. Among the characters as well as the newspapers, plenty of real-life parallels were identified as the film explored the seamy underbelly of commercial pressure on newspapers.

Boman Irani played Konkona's kind but spineless boss with his customary brilliance and all the people in his office looked totally real. Including the desk editor who cut Konkona's copy beyond recognition.

Waak Engliss, Taak Engliss: 15 Lessons In English

You could legitimately ask—why? Why should we talk about the English language in a book on Hindi cinema? You could then also ask, why an English book on Hindi cinema. And that would be the end of the matter...

Well, Bollywood has mostly presented English speakers as caricatures and hence, the need to have well-written dialogues and elegantly composed songs has not been felt often. There have been only a few examples of the sensible, and many nonsensical ones.

In 1878, British Prime Minister Benjamin Disraeli gave a speech in Parliament in which he referred to his bitter rival, William Gladstone.

So, why is this relevant to a piece on Bollywood?

Because Disraeli called Gladstone a 'sophisticated rhetorician intoxicated by the exuberance of your own verbosity'. Exactly hundred years later, Mr Anthony Gonsalves jumped out of an Easter egg with the same line, probably the most famous use of English in Bollywood.

And of course, Mr Gonsalves did not stop there. He backed it up with important theories like the coefficient of linear expansion with juxtaposition of the haemoglobin in the atmosphere. No wonder everybody in Bandra village thought him to be a total dude.

The most famous English song is, of course, the one sung by **Julie** in the eponymous film.

It is a beautiful song, written by Harindranath Chattopadhyay and sung by Preeti Sagar. 'My Heart is Beating' never fails to lift our spirits with its simple words and tune. Harindranath was the brother of Sarojini Naidu so you could attribute the poetry to genetics. The tune was composed by Rajesh Roshan, who is the son of veteran music director Roshan. So you could attribute the melody to genetics as well.

And while the song was being sung by Lakshmi, playing the title role, her on-screen younger sister was hopping and skipping around her. That little sister grew up to become Sridevi.

David D'Costa had only one wish—to speak better English than his son. And he promised his wife exactly that. Soon afterwards, he was framed for his wife's murder and jailed for two decades. In jail, he taught himself English and when he came to his wife's grave after release, he met an upstart of a police officer who looked exactly like him.

Amitabh Bachchan had a verbal duel with Amitabh Bachchan, as the younger one spoke with a brashness and casual accent while the older one spoke with the measured caution of a non-native English speaker. This was the first of many showdowns in **Aakhree Raasta** and the way the two men spoke, it seemed as if they were, well, two different men.

Lagaan had lots of English dialogue and legitimately so. It also had a nice English interlude in the *O rey chhori* song—as Rachel Shelly and Gracey Singh sang their odes of love in parallel tracks. Vasundhara Das sang the English track to perfection and A.R. Rehman majestically merged the operatic flow of *I am in love* with the rustic melody of *O rey chhori*.

Apparently, the English lyrics were written by Farhan and Zoya Akhtar. They were assigned this task by their father—the credited lyricist of the song—to come up with the words very quickly and they did.

It is generally accepted that speaking English is a pre-requisite for a job in a five-star hotel. When country bumpkin Arjun Singh (s/o Dashrath Singh s/o Bheem Singh) was told of this, he immediately proceeded to demonstrate his knowledge of English and the similarities between Bhairon and Byron. And commentaries on cricket.

He got the job—if not for anything else but to just make him stop. And to his maalik, he became the **Namak Halaal**.

Zany lines in English come in droves.

It started way back as Kishore Kumar and Nutan taught each other English in **Dilli Ka Thug**. *C.A.T. Cat maaney billi. M.A.D. Mad maaney paagal.*

Around the same time, in **Howrah Bridge**, you had Helen shimmying in a kimono and announcing her Oriental origins to the world—*Mera naam Chin Chin Choo / Raat chandni main aur too, hello mister how do you do?*

In recent times, **Dhooms 1 & 2**—to get the international feel—zoomed through easy-on-the-ear English lyrics but somebody should have told them while Tata Young is fine, Uday Chopra singing *My Name is Ali* does not really help towards the international marketability of the franchise.

In **Kuch Naa Kaho** (starring Abhishek and Aishwarya—before they got hitched), Javed Akhtar wrote some clever stuff using English letters. *ABBG. TPOG.*

IPKI. Tum POG. For those who haven't got it, read the letters individually.[44]

You are my mind-blowing mahiya... Ajay Devgn was paid the compliment of a lifetime by Shamita Shetty in the film **Cash** as he looked quite nonchalant while she went *crazy with desire.*

In **Tashan**—a film which pretty much defined the phrase 'style over substance'—Kareena was asked to put on blond wigs and wiggle her body as Akshay Kumar complimented her *white white face* and confessed that he wants do *advance booking* at her *dil ke box office.* Wow.

In the annals of the English Bollywood Song (if one such exists in the first place), the person who would get the largest entry would be Annu Malik.

In **Main Khiladi Tu Anadi**, he intoned in the screechy tuneless monstrosity of his voice—'*My Adorable Darling / I think of you every night, every morning...*'

He followed it up with LML and GTH—*Let's Make Love* and *Go To Hell* respectively—in **Haathkadi** (starring Govinda and Shilpa Shetty).

And then, he delivered the knockout punch in the most inane and gratingly bad lyrics of **Waqt: The Race Against Time**—'*Do me a favour / Let's play Holi*'.

Why? Why? Why? Why is playing Holi a favour? Why doesn't Mr Malik do us a favour and stop singing?

But nothing—absolutely nothing—can come close to the great English lyrics in the history of Bollywood that were

---

[44] The bilingual song, therefore, went something like *E bibi ji... Tea peeyo ji... I peeke aai... You peeyo ji...*

written by Indivaar and set to tune by the legendary Bappi Lahiri in a film called **Rock Dancer** (aha—English name too!)...

You are my chicken fry / You are my fish fry
Kabhi na kehna kudiye bye bye bye
You are my samosa / You are my masala dosa
Main na kahoongi mundiya bye bye bye

Wait, where are you going? There's more...

You are my chocolate / You are my cutlet
Main na kahoongi mundiya bye bye bye
You are my rosogolla / You are my rasmalai
Kabhi na kehna kudiye bye bye bye

What poetry! If he had heard all of these, Shelley (Percy Bysshe—not Rachel) would have drowned himself to death. Oh—he did?

6

WE, THE PEOPLE

'Chhaliya mera naam, Chhaliya mera naam / Hindu Muslim Sikh Isaai, sabko mera salaam'—RAJ KAPOOR in **Chhalia**

*N*othing is more inclusive than Bollywood. Cinegoers from all religions and all parts of the country go into a trance witnessing a Muslim lyricist writing a Ramleela song, a Hindu composer churning out a qawwali and lost sons of a Hindu family being brought up by Catholic priests.

And yes, every region and religion of India is stereotyped with equal offensiveness.

◆ Christian Brothers: 12 Depictions of Christianity
◆ Jo Bole So Nihal: 12 Depictions of Sikhs
◆ Bawas in Bollywood: 9 Depictions of Parsis
◆ Crossing the Vindhyas: 10 Depictions of south Indians
◆ The Big Bong Theory: 12 Depictions of Bengalis
◆ East, West, North, South: 8 Regional Superstars

Christian Brothers:
12 Depictions of Christianity

*C*hristians in Bollywood drink a lot (sometimes even running bars), swear in English, pepper their dialogues with 'man', have bombastic names and are by-and-large Good Samaritans.

There have been a large number of priests as well. Usually a solemn person hovering in the background presiding over marriages and the occasional confessional, his dialogues have a profusion of 'my son' and 'Lord *tumko shanti de*'.

Of course, there have been a lot of Foreign Devils (made famous by Bob Christo and Tom Alter, exaggerating their accents) but they were mostly British Oppressors (or The Foreign Hand) and had nothing to do with religion.

The most important signpost of the Bollywood Christian is a suitably polysyllabic name.

Anthony Gonsalves is undoubtedly the best known Christian name in India and even overshadows Vijay Verma, occasionally. Actually, it is probably Amitabh's only screen name which came close to overwhelming his actual name. Post the stupendous success of **Amar Akbar Anthony**, people started calling him Anthony-bhai on the streets. Of course, the added allure of this name came from the fact that it was the name of Pyarelal's (of Laxmikant-Pyarelal fame) violin teacher.

The second most popular Christian name in Bollywood is probably **Bobby** Braganza. She spoke like an Indian teenager, performed a mean dance in a part-Koli-part-tribal outfit although her father (Prem Nath) managed to live up to every single stereotype of the filmi Christian—as he played a heavy-drinking fisherman.

It would be apposite to take up the story of Shiney Ahuja's second film since we have already talked about the stereotype of the benevolent Catholic Father.

In **Sins**, Shiney played the role of a priest (William, if you must know the name) who fell in love with a young woman, impregnated her, got her to abort, married her off to somebody else to hush up the affair and then killed pretty much half the town in a love-crazed spree.[45] He smashed the stereotype of the Catholic priest as well as most tenets of Christianity so violently that there was an avalanche of protests against this Vinod Pande film.

The drunkard is the other Christian cliché in Bollywood, generally seen in a street corner, slurring over dialogue and slobbering over life.

Pran's part in **Majboor** was probably the first time this character had a major role and even got to sing a song about the ill effects of mixing water in bottles of alcohol— *'Daaru ki botal mein kaahe pani bharta hai / Phir na kehna Michael daaru peeke danga karta hai'* And not only the song, he even had a massive say in the climax due to a big clue he held to solving the murder mystery.

The stereotype of the Christian drunkard is so strong that even in a realistic film like **Ardh Satya**, there was a bit part

---

[45] There is a song for this kind of 'murderous rage'... *'Why this kolaveri, di?'*

called Lobo (played by Naseeruddin Shah), a former police officer who turned alcoholic due to the frustrations of the job.

In **Julie**, the social divide shown between a 'cultured' Hindu family and a 'crass' Christian family was rather exaggerated. An engine-driver's daughter fell in love with a Hindu classmate, got pregnant and was promptly accused of 'loose morals'. And of course, because it was a Christian family, they sang songs in English. But thank God for that cliché because we got Preeti Sagar's wonderful *'My heart is beating'*.

If we get into arthouse territory, we have **Albert Pinto Ko Gussa Kyoon Aata Hai**—in which Naseeruddin Shah played the title role of an angry son of a retrenched mill worker. The economic crisis slowly descending on Bombay's thousands of millworkers was sensitively depicted in the film, and Naseer did a stellar job in the part of a motor mechanic.

It is rumoured that Albert Pinto was the name of one of the vendors (caterer/costume/something) from one of the producer's earlier projects, who hadn't been paid. In order to placate him, the lead character was named after him. This story remains tantalisingly unproven, like many of Bollywood's urban legends.

Prahaar is one of those few films to have depicted Indian Christians realistically—with their language, milieu, fears and motivations clearly etched out. Madhuri Dixit gave a stellar performance as Shirley Pinto, the stoic fiancée of an Indian commando, as did the ensemble cast, borrowed from the theatre and all of them directed very well by Nana Patekar.

Baton Baton Mein was set in an authentic Christian milieu and that was part of the novelty of the film but there was nothing in the story that was exclusive to the community. A love story in Bombay peppered with a genial uncle, crazy brother and pestering mother is as cute and relevant today as it was thirty years back. And it painted a loving portrait of India's Maximum City by setting the romantic scenes in local trains, on seasides and amidst cute Christian grannies (Leela Mishra in a floral dress) in drawing rooms.

Bada Din was the first of two Hindi movies Bengali film director Anjan Dutta made on the Anglo-Indian community of Calcutta—the other being **Bow Barracks Forever**.

In the former, Marc Robinson played a young man wanting to make a mark on the music scene as murderous goons, an angry girlfriend (Tara Deshpande) and an irate landlady (Shabana Azmi) descended on him like a ton of bricks. The film was set around Christmas, its name being the Hindi version of the 'big day'.

In the second, a rag-tag group of Anglo-Indian residents of a largish residential block got together in their own eccentric ways to prevent a promoter from taking over their heritage home. Though the intention was to pay an affectionate tribute to the Anglo-Indian community and their resilience, an aggressive love-making scene starring Moon Moon Sen also caught attention.

Moral dilemmas have never been the forte of Bollywood, and Christian moral dilemmas, even less so.

In fact, probably the only one presented was in **Aakhree Raasta**—where David (played by Amitabh Bachchan) went into a church and confessed to crimes he was about to commit. His rationale was that at the end of the three murders he was about to start on, he might not be around for a confessional. The priest broke the sacred oath of secrecy and reported it to the police. He declared that while it was a sin to divulge details of a confession, he was doing so because he considered saving three lives more important.

The police officer (David's lost son—AB in a double role) logically concluded that if the guy was indeed a devout Christian, he would get really upset at the priest's betrayal. And would try to kill the priest as retribution. So he arranged a ring of security around the priest. He probably forgot that it was a Bollywood movie and so David did the most illogical thing in the world. He walked into the police headquarters and murdered his first victim—the Police Commissioner himself.

Honourable Mentions

Ajit's villainy (which grew exaggerated in the subsequent series of jokes) was always centred on a group of henchmen and molls with 'Christian' names, though no allusion was ever made to their religion and Ajit was quite happy with Punjabising the pronunciations. Raabert, Tawny and Mona have been flogged to death, actually.

And finally, we have Commissioner De Mello of **Jaane Bhi Do Yaaro**—who has to be one of the funniest corpses in cinematic history. Though I am not sure if he can be counted as a Christian character, because he was hardly alive.

Jo Bole So Nihal:
12 Depictions Of Sikhs

Probably the only race in India with a sense of humour has to take a lot of rubbish. Putting up with an undending stream of Sardarji jokes cannot be funny.

Bollywood's portrayal of Sikhs in character roles is—as usual—one-dimensional. The Sardar is always the jovial guy breaking into a bhangra at the drop of a hat and running into a fight equally rapidly. Though, there have been many Sardar lead characters in recent times and nearly every A-list star has played one.

One of the earliest Sikh characters in Bollywood was played by Dharmendra in **Jeevan Mrityu**. He was an honest bank employee who was framed for embezzlement and sentenced to prison. When he was released, he was a broken man. Due to a freak incident, he was pronounced dead, giving him the chance to take revenge on his enemies by taking on a different identity. Dharmendra came back as Bikram Singh, a shrewd and calculating Sikh businessman whose agenda was not only to destroy the villains but also win back the love of his fiancée (Rakhee) who had also given him up for dead.

Govind Nihalani made **Vijeta**, a film on the confusion and eventual resolution of a teenager's dilemmas. His career choices, the disagreements with his father, the beginnings of romance, were all dealt with sensitively and realistically.

Kunal Kapoor played the troubled youngster and his real-life father (Shashi Kapoor) carried out his duties on-screen as well. In an interesting piece of detail, the father was clean-shaven while the son maintained the traditional beard and turban. The son did that traditional thing to rebel against his father—ironic.

Easily the most popular actor playing a Sardar on-screen is Sunny Deol.

In **Border**, he played a real-life war hero Major Kuldeep Singh Chandpuri. During the 1971 Battle of Longewala, a small squad of 150 men had resisted a full company of 2,000 Pakistani soldiers, fortified with tanks, from taking over the strategic post. Sunny Deol achieved it on-screen by hollering loudly at the Pakistani commander, demanding the best out of his own men even more loudly and glaring so hard at the Pakistani tanks that they almost melted. Wonder if the real Major did it the same way?[46]

If people had any doubts about the strength, sense of humour and tolerance of Sikhs after **Border**, Sunny Deol returned to dispel all of them—and more—in **Gadar: Ek Prem Katha**. As truck-driver Tara Singh, he sang songs to charm convent-educated girls (mercifully he did not dance). Then he saved a Muslim girl caught in the Partition riots, wooed and eventually married her. After she was forcibly taken to Lahore by her father, he went there and brought her back. Oh—there was the small matter of

---

[46] Sikhs have done stellar duty in the Indian Army and there have been many depictions of the same in Bollywood as well. In a relatively unknown film—**Heroes**—Salman Khan appeared in a cameo as a Kargil war hero.

the Pakistani army in his path so he vanquished them using a good ol' hand pump.

Bonus Movie: He did one more much-publicised turn as a Sikh in **Jo Bole So Nihaal** but the profusion of scantily-clad women on the posters caused too much offence in religious circles and the film had a very limited release due to protest-induced boycotts in cinemas.

A British filmmaker came to India to make a film on the freedom struggle and found a gang of frivolous friends to play parts of revolutionaries. Karan, Sukhi, Aslam and DJ were part of the devil-may-care generation that **Rang De Basanti** sought to portray.

DJ was actually Daljeet, whose mother ran a highway dhaba and whose grandfather was a gurudwara priest. He was a DU student who hung around the university because he didn't have the courage to face the outer world. His language was the Punjabi-infused Hindi that is so common in Delhi. His religion was almost incidental to the plot.

You only realised later on that the group consisted of Hindu, Muslim and Sikh boys but it was done subtly and without any hint of tokenism.

It was as if the film was made for the return of Congress to power in 2009. Every paper in this land went completely gaga over Manmohan Singh's second term in office and dubbed him **Singh is Kinng**.

Akshay Kumar rocked the box office with a film that was fabulously inane, a negative that Akshay and his favourite directors have not only converted to a positive but raised to an art form. A Punjabi village bumpkin's trip to Australia (via Egypt to sing a song) and transformation into becoming the 'Kinng' of the underworld was as fantastic as they got. But if you wanted realism, you would do well to avoid Anees Bazmee movies. The story was just an excuse to wrap around the gags, hit songs and Katrina Kaif around Akshay. So that's what happened and even Snoop Dogg appeared to pay homage to the Singhs—Happy, Lucky, Mika, Guruji et al.

> *Outrage Alert*: Akshay's designer-trimmed beard attracted the ire of Sikh religious leaders and the star had to placate them.

Love Aaj Kal traced the changing face of love, yesterday and today. In the modern day, Jai (Saif Ali Khan) and Meera (Deepika Padukone) broke up a near-perfect relationship to pursue their dream careers. This was completely incomprehensible to middle-aged Sikh restaurateur, Veer Singh (Rishi Kapoor), who had travelled the breadth of the nation for one glimpse of his beloved. Their stories inter-cut each other and Saif also played the younger Veer Singh, the rowdy who transformed to win his love.

Could Veer Singh have been something else instead of a Sikh? Probably, but it helps because the moment you show a Sikh, the stereotype of large hearts takes over. And love stories are all about large hearts. Yesterday, today and tomorrow.

Enterprising Sikhs have travelled halfway across the globe to set up thriving businesses. One of the first such outposts was London, where Southall can easily be mistaken for a town in Punjab. This is the area where **Patiala House** was located.

Apparently based on the life of Monty Panesar, this was the story of a Sikh boy (Akshay Kumar) who passed up the chance to play for England because his autocratic father (Rishi Kapoor) refused to allow him to represent the 'enemy'. His father, having borne the brunt of extreme xenophobia when he had first come to the country (UK), had developed bitterness towards his adopted country.

Harpreet Singh Bedi did not want to waste time doing an MBA. His ambition was to become **Rocket Singh: Salesman Of The Year**.

True to the industrious nature of his race, he plunged headlong into a job—that too, in action-packed sales. As a salesman for computer firm AYS Corporation, he was exactly what we know Sikhs to be—honest and hardworking, jovial and jugaadu. Starting from the Guru Nanak wallpaper on his computer to the turbans to the slightly Punjabi accent, Ranbir Kapoor got the nuances of a young Sardar just perfect.

And no, the stereotypes of Sardarji jokes weren't true either since he wasn't short of brains. '*Mere number kum hain, dimaag nahin...*'

At least one entry in the list has to be a girl who is a 'Sikhni from Bhatinda'—Geet Kaur Dhillon, played by Kareena Kapoor in **Jab We Met**. As the hyper-talkative, super-gregarious Punjaban, Kareena made the role her own and gave the character depth. Her mannerisms, her slight accent, her clothes were straight out of small-town Punjab.

Harpreet Singh Bedi, with his grandfather

Her entire family—including Dara Singh as her strict grandfather—was excellent and the ensemble gave the film its warmth.

Amitabh Bachchan has played a Sikh character in just a couple of not-so-great movies. In Mehul Kumar's **Kohram**, he played Colonel Balbir Singh Sodhi who went underground after an assassination attempt on a corrupt home minister and reappeared in a clean-shaven avatar.

He played another Sikh soldier—Major General Amarjeet Singh—in **Ab Tumhare Hawale Watan Sathiyon.**

Baby Sardars must have been certified by the *Guinness World Records* as the cutest species on earth. Nothing epitomised this cuteness better than the silent Sardar kid in

Kuch Kuch Hota Hai, who went about counting stars and kissing girls without speaking a word. Parzan Dastur, who played the kid, became an overnight sensation and his last scene entreaty for Kajol to stay back (*'Tussi na jao'*) became a catchphrase. Karan Johar—the king of emotions—just knew nobody but a cute Sardar kid could pull this off.

Bawas In Bollywood: 9 Depictions Of Parsis

*I*t's true that Parsis are not very visible people. But Bollywood does worse than make them invisible. Every time a member of the minority community appears on screen, more often than not, he or she is a caricature. Of all stereotypes, the Parsis are probably the worst hit.

The men are always shown wearing the traditional black hat and a white bandgala coat, driving a vintage car loaded with a large family. The women wear sarees worn in the traditional style and carry Japanese hand fans. They speak in an accent with all their 'T's pronounced hard, and use a whole lot of '*dikras*' in their conversation. Has anyone met a Parsi like that in real life?

Khatta Meetha is probably the movie which has the highest number of Parsi characters ever.

A loose remake of **Yours, Mine and Ours**, it had two single parents, Homi Mistry (Ashok Kumar) and Nargis Sethna (Pearl Padamsee), marrying each other and uniting their gigantic families to make a family of oh-my-God proportions. Firoze, Freni, Fardeen, Peelu, Russi, Jaal and Fali went about doing the usual sibling rivalry stuff before The Great Family Bonding happened.

None of the on-screen Parsis spoke in any kind of exaggerated accent and even their clothes were quite regular. In fact, probably the only reason the lead characters were made Parsi was to take recourse to the liberalism of a community that allows a second marriage between two elderly people.

Pestonjee was the story of two good friends—Naseeruddin Shah and Anupam Kher—who fell in love with the same woman (Shabana Azmi). One sacrificed his love for the other. Sounds likes standard-issue Bollywood love triangle, doesn't it? Except that there was a twist in the tale when the sacrificer returned to meet the couple after some years and found out that his friend was having an extramarital affair.

Directed by Vijaya Mehta, this is what was called 'art film' in the 1980s and had a different mood and tempo from Bollywood. The three lead actors' acting credentials were never in any question; they got under the skin of their characters effortlessly, and returned one of the most authentic depictions of Parsis on screen.[47]

Many films have had cameos of slightly batty Parsi characters but I would choose only one—**Muqaddar Ka Sikandar**—where the character was not a real Parsi but a fake one, making the imitation way more outrageous.

In a zany sub-plot, budding lawyer Vinod Khanna decided he had to help a young girl elope (which would help his case in a convoluted way). He 'infiltrated' the girl's house as a gate-crashing Parsi guest, in complete (aforementioned) costume. And as if that wasn't enough, he chose to bring along Ram Sethi (veteran character actor, playing a character called Pyarelal Aware) as his daughter (dressed in Parsi drag).

---

[47] *Trivia Alert*: The cast includes one Kiran Thakursingh–Kher in one of her earliest film roles–then newly married to Anupam and not yet transformed to Kirron.

Wait—it got better! Oranges were used to create certain parts of the female anatomy and eventually the girl eloped and Vinod Khanna abandoned his Parsi accent, clothes and mannerisms.

Deepa Mehta depicted the tensions of Partition in **1947 Earth** through the eyes of a little girl from a rich Parsi family. The retinue around her mansion—the maid, the masseur and the ice-candy man—were from the two sides of the divide and their relationships in the context of romantic and political developments were seen from a 'neutral' point of view.

The original novel (*Ice-Candy Man*) was written by a Parsi,[48] who co-wrote the screenplay as well, and the film had the Parsi community as an interesting backdrop to the Hindu-Muslim relationships. Rahul Khanna and Aamir Khan turned in great performances as the suitors of Nandita Das.

Parzania too had a Parsi family caught in the crossfire of Hindu-Muslim riots, this time the post-Godhra riots of 2002 Gujarat. A poignant tale of a Parsi boy, lost in the riots, and his parents' attempts to find him did not find too much of a commercial audience due to its bleakness. It did not help matters when the Gujarat government decided to ban the film for—what they felt was—an unfair depiction of the communal situation.

Naseeruddin Shah was his customary excellent self as the father, while Sarika—making a Hindi film comeback after her separation from Kamal Haasan—turned in a

---

[48] *Trivia Alert*: In the last scene of the film, the author (Bapsi Sidhwa) appears in a brief cameo as the grown-up version of the little girl.

surprisingly touching performance as the mother who had lost her son.

As **Munna Bhai MBBS** chugged along to become a pan-India success with its formula of love, fresh air and hugs, it also brought on two of the most noticed Parsi characters in Bollywood—Dr Rustom and his carrom-playing dad.

Dr Rustom (played by a real-life Parsi, Kurush Deboo) looked exactly the part of a brilliant doctor prone to the occasional bouts of madness. His accent was authentic without going overboard and he stayed in a house with large balconies—something only Parsis have access to, in Bombay. His juice swigging, carrom-flicking father did not utter a single word in the film but managed to exude Parsi-ness through his vest and cap.

As a vehicle for star Saif Ali Khan trying his hand at acting, **Being Cyrus** succeeded admirably at telling a tight story well and not letting the star overpower the rest of the cast. Saif reciprocated by doing a great job of playing Cyrus Mistry, a mysterious guest in the extended Sethna family. Naseeruddin Shah as the doped artist Dinshaw, Dimple Kapadia as his high-strung wife Katy, Boman Irani as the brother with the persecution complex and Simone Singh as Boman's wide-eyed child-wife were all spectacular in bringing alive an eccentric Parsi family.

That the director (Homi Adjania) and co-screenwriter (Kersi Khambatta) were both Parsis probably helped the milieu to be bang-on accurate, apart from the story being a very interesting thriller.

In Mani Ratnam's **Guru**, the aristocratic Anglicised Parsi was the villain. The Contractors represented the old money of Bombay, blocking the entry of new entrepreneurs into the textile-trading community. They had swanky cars, swish suits and clipped accents, along with the confidence of old money. With those, the Contractors (junior played by Arjun Bajwa, senior played by Dhritiman Chatterjee) tried to block Gurukant Desai's meteoric rise to industrial superstardom.

But the author-backed Bollywood hero is like an idea whose time has come. Nobody can stop it.

And finally, we have to talk about the Greatest Film Ever Made—**Sholay**—and there was a Parsi there as well.

Remember the engine driver in the train that got attacked by dacoits in Jai and Veeru's introduction sequence? Well, that was Mushtaq Merchant looking suitably harassed by the attack of the northies in his domain, but doing a decent job of cranking up the speed and providing Veeru with liquor.

Of course, the twist is that he was the only person to have a double role in **Sholay**. Remember a thin figure who screamed and jumped up and down as Jai-Veeru drove off in the double-carrier bike of '*Yeh dosti*'? That was Mr Merchant again—as he played the guy whose bike gets stolen by the heroes. There was a full sequence devoted to the theft but that got chopped at the editing table.

Just what I said... they are always on the sidelines!

Crossing The Vindhyas:
10 Depictions Of South Indians

When you have a story of long-lost brothers, natural and unnatural calamities, rich fathers and poor lovers, to tell in less than three hours, elaborate characterisations become a sort of waste of time. Ergo, stereotypes.

South Indians are dark. They wear white mundus or checked lungis. They have an accent thicker than coconut chutney. And they are either part of the intelligentsia or the mafia. All of the above, more often than not, contribute to the character becoming a comic sidekick.

But sometimes, the character becomes memorable—the accent notwithstanding—and is not a sidekick.

Some of them are still funny, though.

Mehmood is the worst offender in this category. With his exaggerated accent and flailing lungis, he imprinted the stereotype on the Bollywood audience's mind. Though, the film that is most famous for a south Indian character is such a comic masterpiece that you can't stop laughing long enough to feel offended.

As the music maestro Master Pillai in **Padosan**, he was the perfect foil to Kishore Kumar's histrionics. Add to that Manna Dey's classically trained voice belting out a Carnatic version of 'Ek chatur naar' and you had mayhem.

The character was the 'villain' of the piece, made fun of, given a ridiculous 'get-up' and vanquished in the battle for Saira Banu's attentions.

No wonder they don't like to speak Hindi south of the Vindhyas.

While the north Indian tendency is to lump all south Indians together as Madrasis, there's life beyond Chennai—as hot and spicy Hyderabadis would tell you. Theirs is the only south Indian city where people speak a decent smattering of Hindi—though with a distinctive '*dakhni*' accent. Many characters have imitated that but none better than the ever-helpful, film-crazy auto-driver who called himself **Hero Hiralal**!

A Mumbai film crew landed up in Hyderabad and our hero fell in love with the heroine. Thanks to a completely predictable plot, rather shoddy production values and zilch star power (despite major acting talents), the film sank without a trace. Pity nobody heard Naseeruddin Shah getting the dakhni accent bang-on right...

What a tragedy it is that the holder of a Master's degree from Kerala University would be selling coconuts on the streets of Bombay. That is exactly what Krishnan Iyer, MA (pronounced Yem Yeah!) did in (the older) **Agneepath**. When he wasn't saving mafia dons from assassinations, that is.

Hardworking and honest, he was also a proud member of his community, evident by his invoking the names of the (then) President R. Venkataraman as well as C.V. Raman and S. Radhakrishnan to prove his community's intellectual superiority.

Mithun Chakraborty won a Filmfare Best Supporting Actor award for this film—in which he apparently took the help of a Tamil spot boy for specific words. The accent in which he spoke Hindi was entirely his own, though.

Note: In the hullabaloo over Krishnan, we tend to forget the other south Indian in the film—villain

Anna Shetty (played by Deepak Shirke), whose accent was also as thick as they got.

When Kamal Haasan debuted in Hindi, he had a thick Tamil accent. This disadvantage was turned into the plot of **Ek Duje Ke Liye**—where south Indian Kamal and north Indian Rati Agnohotri were kept apart because of their cultural differences.

The culture, the language and even eggs were causes of friction between two warring neighbours from different sides of the Great Indian Divide. Kamal Haasan's character learnt Hindi during the course of two songs, of which the more innovative one was composed entirely of Hindi film names sung to tune.

The most common moniker of south Indian characters in Bollywood is—you guessed right—Anna. And if you thought that's easy to remember, then you certainly won't forget the original Anna Seth, played with chilling perfection by Nana Patekar in **Parinda**.

Anna had no accent, no obvious dressing preferences and yet the set design of his house screamed out the origin of the character. The pantheon of gods, the swings, the puja rituals, even the incense-stick holders—all of them were distinctive enough. And by that, the film replicated the stories of people who came in from all over to Mumbai and eventually made it big, sometimes in Bollywood, sometimes in business and sometimes in the underworld. Real-life dons like Varadarajan Mudaliar and filmi dons like Velu Naicker made the cut. So did Anna Seth.[49]

---

[49] *Trivia Alert*: The 'corpse' in Anna's factory in the very first scene was Vidhu Vinod Chopra.

The Iyer must marry another Iyer—Old Jungle Proverb.

In the frothy romantic comedy **Hum Hain Rahi Pyar Ke**, this was probably not the intended message but that's what is relevant to the topic at hand.

Mr Iyer decreed that his daughter—Vaijayanthi (played by the forever-bubbly Juhi Chawla) would marry a boy from the community (and he even found a classical dancing pansy to fit the bill). Vaijayanthi had other plans and ran off to become the governess of a handsome bachelor's (Aamir Khan) nephews and nieces.

The mayhem that followed was interspersed with Carnatic music, Tamil-accented Hindi and several stretches of Tamil dialogues—spread between the heroine and her father. A part of it was also high-quality Tamil wisdom. When Mr Iyer was asked what was wrong with Aamir for marriage with his daughter, he said with all honesty—'*Buraai kuch nahin. Woh achha chhokra hai.* But he's not an Iyer.' Can't argue with that.

To counter the muscle and guts of the Mumbai underworld, you need a logical, calculating mind. And as the foil for Chandru and Malik in Ram Gopal Verma's **Company**, we had Commissioner Sreenivasan—played by Mohanlal. Said to be modelled on real-life Mumbai Police Commissioner D. Sivanandan, this character was all logic and seemingly slow. Yet, behind the calm demeanour and Malayali accent was a steely resolve. Sreenivasan fought the battle effectively and towards the end of the film, he was eased out and made the head of the Police Training College. And the cerebral cop was supposed to be writing a book on the Mumbai underworld—called *Company*.

Note: Mohanlal returned as a police officer in yet another RGV film—unfortunately, **Ram Gopal Verma Ki Aag**—where he played Inspector Narasimha, the encounter specialist. No mention of his origin was made but with his accent, it was very difficult to think of him as, say, a Gujarati.

Named after one of the funniest movies of all times, the 'Golmaal' franchise has become amazingly and inexplicably successful. One of the reasons for this is probably the avalanche of spoofs the makers unleash on us. Every character and every scene seem to be designed around taking somebody's trip. Thus, it seems almost normal when you have Celina Jaitley playing a south Indian woman by the name of Meera Nair in **Golmaal Returns**. Sigh.

As Shreyas Talpade's wife in the film, she went around in heavy Kanjeevarams, spewing *aiyo ramas*. Everybody in the film was trying to be funny, and while the stereotypes were hackneyed, the choice of the name was quite inspired.

The image of the reclusive mathematical genius was initiated by Srinivas Ramanujam—and that image has been propagated with a clear south Indian feel. But it is not a common image in Bollywood. The Bollywood hero has never been too comfortable with the Binomial Theorem.

One exception to this rule is Venkat Subramaniam, played by Amitabh Bachchan in **Teen Patti** (probably inspired by the name of one of the scriptwriters: Shivkumar Subramaniam). He played the maths professor, out to redefine the laws of probability. And when he tried to prove his theory in real casinos, all hell broke loose. Some shades of the Kevin Spacey-starrer **21**, Ben Kingsley in a small role and the presence of Amitabh Bachchan, could not salvage the many unconnected elements in the film, which collapsed in a heap.

If we manage to get past the special effects of **Ra.One** and look at the geek who came up with this video-game super-villain, we find he is Shekhar Subramaniam!

Shah Rukh Khan played a Tamil video-game designer who loved giving deep, meaningful advice to his son and eating noodles with curd! By professing this love for curd-noodles and interspersing his dialogues with Tamil phrases (most notably, *inge vaa*), SRK managed to piss off almost everyone in the southern part of the country. When his alter-ego was in serious trouble, a south Indian superstar came to the rescue but even that wasn't enough to placate them.[50]

Though, keeping in mind the audience to the north of the Vindhyas, he called his wife a term of Punjabi endearment—*Chammak Challo*...

---

[50] Even in **Om Shanti Om**, SRK did a manic spoof of a south Indian hero by fighting stuffed tigers in fight scenes and again peppering dialogue with a faux-southie phrase ('*Yenna rascala!*').

The Big Bong Theory: 12 Depictions Of Bengalis

*A*s a much-forwarded internet joke goes, one Bengali is a poet. Two Bengalis are a film society. Three Bengalis are a political party. Four Bengalis are—well—*two* political parties. As far as stereotypes go, this is at least intelligent, which is not what can be said about most Bollywood stereotypes. As far as Bengalis go, they are more fortunate than the south Indians in portrayal but then there are fewer Bengali characters as well.

One of the earliest Bengali characters in popular Hindi cinema was the eponymous Miss Chatterjee, who was the subject of Johnny Walker's attention in the song *Suno suno Miss Chatterjee* (from the film **Baharen Phir Bhi Aayengi**). Ostensibly set in Calcutta, the song moved from Victoria Memorial to trams to a nameless garden where 'modern' young men and women were dancing the twist. But that did not stop the inimitable Johnny Walker from wooing his Bengali girlfriend with many words that (apparently) rhymed with Chatter(jee)—for example, Matter, Better, Letter!

The massive cosmopolitan cauldron that is Mumbai is home to north Indians, east Indians and even some west Indians (not Kieron Pollard's compatriots). And no film brought this fact home better than the one dedicated to the city—**Anand**. The trio of friends consisted of a Marathi, a Punjabi (recently migrated from Delhi) and a Bengali (presumably settled). And the most famous Bong nomenclature was born.

Dr Bhaskar Banerjee a.k.a. Babumoshai—in Rajesh Khanna's famous lilt—was the archetypal Bengali. Mercifully without a Bong accent, he was the typical intellectual Bengali who wrote long literary diaries while his friend, Dr Prakash Kulkarni, was minting money at his private nursing home. He was also prone to murmuring poetic sweet nothings to his sweetheart that were thoroughly decried by the big-mouthed Punjabi, Anand Sehgal.

The affectionate and accurate portrayal was brought about by the Bengali director (Hrishikesh Mukherjee), who based the relationship on his own friendship with the iconic garrulous Punjabi, Raj Kapoor.

In **Do Anjaane**, Amit and Rekha Roy (played by the real-life Amit and Rekha) were happily married though Rekha's ambition (and Amit's lack of it) caused some friction. In walked a *kabab mein haddi* (Prem Chopra, strangely named Ranjit Mullick).[51] Soon, Amit was thrown off a train (by Prem, who's never up to any good) and the grieving Rekha became a superstar. If that wasn't enough drama for you, Amit Roy came back as a Punjabi producer willing to produce Rekha Roy's next film.

The story was set in Calcutta but no overt Bongness was displayed till we realised that Rekha was a Bengali superstar and her iconic role was an '*ek-chutki-sindoor-ki-keemat*' kind of part in a film called **Potibrata** (Pativrataa, to the rest of the country). And then, to counter the Punjabi producer's immaculate Hindi, a Bengali director

---

[51] Ranjit Mullick is the name of a well-known Bengali actor.

Mr Sanyal (played gleefully by Utpal Dutt) emerged and you had more Bengali accent than a Pranab Mukherjee Budget speech.[52]

In Kamal Haasan's 'magnum opus' **Hey Ram**, the film opened with his character returning from an archaeological dig in the subcontinent's oldest town (Mohen-jo-daro) to the second oldest (Calcutta). He was greeted by his wife, Aparna—the archetype of the sexy Bengali woman in a traditionally worn saree, with a large bindi, larger eyes and a husky voice to die for.

Without offering any explanation as to how a south Indian archaeologist married a Bengali schoolteacher, Kamal Haasan dived under the sheets with her—and nobody complained. As the languorous love-making scene unfolded, Rani Mukherjee recited verses from Jibanananda Das—a famous Bengali poet—in her Juhu-accented Bengali and broke many hearts by dying soon afterwards.

> *Note:* Contrary to popular belief (emanating from the promos—seen by considerably more people than the film itself), Rani Mukherjee was raped and killed in the post-Partition riots and did not die from Kamal biting her on the bum.

What do you call an alcoholic, eccentric, charismatic Bengali? Uffoh, you idiot—not Ritwik Ghatak. I meant in the movies.

---

[52] *Trivia Alert*: Yet another iconic Bengali, Mithun Chakraborty, made a debut in a bit part in the film—as a neighbourhood tough in Amit and Rekha's locality.

Yes, **Devdas** Mukherjee is the man—arguably the most popular Bengali character in Bollywood. In the better-remembered, more opulent Sanjay Leela Bhansali version, Shah Rukh Khan tripped his way through in a dhoti and kurta (which Bengalis, curiously enough, call a 'panjabi) in supposedly rural Bengal first, and Calcutta's red-light district later on. Sanjay Leela Bhansali's knowledge of Bengali culture and language was limited to one word as Aishwarya Rai went *Issshhhh...* at varying levels of pitch and volume.

One is at a bit of a loss to understand the reason why even the Punjabi audiences liked (the kurta bit notwithstanding) this sissy drunkard who couldn't choose between two gorgeous women. After all, they don't really get the difference in the northern parts of the country—'*Chandramukhi ho ya Paro, ki farq painda yaaro...*'[53]

In **Parineeta**, Saif Ali Khan played the Bengali to the hilt by wearing batik kurtas (a.k.a. 'panjabis'—see above), driving around Victoria Memorial, singing romantic songs and taking the Toy Train to Darjeeling. He was Shekhar Roy, the son of the Bengali millionaire Nabin Chandra Roy. And his childhood sweetheart was Lolita—which can only be described as the Second-Most Typical Bengali Name of All Times (losing the top spot to Paromita, probably). Soon, we had Sanjay Dutt walking in as Girish Sharma. If his name wasn't typically Bengali, his costumes, attendance and dance at Durga Puja pandals clearly were.

---

[53] Hat Tip: Sujoy Ghosh's **Jhankaar Beats**, where this line was used.

Between the three of them and 1960s Bengal, you had an encyclopedia of Bongness that would have been a cakewalk for the director, Pradeep Sarkar, to create. [54]

Bongness, exemplified by this Durga Puja celebration

An idealistic student leader taking on the entrenched political leadership of a state is the stuff legends are made of. Add to that a migrant henchman helping out the politicos and a frivolous youngster who realises the power of democracy—and you have **Yuva**.

As Michael Mukherjee, Ajay Devgn was the charismatic student leader of Presidency College who was not beyond

---

[54] *Trivia Alert*: Saif's father's role was played by Sabyasachi Chakraborty, who has played Feluda (Satyajit Ray's detective) in several Bengali films.

solving dense mathematical problems on police lock-up walls. While the faux Bengali accent was completely missing in his case, it was there in super-exaggerated form in the voice of Prosenjit Bhattacharya (Om Puri)—the slimy neta. Set in the fiery backdrop of Calcutta, the language of the film had to be the lingua franca of revolution.

In **Mumbai Matinee**—one of the low-budget, off-beat efforts—we met Debu (Debasish) Chatterjee, billed as a 'thirty-something virgin' on the lookout for some 'action'. As is the norm in sex comedies, our mild-mannered hero got caught in unwitting adventures including an encounter with a sexologist baba, an inadvertent part in a porn film and eventually, a run-in with a Bengali police officer.

The language of Rahul Bose's character would have remained immaterial to the story if not for the aforementioned police officer. In a completely over-the-top comic scene, the police officer arrested Debu from a brothel and proceeded to lecture him on the collapse of Bengali moral fibre—in theatrical Bengali. Rahul Bose's feeble attempts to explain himself were lost in the high-pitched monologue. *Maa go...*[55]

When **Guru**kant Desai hit a roadblock in his quest to become India's biggest industrialist, he was helped by an idealistic newspaper editor. When he bent a few rules to get ahead, it was the same editor who took him on.

Manik Dasgupta (played by the forever versatile Mithun Chakraborty) was the upright newspaper editor,

---

[55] (Theatrical) Bengali invocation of the mother akin to the Marathi '*Ai la*'.

who was always fair—even if it meant going hammer-and-tongs after his loved ones. While the character was based on a real-life media baron, Mithun gave it some deft touches of eccentricity—like lapsing into Bengali in the middle of a diatribe. While the model for the role wasn't Bengali, the language didn't seem out of place. After all, some of the best-known editors in this country are Bengalis.

Why would two brothers controlling a betting syndicate in Mumbai be Bengali? Why would their third brother be called Mikhail? Why would their idea of fun be firing empty shots at people? There was no reason whatsoever behind what were probably the most eccentric Bengali characters in Bollywood.

In **Kaminey**, three Bengali actors—Deb Mukherjee, Rajatabha Dutta and Chandan Roy Sanyal—played the three manic brothers with hand-rubbing glee. AK-47s, missing cash, drugs and, the crowning moment of the film—the *Dhan Te Nan* song sequence—all had one of the three Bongs in it. Bongs rule, don't they?

The last two characters in the list come together.

They were both corporate professionals—grappling with workplace pressures and personal issues in style. One was an MBA and the other an architect. Nothing ruffled their perfectly tailored suits and they cut a sexy figure blowing smoke in the face of their business rivals. They had none of the 'distinctive' traits of Bengali—except for their names.

Ladies and gentlemen, please put your hands together for Nishigandha Dasgupta (**Corporate**) and Shonali Mukherjee (**Karthik Calling Karthik**).

Honourable Mention

In **An Evening in Paris**, a Bengali heroine pranced around in a bikini and a Bengali water-skiing instructor called Deepak Sen landed up. Shammi Kapoor put exaggerated roundness on his syallables to play a Bengali cameo before eschewing it to sing hit songs in the voice of Mohammed Rafi.

East, West, North, South: 8 Regional Superstars

*T*he Indian film industry is not about Bollywood. Every state of India has its own homegrown superstar(s) with massive fan followings. Many of these stars' regional language releases get national attention and international releases. In terms of remuneration, many of these stars eclipse their Bollywood counterparts and words fail to describe the hysteria they generate. And at different points of time in their careers, they have attempted to reach a pan-Indian audience with varying degrees of success.

Uttam Kumar

Uttam Kumar—the leading star of Bengal—made his Bollywood debut by producing and starring in a romantic drama—**Chhoti Si Mulaqat**—in the late 1960s. It had all the right trappings including Uttam's dashing looks and undeniable charm, Vyjayanthimala and a very good music score by Shankar-Jaikishan but did not fare well commercially. Like all inexplicable failures, this too had a conspiracy theory that the big guns of Bombay did not want Uttam Kumar to succeed. Post this failure, he never did a conventional leading-man role in Bombay again and returned to rule Bengal.

Much later in his career, he did Shakti Samanta's **Amanush** (made in both Hindi and Bengali) as well as a strong supporting role in Gulzar's **Kitaab**. By this time, he wasn't the dashing hero and more of a character actor.

The last Hindi release before his death was Manmohan Desai's **Desh Premee** where he—as Paran Ghosh—was one of the leaders of slum Bharat Nagar, all of whom lived in an atmosphere of intermittent animosity, and received advice from Amitabh Bachchan.

Rajnikanth

The word Superstar has got intrinsically linked to the adopted name of Shivaji Rao Gaekwad as his legend has spread far beyond the states in which his language is spoken. As he became the biggest Tamil superstar by the early 1980s, he made his Hindi film debut in **Andhaa Kaanoon** and in the company of of Amitabh Bachchan, he proceeded to polish off his father's three killers wearing black leather jackets, red eyes and large nostrils.

While the film was a big hit, Rajni did not really follow it up with anything big, and some pretty forgettable action films characterised his output in the 1980s. Most of them managed to tell the stories in their titles—**Jeet Hamaari**, **Dushmano Ka Dushman** and **Insaaf Kaun Karega** for example.

During this, he had developed a reputation for doing cool things with cigarettes and sunglasses. This was exploited to the fullest in **Geraftaar**—where he was Inspector Hussein in a guest appearance, but people went asthmatic whistling through his entire role—which ended with him lighting a cigarette while he was about to be killed).[56]

---

[56] An article about Rajnikanth in *Slate* magazine says, 'Putting his sunglasses on is an operation as complex as a Vegas floorshow.'

He did some more roles—bit parts, compared to his southern output—in not-so-notable films like **Bhagwaan Dada**, **Asli Naqli**, **Uttar Dakshin**, **Bhrashtachar** and **Farishtay**. He did a delightfully comic turn as taxi-driver Jaggu in **Chaalbaaz**. If there was ever a north-south fight to the death, it had to be Rajni vs Sunny Deol—in which Sridevi won.

This was followed by **Hum**—a triple combo knockout punch—with him, Big B and Govinda playing to the gallery. The scene with Rajni's Bat-dance and his *'Beteylal, teen se bhale do, do se bhala yek'* dialogue is still a cult favourite. Interestingly, the film's biggest draw was supposed to be Amitabh, but in Ooty, where the film was being shot, crowds routinely landed up to touch Rajni's feet and get infants blessed by him.

After that, he did a few more forays as primarily strong character roles in some really weak films, learnt his lesson and returned to breaking records in Tamil.

When one sees his friendship with the Big B, one hopes that the two will act together in an epic, and we can all die in peace after that.

Kamal Haasan

The other Tamil star is considered more of an 'actor' and has wooed the national audience with a mix of dubbed versions of Tamil films and starring roles in important films.

His initial films were big solo-hero successes, starting with **Ek Duje Ke Liye**—which exploited this south Indian background for the story of a north-south romance. All the stereotypes of Tamil language and culture were duly poked fun at and the film went on to become a huge hit on the back of a brilliant score. After that, he had another rocking music score in **Sanam Teri Kasam** that again became a hit. He followed this up with **Sadma** (remake of a Tamil hit that established both him and Sridevi as hugely talented stars), and **Rajtilak** (a lost-and-found period potboiler). And as if that was not enough, he had an author-backed role in **Saagar** that should have established him as an A-list star in Bollywood.

But—quite inexplicably—he never did any leading role after that and only returned with directorial ventures in the last decade or so. Some of them were cute (**Chachi 420**), some convoluted (**Hey Ram**) and some plain bad (**Mumbai Express**). What a pity we didn't get more of Kamal the actor.

Mohanlal

Mohanlal—the leading light of Malayalam cinema—is not the conventionally handsome film hero and his accent is rather distinctive, to put it politely.

He took on the Mumbai underworld as Police Commissioner Srinivasan in **Company**. A cool, calculating cop who hunts with his brain was a role he sunk his teeth into and the manic energy of the dons found an interesting counterpoint in his slow gait.

Buoyed by this success, Mohanlal returned to work with the same director and an even bigger star cast in a remake of the Greatest Film Ever Made. That film was—tragically— **Ram Gopal Verma Ki Aag**. Everything associated with that movie got blasted into small pieces and poor Mohanlal was no exception. Inspector Narasimha (equivalent of Thakur in the original) was seen as a caricature at worst and ignored at best.

He has not come back since. And we can only blame Ramu for that.

Chiranjeevi

If Rajni is Superstar, Chiranjeevi is Megastar and Supreme Hero.

Blessed with a mouthful of a name (Sivasankara Varaprasad Konidela), he ruled the Telugu filmdom as Chiranjeevi—with a fan-following as large and mad as it got. His Bollywood debut was in **Pratibandh**, as a trigger-happy cop out to protect the chief minister from the evil machinations of Spot Nana (played by Rami Reddy, who's got to be the Most Deadpan Villain of All Times). With kick-ass action and some giggly relief in the form of Juhi Chawla, the film was a reasonable success and it surely paved the way for more of the same.

That 'more' came in the form of **Aaj Ka Goondaraaj**—the standard issue clanger the '90s were notorious for—which sank without a trace (or maybe with some trace but we don't know for sure).

He came back as **The Gentleman**, which was the remake of a Tamil film called—well—**Gentleman** and the significance of the additional THE was lost on pretty much everybody. Directed by Mahesh Bhatt in the period when he was simultaneously directing some six films at any point of time, it did quite disastrously.

And that was the last we heard of Chiru in this part of town.

Nagarjuna

Telugu superstar Nagarjuna made an explosive—albeit deadpan—national debut in Ram Gopal Verma's **Shiva**. The story of a regular student becoming a vigilanté to resist the force of a local don was steeped in reality. The choreographed violence and the intentionally jagged filmmaking style made the film achieve some sort of cult status.

The director-star duo got together to remake one of their Telugu films in Hindi. In **Drohi**, Nagarjuna continued his deadpan act as a hit-man finding love and escaping his past. This theme did not work but RGV perfected it by the time he made **Satya**.

Soon after this, Nagarjuna made two forays in quick succession. **Khuda Gawah** was the glamorous role where he took on a parallel track (originally slated for Sanjay Dutt) of romance and some bravado. **Zakhm** was a shorter but critically acclaimed role, where he played a film director who sired an illegitimate son with his mistress.

His last two Hindi films have been **Agni Varsha** (an ancient play adaptation, where he was seen getting into a clinch with the forever-hot Raveena Tandon) and **LOC Kargil** (where he must have been one of the soldiers but nobody—including J.P. Dutta—can confirm this). The former got lost in the theatres and the latter got lost in the interminable cast.

Ravi Kissen

Bhojpuri has become the latest regional film industry to become big and its great white hope is Ravi Kissen—who has become hysterically famous all over India thanks to his appearances on *Bigg Boss*. His cultivated image of a buffoon, however, hasn't helped him to get lead roles.

He has worked with critically acclaimed directors like Shyam Benegal **(Well Done Abba)** and Mani Ratnam **(Raavan)**. He has appeared in a wide variety of roles too, though most of them seem to have been extended bit parts. In **Luck**, he was a libidinous crook. In **Tanu Weds Manu**, he was the UP goon out for a scrap. His most recent outing has been in **Chitkabrey**, where he played a ragging victim out to settle scores, though his purported nude appearance garnered more comment than this performance.

Which brings us to the most successful crossover of them all.

A man started in Tamil cinema, acquired incredible acclaim and commercial success, had his works dubbed and released in Hindi and, after the unprecedented success of that, made a national debut, became wildly popular and is now an international superstar.

Ladies and gentlemen—keep listening to A.R. Rehman.

7

THOSE MAGNIFICENT MEN AND WOMEN

'But what if I repeat myself? So does history.'—
SHAH RUKH KHAN

In the end, it is all about the stars.

Some of these stars started small and then exploded. Some of them came from illustrious families. Some ruled the universe before they ruled our hearts. Some of them are so big that award ceremonies are meaningless without them. And yet they are so close to us that we call them by their nicknames. Some of them have urban legends around them.

And some of them are like God. With a capital B.

- ◆ Starting Small: 12 Low-Profile Debuts
- ◆ Heartbreak Hotel: 13 Unlucky Star Children
- ◆ Pride of India: 15 Miss Indias
- ◆ 12 Star Nicknames
- ◆ Pehli Mulaqat: 5 Famous First Meetings
- ◆ Baar Baar, Lagataar: 16 Stars with Hattricks at Filmfare Awards
- ◆ What's In a Name: 9 Stars Appearing On-Screen with their Real Names
- ◆ QS Cutie: 18 Early Films of Aamir Khan
- ◆ Nishabd: 10 Silent Scenes of Amitabh Bachchan

Starting Small: 12 Low-Profile Debuts

*A*lot of actors from film families have either stood in for others or have been pushed into small scenes. This is obviously before their 'launches', which are a little better planned and publicised, not to mention more anticipated.

Raj Kapoor's three children appeared in the immortal love song *'Pyaar hua ikrar hua'* of **Shree 420**, looking tremendously cute in their raincoats and umbrellas as the lyrics prophetically declared that the RK lineage will ensure the show goes on— *'Hum na rahenge, tum na rahoge / Phir bhi rahegi yeh nishaniyaan'.*

Rishi, who was the youngest of the three, was bribed with chocolates by Nargis to shoot in the rain.

Sanjay Dutt had a brief screen appearance before he made his 'formal' debut in **Rocky**. He appeared in **Reshma Aur Shera** (produced by Sunil Dutt) as a sidekick to the main singer in a qawwali. He was there (with his trademark goofy smile) clapping in the standard qawwali style (open-palms-wide-rotate-palms-in-opposite-directions-clap-delicately).

Aamir Khan's first movie role was that of the child version of his youngest uncle (Tariq) in their home production, **Yaadon ki Baaraat**. He appeared in the title song, during which he excused himself to take a leak. Apparently, the entire family teased him about that for a long time.

Aamir's nephew, Imran Khan, carried on this family legacy by appearing as the kid version of his uncle in two home-production blockbusters—**Qayamat Se Qayamat Tak** (in a virtually invisible role) and **Jo Jeeta Wohi Sikandar** (a substantial role, including a beautiful song).

Hrithik Roshan's dancing skills were evident from a very early age as he danced alongside Sri Devi and Rajnikanth (wow!) in **Bhagwaan Dada**. He also acted in a film called **Aap Ke Deewane**.
    Both the films were produced by his father and the former was directed by his grandfather.

Even when it is not a home production, if a star-child is present on the location and looks cute enough, the temptation is great for the producer to (a) save money by shoving the kid in and (b) thereby earn brownie points with daddy. This is probably what happened when Bobby Deol was requisitioned to play the junior Dharmendra in Manmohan Desai's **Dharam Veer**.

In the early scenes of **Kabhi Khushi Kabhie Gham**, Jaya Bachchan was seen playing with her kid son, who grew up to become Shah Rukh Khan in the film. Then a toddler, Aryan Khan was recruited to play his real daddy's kiddie version there.

While **Dilwale Dulhania Le Jayenge** was strictly not his home-production, Karan Johar still played an important part in it (as assistant to Aditya Chopra) and even in the cast. He played Rocky, SRK's chubby friend. Though, even this was not his acting debut.

Karan Johar's first acting assignment was in a TV serial of the 1980s called **Indradhanush**—in which a gang of schoolboys inadvertently built a time machine. He played a bumbling friend of the hero. In one scene, when the hero was wondering how to make a computer chip, he good-naturedly offered his bag of potato wafers.[57]

The **Mr India** gang comprised at least two later stars— Aftab Shivdasani (who had earlier been seen as the Farex baby) and Ahmed Khan (who is a choreographer and has directed **Fool 'N' Final** in recent times). Ahmed showed promise right at the beginning, when he breakdanced through his role in **Mr India.**

Before he achieved fame as the yodelling gypsy of *Mehbooba Mehbooba* (in **Sholay**), Jalal Agha made a regal debut in one of the greatest epics of Indian cinema as one of the most famous characters of Indian history. He was the young Shahzada Salim in **Mughal-e-Azam.**

Just as surprising is the kid who played the role of the young Ashok Kumar of the landmark hit of the 1940s— **Kismet**. Mehmood debuted and later came back to become one of the most famous comedians of Hindi cinema.

And as a sort of ending, it would be interesting to showcase the lowest-profile debut of a member of the highest-profile family of Bollywood.

---

[57] SRK's other friend in **DDLJ** (Robby) was played by Arjun Sablok, who went on to direct **Na Tum Jaano Na Hum** and **Neal 'N' Nikki**. In hindsight, he should have stuck to acting.

Shweta Bachchan Nanda made an appearance in the Greatest Film Ever Made, while she was still unborn. Jaya Bachchan was pregnant with her while shooting for **Sholay** and the make-up crew had a tough time making the glowing Jaya look like a lifeless widow in the film.

Heartbreak Hotel:
13 Unlucky Star Children

*K*apoor. Bachchan. Deol. Roshan. Khan.
The Bollywood firmament is crowded with stars of the same surname, perpetuating fan followings across generations, wonderfully symmetrical photos-ops and casting possibilities. But there have been so many who didn't make it. So many whose debuts were bankrolled by their fathers who were great judges of audience taste, and yet collapsed.

What happened to them?

Kumar Gaurav

The son of Rajendra Kumar a.k.a. Jubilee Hero tops the list. A decent actor with chocolate-boy looks, he was supposed to pose a challenge to Bachchan's throne. Sadly (and inexplicably), **Love Story** remained his only hit.

He did several promising movies after that, all of which flopped. When he did act in (and produce) a hit—**Naam**—his brother-in-law[58] garnered all the praise. More than a decade after his debut, Rajendra Kumar made a last-ditch attempt with a film called **Phool**, with Madhuri Dixit opposite his son but that sank as well.

Later on, he acted in **Kaante**—a pretty decent performance—but that was not enough to resurrect his

---

[58] Kumar Gaurav is married to Namrata, Sanjay Dutt's sister.

career. When last heard, he had acted in an English film (**Guiana 1838**) and garnered some praise for it. But right now, he seems to be too old to be the hero's friend and too young to be the hero's father.

Rajiv and Kunal Goswami

Manoj Kumar's son Rajiv Goswami was paired opposite Meenakshi Sheshadri in **Painter Babu**, a film—needless to say—produced and directed by his dad.[59] It would be fair to add here that the only thing more tragic than the plot was the direction. While not in the league of the Worst Films of All Time (which was achieved in a later film by Manoj Kumar—**Clerk**), his dad's direction was probably why poor Rajiv sank without a trace.

Rajiv has a younger brother called Kunal, who was the hero of **Kalakaar**. But the music of the film (especially the fantastic '*Neele neele ambar par*') overshadowed everything else in the film, including Kunal. Later on, he was the lead in **Vishkanya** where Pooja Bedi's venomous vibes administered a lethal shot to his career.

Suneil Anand

Dev Anand launched his son, Suneil, in a film called **Anand Aur Anand**. It is one of the best examples of unintended hilarity in Hindi cinema—where Suneil was chased by drunken elephants in the climax. The film could have also been called 'Sharaabi Meets Haathi Mere Saathi'. Later, Suneil wrote, directed, produced and acted in a film called **Master** on a martial arts theme, where the hero was

---

[59] See chapter on Artists for plot details, if you are into masochism.

framed and imprisoned in Hong Kong. He learnt kung fu from a fellow inmate and took revenge when he was released. There was, however, no mention of the trademark dialogue of kung fu films—'*Kiyaah Choo Mash-tah Sinchuang Kung Pao Mash-tah Honourable Mash-tah*'. Probably that's why it failed.

Sanjana, Karan and Kunal Kapoor

Sanjana Kapoor was the first Kapoor woman to act in movies, much before her cousins Lolo and Bebo joined the party. In **Hero Hiralal**, she played a film star falling in love with a Hyderabadi auto-driver. But an extremely crappy climax and Sanjana's obvious inability to look like a plump, made-up matinee idol spelled doom for this movie. She also acted in **Junoon** and **36 Chowringhee Lane**—both her father's productions—as a child artiste. She continues to be a leading theatre actress and producer, who brought back the buzz to Prithvi Theatre almost single-handedly.

Karan Kapoor found stardom as the male face of Bombay Dyeing. As a blonde hunk, he was a very successful model when he made his Bollywood debut in **Sultanat**. He was cast opposite Juhi Chawla (in her debut role as well) and got completely overshadowed in the fisticuffs between Dharmendra and Sunny Deol in the middle of a desert sultanate.

He also starred in **Loha** and **Zalzala**, both of which starred Dharmendra, making them co-stars in hundred per cent of Karan's Hindi films, which weren't too many (read: 3) due to his foreign-accented Hindi and very furniture-like acting.

Kunal Kapoor was launched in **Vijeta**, set during the 1971 Indo-Pak War about a complex father-son relationship (played by Shashi and Kunal respectively). He was a young air force cadet with a budding romance to nurture and an impending war to fight. Directed by Govind Nihalani, the film garnered a lot of critical acclaim and Kunal did a few small roles thereafter, before vanishing.

Faisal Khan

Aamir Khan and his brother Faisal Khan 'debuted' in the same film. In **QSQT**, Faisal was there as a sidekick of a side-villain (played by Makrand Deshpandey) who tried to molest Juhi Chawla. He helped reduce the family's junior artiste budget again in **Jo Jeeta Wohi Sikandar**, where he was a Xavier's student.

Faisal got a proper launch in **Madhosh** (produced by dad Tahir Hussain)—opposite another newcomer, Anjali Jathar. Despite heavy promotion and pretty good music, the film tanked.

His perfectionist brother got him a second lead in **Mela**, a very meaty role for someone with one flop. Despite very good action and competent acting, **Mela** did nothing for Faisal. Come to think of it, neither did it do anything for Aamir.

In recent times, Faisal was diagnosed with schizophrenia and had fallen out with Aamir.

Puru Raaj Kumar

Raj Kumar's son, Puru, made his debut in a film called **Bal Bramhachari** opposite the super-successful Karisma Kapoor, directed by Prakash Mehra and with no apparent help from his dad. This means Raj Kumar cannot be blamed for the devastation of distributors brought about by the film.

He followed it up with a villainous act in the film called **Hamara Dil Aapke Paas Hai**, where he raped Aishwarya Rai only to be beaten to a pulp by Anil Kapoor—not for the rape, but for offering to marry Ash to atone for the rape. Yes, that was the plot. And Happy Women's Day. He has also acted in **Umrao Jaan**, **LOC Kargil** and a few films in small roles but is nowhere near reaching the eccentric stardom of his father.[60]

Armaan Kohli

Rajkumar Kohli is one of the moderately successful producer-directors of Hindi cinema—with several moderate B-grade successes to his credit. His son—Armaan Kohli—is a contender for the world record for the maximum number of launches (relaunches?) of an actor by a relative.

He debuted in a film called **Virodhi** way back in the 1990s and has been seen in several of his dad's productions. This trend ended with a film called **Jaani Dushman—Ek Anokhi Kahani**[61], where he played a snake (*ichchhadhari naag*) and proceeded to kill almost the entire star cast, which included but was not restricted to Sunny Deol, Sonu Nigam, Aditya Panscholi, Sunil Shetty and Aftab Shivdasani. A filmful of heroes polished off by a relative newcomer—only an indulgent dad would agree to make this script.

---

[60] Raj Kumar's daughter is Vastavikata, who has recently appeared in a film called **Ei8ht Shani**. With a name like that, we cannot pretend that it will be easy for fans to scream out her name.

[61] *Trivia Alert*: Rajkumar Kohli directed another film called **Jaani Dushman** in the mid-'80s—again a multi-starrer which was about a psychotic King Kong kind of monster, which went about killing brides to avenge his wife's infidelity.

Sanjay Kapoor

The youngest brother of Boney and Anil debuted in a film in production for an inordinately long time, **Prem**. He starred opposite Tabu (also in her debut) and lip-synced to what went on to become the National Anthem of Constipation—*Aati nahin, aati nahin.*[62] Sanjay's brother bankrolled his forays in several big-budget movies opposite really big-ticket heroines—including Madhuri Dixit in **Raja**.[63]

Sanjay acted in several films outside the Kapoor banner as well—most notable among them being **Chhupa Rustam** (opposite Manisha Koirala and Mamta Kulkarni), **Qayamat** (as a villain in a copy of **The Rock**), **Sirf Tum** (opposite Sushmita Sen) and his crowning glory **Kal Ho Naa Ho** (as the gorgeous Sonali Bendre's husband). He threatens to (and does) surface once in a while in reasonably visible movies (**Luck By Chance**, for example) so there is still some time before we can give him a Lifetime Achievement Award.

Uday Chopra

The world record for the maximum relaunches by the family is a difficult one to decide when Uday Chopra also enters the fray. He was launched by his family in **Mohabbatein**—as a happy-go-lucky student out to woo a girl.

Of the ten-odd films he has done, only two (**Charas** and **Supari**) have not been made by family or friends. The scathing reviews he has got and the terrible box-office fate

---

[62] There is another school of thought which feels that *Dum maro dum* is the Constipation Anthem, and *Aati nahin* is merely the National Song.

[63] Both the Kapoor brothers have the dubious distinction of acting in films named after them but being more famous for Madhuri. Anil's effort is **Beta**.

of his solo ventures have done nothing to cramp his style. His doting daddy and brother have continued to express faith in him, with top actresses opposite him and lavish budgets backing each one of his films.[64]

Mahakshay Chakraborty

The industry waited with bated breath for the launch of Mahakshay Chakraborty a.k.a. Mimoh[65] in a film named after one of his father's biggest hits—**Jimmy**. The multiplexes were unmoved, and reports from the smaller centres—which have worshipped his father—were lost in transit.

He has made another attempt with **Haunted**, India's first 3-D horror movie but people were horrified in an unintended sort of way. The box-office collections of the film have ensured that horror films, 3-D films and Mahakshay are not coming back in a hurry.

But the industry awaits...

---

[64] His love interest in **Mohabbatein**—Shamita Shetty—has retired from films and taken on interior decoration. A few days after her announcement to this effect, Uday too 'retired' (though he's slated to appear in **Dhoom 3**)—thus coinciding both their entries and exits.

[65] Mimoh is named after his father's two idols—**MI**chael Jackson and **MOH**ammed Ali.

Pride of India: 15 Miss Indias

*T*hey say that if you're not born in the filmi fraternity, the only way to get in is to become Miss India. In fact, for the female Bollywood aspirant, that's the more common way in. Over the years, many Miss India winners have made their way into Bollywood with varying degrees of success.

And it has been happening for a very long time. In the earliest days of Miss India, the winners usually hit the ramp, but from the 1980s onwards—when there was increased visibility of the winners—Bollywood lapped them up.

Persis Khambatta

Year of crowning: 1965

Early mark: Her debut was a rather intriguingly named movie called **Bambai Raat Ke Baahon Mein**, directed by K.A. Abbas.

Biggest claim to fame: Not in Bollywood. She moved to Hollywood as probably the first Indian crossover and starred in a shaven-head role in **Star Trek: The Motion Picture**. Acted in several other films, though none was very high-profile.

Other notables: Wrote a coffee-table book *Pride of India* on the Miss India pageant down the ages.

Currently: Unfortunately, she died of a heart attack in 1998.

Swaroop Sampat

Year of crowning: 1979

Early mark: Hrishikesh Mukherjee's **Naram Garam**, where she was part of a really unusual love triangle involving

Amol Palekar and Utpal Dutt... don't ask, just see the movie.

Biggest claim to fame: Her most-loved role came in TV serial **Yeh Jo Hai Zindagi**, which entertained middle-class India for a long time and still lives on in reruns and DVD sets.

Other notables: None really unless you count a bikini scene of hers from the movie **Karishmaa** that went 'viral' and still logs in many views on YouTube.

Currently: Married to Paresh Rawal and settled into happy domesticity. No plans of returning.

Sangeeta Bijlani

Year of crowning: 1980

Early mark: As one of the three leads in **Tridev**, she got noticed because of the sheer magnitude of the film's success if not for the length of the role.

Biggest claim to fame: Sadly, not quality but quantity. She had an astonishing twenty releases in her seven-year career and nine in one year (1991) alone. Actually, her moment in the sun—if you can call it that—was when the married Mohammed Azharuddin ditched his first wife to marry her.

Currently: Still married to Azhar, who's now an MP. Seen often at Page 3 parties.

Juhi Chawla

Year of crowning: 1984

Early mark: Didn't get noticed in her first film, **Sultanat**. Her second Hindi release was **Qayamat Se Qayamat Tak**, which marked the resurgence of romance in Bollywood and sealed her place as an A-list heroine.

Biggest claim to fame: Probably **QSQT** but Juhi has a whole lot of very big hits to her credits, going all the way from David Dhawan (**Bol Radha Bol**) to Nagesh Kukunoor (**3 Deewarein**). She's easily the most successful Miss India in Bollywood.

Other notables: Along with Shah Rukh Khan and her husband Jay Mehta, she is a producer (though not majorly successful yet) and businesswoman (again, not majorly big-league considering they own Kolkata Knight Riders).

Looking forward to: Lots of ads for snack food and cheering at KKR matches. And occasional 'interesting' roles like the ones in **I Am** or **Luck By Chance**.

Sonu Walia

Year of crowning: 1985

Early mark: **Khoon Bhari Maang**, where she was a top model and the villain's moll (with a heart, though). She was 'defeated' by Rekha in a modelling competition as well as in securing Kabir Bedi's advances.

Biggest claim to fame: Again, quantity over quality. She has acted in fifteen indistinguishable films in her three busiest years (1989–91) and twenty-six overall.

Looking forward to: Settled in the US with her hotelier husband. No plans of returning.

Madhu Sapre

Year of crowning: 1992

Early mark and biggest claim to fame: The one and only film she has done—**Boom**. Katrina Kaif, Padma Lakshmi and Madhu Sapre had their collective professional obituaries written with this one film (and for good reason, too). Only Katrina was able to rise after that. Madhu has never acted in a film again.

Other notables: Highly controversial ad for Tuff shoes that featured her and (then-beau) Milind Soman wearing only sneakers, a python and each other.

Looking forward to: Lives in Italy with her husband. Hopefully, she's not planning anything like **Boom** again.

Namrata Shirodkar

Year of crowning: 1993

Early mark: If you call **Mere Do Anmol Ratan** and **Hero Hindustani** that.

Biggest claim to fame: As the golden-hearted prostitute in **Vaastav**, opposite Sanjay Dutt (whose career was resurrected after that).

Other notables: Sister of Shilpa Shirodkar and grand-daughter of actress Meenakshi (who appeared in India's first swimsuit scene), Namrata has been eye-candy in several not-so-notable movies.

Looking forward to: Married to Telugu actor, Mahesh Babu. No plans of returning.

Sushmita Sen

Year of crowning: 1994

Early mark: Her debut film, **Dastak**, was about a Miss Universe being stalked by an obsessed fan. It generated an unprecedented buzz but did not do too well.

Biggest hit: **Main Hoon Na**, where she appeared like a typical Yash Chopra heroine.

Other notables: Mainly off-screen romances and assorted gossip haven't really helped us focus on her body of work. The occasional comic role (**Maine Pyar Kyun Kiya**) and 'acting' role (**Chingaari**) have got noticed.

Looking forward to: A long-standing ambition to produce and star in a film on the Rani of Jhansi, which may have some autobiographical shades if she has her way.

Gul Panag

Year of crowning: 1999

Early mark: **Dhoop**, a short-and-strong performance in a serious film.

Biggest hit / claim to fame: Has acted in mainly offbeat films, the most acclaimed of which is **Dor**. She played a woman whose husband stood accused of murder and only an impossible task could free him.

Other notables: Another realistic performance in **Manorama Six Feet Under** and a sassy role in **Turning 30**.

Looking forward to: A happy married life and some more interesting roles, maybe. At her wedding, the baaraat arrived on Royal Enfield Bullets. As @gulpanag, she is one of Bollywood's earliest adopters of Twitter.

Lara Dutta

Year of crowning: 2000

Early mark: Her debut film, **Andaaz**, pitted her against Priyanka Chopra (whom she beat to become Miss India). Not a huge commercial success, it was in the news for the casting and costumes.

Biggest hit: Probably David Dhawan's **Partner**, opposite Salman Khan.

Other notables: Hysterical roles in comic capers like **Bhagam Bhag**, **Masti**, **No Entry**, etc.

Looking forward to: A happy married life with Mahesh Bhupathi. More films from her production house, Bheegi Basanti, whose first release was **Chalo Dilli** (where she starred opposite Vinay Pathak).

Celina Jaitley

Year of crowning: 2001

Early mark: Skimpily clad as Fardeen Khan's arm-candy— **Janasheen**. Got completely overshadowed, as is the norm in home-productions of male stars.

Biggest hit / claim to fame: Probably **Golmaal Returns**.

Other notables: Smallish roles in multi-starring comedies like **No Entry**, **Thank You**.

Looking forward to: A happy married life with hotelier Peter Haag and her twin sons, Winston and Viraaj.

Neha Dhupia

Year of crowning: 2002

Early mark: In **Qayamat**, where she was the woman from Ajay Devgn's past and did a bikini scene (as she was probably expected to do so, with her Miss India 'background').

Biggest claim to fame: **Julie**. Her dare-bare act as a prostitute on a mission got a huge number of eyeballs. This was amplified by her comment—'In the industry, only sex and Shah Rukh sell.'

Other notables: Some roles in offbeat films like **Phas Gaye Re Obama** and **Dasvidaniya**. Large number of small roles in multi-starring comedies.

Tanushree Dutta

Year of crowning: 2004

Early mark: **Chocolate**, a faithful and yet uneven remake of **The Usual Suspects**.

Biggest hit: Probably, **Aashiq Banaya Aapne**—which also got a lot of publicity because of her clinches with Emraan Hashmi.

Other notables: If that's what you call the usual glam-girl in thrillers or comedies.

Puja Gupta

Year of crowning: 2007

Early mark: An obscure offering—**Kehtaa Hai Dil Baar Baar**—which didn't get her fame or fortune.

Biggest hit / claim to fame: **FALTU**, which was famous for the ultimate party anthem '*Chaar baj gaye lekin party abhi baaki hai*'.

Other notables: None yet.

12 Star Nicknames

Stars are usually known by flattering epithets (Big B) and jazzy initials (SRK). Sometimes, their names shorten (Sallu) or morph (KJo) into something that rolls off the tongue easily. But what do their friends call them? Their parents? Their relatives? What were they called before they became stars?

Pancham

Probably the most famous nickname in Bollywood, R.D. Burman's name had several stories behind it.

The most credible version is the one in which he was named by Ashok Kumar because he was unable to sing the fifth note (pa) right during the rehearsal of a song (*Dol rahi hai naiya* for the film **Shikari**) at home.

That makes it the perfect nickname: a completely insignificant event bringing about a name that stayed throughout one's life and beyond.

Dadamoni

Literally meant 'a jewel among brothers'. That's what Abhash Kumar (a.k.a. Kishore Kumar) and Anup Kumar Ganguly called their elder brother, then a superstar of Hindi cinema—Ashok Kumar, the man who gave RD his nickname.

Munna

Amitabh Bachchan has been called The Big B, Amit and Lambooji—by various people.

But his most affectionate nickname was the one given by his parents. The Star of the Millennium was their little boy—Munna.

Dabboo. Chintoo. Chimpoo. Lolo. Bebo.

The Kapoors have a penchant for silly nicknames. But then, what is a nickname if it is not silly? Randhir, Rishi, Rajiv, Karisma and Kareena respectively.

VD

Veeru Devgan's eldest son was named Vishal when he was born. When he was about to be launched by his father in a film called **Phool Aur Kaante**, his name was changed to Ajay. But for his old friends, he is still known by the initials of his birth name.

Baba

Sanjay Dutt is known for his heart of gold by friends across the industry—from superstars to spot boys. And as the son of a big star, he was first known to them as a little boy who came to the sets as Sanju-baba. They still call him Baba.

Chichi

Govind Ahuja was derogatorily referred to as the *Virar ka Chhokra* when he started acting in movies. The south Bombay journalist lobby turned up their noses even more when they heard his nickname. But Govinda is still going strong.

Guddu. Duggu.

Bollywood's actor-director combo with a hundred-per-cent success ratio is the father-son duo with reflective nicknames—Rakesh and Hrithik Roshan respectively.

Bosky

Rakhee and Gulzar's only daughter—Meghna—has a pet name, Bosky. And Gulzar's bungalow in Bandra is called Boskyana.

Rinku

Sharmila Tagore. And if it is of any interest, her sister's nickname was Tinku.

Koko. Bonnie. Tito.

Silly, meaningless names. The only thing that explains them is the race to which the three belong. Who else but Bengalis would give such silly names to women as beautiful as Konkona Sen Sharma, Bipasha Basu and Sushmita Sen?

Piggy Chops

During the shooting of **Bluff Master**, Abhishek Bachchan named her Piggy Chops and the name stuck within the unit. However, when it was time to give her credit for the cameo in **Taxi No. 9211**, producer Rohan Sippy put it as the nickname and it entered national consciousness.

Pehli Mulaqat:
5 Famous First Meetings

*H*indi films would be nothing if not for the legends surrounding most of them. All the stars, all the movies, all the hits would have come to nought if you did not have that hanger-on who claimed to be there when it all happened.

I think one of the greatest heroes of Bollywood is the guy who stopped Amitabh from boarding the train to Allahabad after his twelfth flop. That man also introduced him to Prakash Mehra who was looking for an actor for a film called **Zanjeer**.

There is no such guy? What rubbish? In fact, that guy was featured in a scene in **Rangeela**, where he recounted this story. That guy was Neeraj Vohra? That guy was *played* by Neeraj Vohra. He actually exists. No, really.

Of all the legends around the stars, the most interesting ones are about the first meetings. There is an element of suspense and drama around these. Thanks to our predisposition towards astrology, there is something inherently attractive about a chance meeting between two Masters of the Universe.

STATUTORY WARNING: Some of the stories have been embellished by the author's imagination.

Guru Dutt & Dev Anand

Dev Anand was an employee of the Indian Postal Services. During the war, he worked as a censor and read hundreds of letters daily to edit out passages unwanted by the government. While doing this boring job, he was completely taken aback by the passionate fan letters addressed to film stars and dreamt of getting some letters like that himself.

One day, his dhobi returned his laundry in which there was a shirt which was not his. Same size but definitely not of the same sartorial elegance Dev was used to. On enquiring, the dhobi speculated that the shirt could belong to this other fellow—who lived in the same chawl—who was working on odd jobs at Prabhat Talkies. To get a little dope on the film industry, Dev decided to take the shirt back to the owner himself. And became so thick with Gurudutt Shivshankar Padukone that very soon, the most famous pact of Hindi cinema was made... if Dev produced a film, Guru would direct it. If Guru produced one, Dev would star in it.[66]

Balraj Sahni & Johnny Walker

Badruddin Jamaluddin Qazi was a conductor with the Dadar depot of BEST. His standard routine consisted of entertaining passengers while handing out their tickets. A stammering lover proposing to his girlfriend for Mr Braganza. An out-of-tune singer doing a ghazal for Mrs Apte. A drunkard getting harangued by his wife for Mr Sahni. Balraj Sahni, that is.

Balraj Sahni was working on a script for a film called **Baazi**—most parts of which were filled except for one of a comedian. He was impressed enough by Badru's antics to fix up an appointment for him with the director, Guru Dutt.

---

[66] For the record, Dev kept his part of the bargain with **Baazi**. Guru did not.

On the day of the meeting, Badru staggered into the room completely drunk, proceeded to fall over furniture and almost kissed the studio receptionist, Miss Lobo. Only when the director was about to call the police, did he confess that he was acting. Thanks to his drunken turn, when the time came to decide a screen name (B.J. Qazi is not what screen legends are called), Guru Dutt unilaterally decided to infringe on the copyright of the world's most famous brand of Scotch whiskey. And for generations after that, Indians thought that Johnny Walker did drunken roles so well that they named a whiskey after him.

Raj Kapoor & Nargis

Baby Nargis had acted in a few films as a child artiste. She grew up to be a raving beauty and acted in a few forgettable films as well.

During that time, Prithviraj Kapoor's eldest son was getting on everyone's nerves on the sets of a film where he was the clapper boy. (It is a common filmi family tradition to send the new-generation kiddos as assistants to directors who could not refuse them.) There were rumours that the clapper boy took more time to get ready than the hero.

Anyway, Raj decided that there were better films to be made, cocked a snook at his bosses, used his father's clout to get financing and even got a script written. To save some money, he decided to act in the lead role himself. By this time, he had screen-tested many girls for the lead role and did not like any. Just when he was getting really impatient, he happened to see some footage of Nargis and decided that the girl had some magic. An appointment was fixed and young Mr Kapoor went off to meet the girl.

Either Ms Nargis did not know the director's time of arrival or she could not care less, she was busy in the kitchen when the door was knocked on. Actually, she was frying some stuff in besan—with her hands wrist-deep in the batter. With no servants around, she ran and opened the door herself. Tousled hair, hands in a mess... but she was very impressed by the light-eyed, fair-skinned good looks of Mr Kapoor. And in a dazed manner, when she used the back of her hand to push back a few strands of hair from her forehead, she smeared some besan on to her hair.

Mr Kapoor remembered this scene for the rest of his life and immortalised it in his teen-romance **Bobby**.

Satyajit Ray & Sharmila Tagore

Ray developed a reputation for giving chances to newcomers right from his first film. He did not really have a choice during his first film, **Pather Panchali** as none of the actors of Bengali cinema then fitted the bill for any of the roles—and more importantly, he did not have the money to pay any of them.

When he was testing actresses for the role of Aparna in **Apur Sansar**, it turned out to be one long haul with none of the hopefuls having the innocence, beauty and sensitivity needed for the role.

When a common friend told Ray of a fourteen-year-old who was distantly related to Tagore, he wanted to refuse but could not do so because of his 'bhadralok' upbringing. His worst fears were confirmed when the girl in question landed up in a short yellow frock and a fringe cut. But something must have come through in her English diction, because Ray asked his wife to take the girl inside, tie her hair in a bun using a wig and dress her in a traditional saree.

And that's when Sharmila Tagore became Aparna. At the end of her journey, she went on to become the biggest star of Bollywood.

Ramesh Sippy & Amjad Khan

The offices of Sippy Films had a room which was ostensibly for their story department. In 1972, the story department was all but disbanded as the scion of the company—Ramesh—was always closeted with two Muslim boys of the same age (which was very young, by filmi standards). Salim Khan and Javed Akhtar were given full use of the story room as they were working on a two-line story idea commissioned by G.P. Sippy. 'A police officer's family is massacred by a dacoit. To take revenge, the officer takes the help of two small-time crooks.'

Of the four characters mentioned in the two lines, three had already been cast. And as the screen-writer duo worked towards the climax of the screenplay, they realised that the dacoit was turning out to be the most charismatic of the lot. And with two major stars of the day slated to play the police officer and one of the crooks, the actor playing the dacoit had to match up to them. All major villains of the day were evaluated and rejected for lack of menace. Danny Denzongpa was almost signed on but he withdrew because he was committed to do Feroz Khan's **Dharmatma**.

At this point, Satyen Kappu recommended to Salim Khan a young actor who was acting in an IPTA production with him. Salim saw the actor and asked him to come and meet Ramesh Sippy for a role that would be the finest of the film.

When the actor walked into the dimly-lit story room, Ramesh Sippy was lying on a mattress on the ground with his back to the door. Hearing a voice, he turned around and looked up to see a guy who was medium in build but because of Ramesh's perspective from the floor, looked like a menacing figure who loomed across the entire frame of the door. Ramesh Sippy turned around and met Amjad Khan for the first time.

After that first meeting, Amjad went back and returned for the screen test in army fatigues, with blackened teeth and a grubby, bearded look. Now, Ramesh Sippy met Gabbar Singh for the first time.[67]

---

[67] Acknowledgements are due to Anupama Chopra, who recounted the story of this meeting in her bestselling book, *Sholay: The Making of a Classic*.

Baar Baar, Lagataar: 16 Stars With Hat-tricks At Filmfare Awards

*F*ilmfare Awards have been around for six decades. It has had its shares of controversies and allegations of biases towards various stars at different points of time. Also, without the benefit of hindsight, the jury has sometimes chosen poorly, making the awards list look quite awry a few years on. But for its sheer longevity, Filmfare is still the prize every filmwallah aspires for.

It is also a great indicator of the extent to which certain people ruled the roost in a certain era. The biggies of Bollywood are all on that list. But how does one identify the *real* doyens in each category?

One criterion is to find people who have done hat-tricks. Only a fantastic mix of talent, speed and luck allows you to win three years in a row. But thanks to the exclusive star system of Bollywood, there seems to be a pretty large number of people who have been there, done that.

Best Director

Given the prolonged involvement a director has (or should have) with a film, churning out one award-winning film a year for three years should be quite impossible. As surprising as it might sound, this is the category where we have—not one, but—two hat-tricks!

Iconic director Bimal Roy did his first trio in the first three years of the Awards as **Do Bigha Zamin**, **Parineeta** and **Biraj Bahu** won (between 1953 and 1955). There was a gap of two years when V. Shantaram and Mehboob Khan put a foot in the door but Roy returned in 1958—60 with **Madhumati**, **Sujata** and **Parakh**.[68]

To put his achievement in perspective, no other director has won it in even two consecutive years. Very soon, we won't have directors who make even six films in their entire careers.

Best Actor

This one is expected since Dilip Kumar ruled the Best Actor category like his own backyard in the early days of the Award.

In the first ten years, he pocketed the Best Actor trophy five times including a hat-trick from 1955 to 1957 for **Azaad**, **Devdas** and **Naya Daur**. In doing this, he beat off stiff competition like Raj Kapoor in **Jagte Raho** and Dev Anand in **Munimji**. In fact, the stiff competition carried on for quite some time as the trio of Raj-Dev-Dilip were the three Best Actor nominees in five different years.

Four superstars—Rajesh Khanna, Amitabh Bachchan, Naseeruddin Shah and Shah Rukh Khan—have won the Best Actor Award twice in a row. But we are still awaiting the hat-trick.

---

[68] Inertia must surely count for something because Bimal Roy won it for **Parakh** (clearly not one of his best films) in 1960 by beating K. Asif who was in the running with a film called **Mughal-e-Azam**.

Best Supporting Actor

Bollywood's forte seems to be the underdog. The guy who gets hammered for a large part of the film returns to beat the shit out of his tormentors. And for a large part, life imitates art. Abhishek Bachchan seems to have followed in the footsteps of his illustrious father in this regard. The Big B waited for his thirteenth film (**Zanjeer**) to hit box-office gold. Junior B waited till his fourteenth film to get commercial and critical acclaim in Mani Ratnam's **Yuva**. After **Yuva** in 2004, he did the supporting act to his father in **Sarkar** and to King Khan in **Kabhi Alvida Naa Kehna**— to complete the hat-trick.

Big B had won three Supporting Actor awards in all. Junior equalled him in three years.

And what about Best Actor in a leading role? Well, Big B leads 5-0 on that one.

Best Music Director

The Music category sees the most number of reigns. Music, lyrics and voice—all categories have winners of three consecutive awards. And the big daddies of Bollywood—the music directors—have won the most.

Two have won four in a row.

No surprises when I say Laxmikant-Pyarelal did it in the late 1970s. And even less so when I name A.R. Rahman (in the late 2000s). LP, the longest playing record in the industry, won it for four rocking tracks—**Amar Akbar Anthony**, **Satyam Shivam Sundaram**, **Sargam** and **Karz**. And Rahman sealed his supremacy with **Rang De Basanti**, **Guru**, **Jaane Tu Ya Jaane Na** and **Delhi 6**.

Shankar-Jaikishan is currently (after the 2011 awards) the joint holder of the maximum number of awards won—nine. Known to be the melody-makers of RK Films, their hat-trick tragically includes **Mera Naam Joker**—the studio's biggest failure, which nearly drove Raj Kapoor to bankruptcy. The other two films were **Pehchaan** and **Beimaan**.

In the early 1990s, when purists were lamenting the death of melody and originality, in walked Nadeem Shravan. And for several years, they could do no wrong. They manufactured hit songs by the dozen throughout the decade, but their hat-trick happened in the first three years of their careers. **Aashiqui**, **Saajan** and **Deewana** were the films that rocked—jhankaar beats notwithstanding.

Best Lyricist

Gulzar has won a Best Lyricist prize ten times. Javed Akhtar has won it for eight. They have not managed to do three in a row. The person who did it never won a Filmfare Award again.

Shakeel Badayuni's trio of hits—running from 1960 to 1962—was a swan-song like no other. The title song of **Chaudvin Ka Chand**, *Husnwale tera jawaab* (**Gharana**) and *Kahin deep jale kahin dil* (**Bees Saal Baad**) were the three offerings of Shakeel that became award-winning songs.

Best Playback Singer (male)

It seems a little unfair that Kishore Kumar does not have the longest-winning streak in male playback singing. His longest unbroken reign was four when he won for *Pag ghungroo* (**Namak Halaal**), *Humein aur jeene ki* (**Agar Tum Na Hote**), *Manzilein apni jagah* (**Sharaabi**) and *Saagar kinare* (**Saagar**) between 1982 and 1985.

But it sounds almost providential that he also won the prize in 1980 (for *Hazaar rahein* from **Thodisi Bewafaii**) and would have had a double hat-trick if his own son hadn't beaten him in 1981. Amit Kumar had chart-topping numbers from **Love Story** and beat his father—only to never win again.

The quirky genius with a curious record at the Filmfares

Poetic? Tragic? You decide.

So, who does have the longest winning streak? Nope, it is not Mohammed Rafi either—who doesn't even have a hat-trick to his name.

The only singer to have five—five!—continuous awards is Kumar Sanu. And quite ironically, he earned his early bread by doing covers of Kishore Kumar classics. He shrugged off jokes about a nasal voice and his winning graph became identical to Nadeem-Shravan's with *Ab tere bin jee lenge hum* (**Aashiqui**), *Mera dil bhi* (**Saajan**) and *Sochenge tumhe pyaar* (**Deewana**). He added two more to his kitty with *Yeh kaali kaali aankhen* (**Baazigar**) and *Ek ladki ko dekha* (**1942 A Love Story**).

What we don't know for certain is whether he stopped winning or—as he claimed—withdrew from competitive awards. What we do know is that he was grateful enough to name his bungalow Aashiqui.

Best Playback Singer (female)

The ultimate diva—Lata Mangeshkar—competed in a general playback singing category for both male and female singers. She withdrew from competitive awards soon after.

Among the rest, four singers have done hat-tricks.

Three of them can be considered absolute equals—in talent and popularity. Anuradha Paudwal won it for **Aashiqui**, **Dil Hai Ke Manta Nahin** and **Beta** (from 1990 to 1992). Kavita Krishnamurthy did it for **1942 A Love Story**, **Yaraana** and **Khamoshi** (from 1994 to 1996). Alka Yagnik came to the party last with **Taal**, **Dhadkan** and **Lagaan** (from 1999 to 2001). See—one after the other, in a perfect queue!

And the fourth one? She is a little ahead of these three... also, she has won four awards in a row for **Caravan**, **Hare Rama Hare Krishna**, **Naina** and **Pran Jaye Per Vachan Na Jaye**. She is the one and only—Asha!

Best Actor in a Comic Role

This award has had a patchy stint. For a character as regular as the Bollywood comedian, this award was given regularly only from 1989 onwards and was wound up after 2006.

In 1989, Anupam Kher converted the solo award into a joint one. Awarded for **Ram Lakhan**, he called his on-screen partner Satish Kaushik on stage and shared the prize with him. Two years later, he started a hat-trick and picked up awards for **Lamhe**, **Khel** and **Darr**. He returned for a fifth time to pick up an award for **Dilwale Dulhania Le Jayenge** and be remembered as one of the greatest comic actors of Bollywood.

And to think, the role that brought him fame (and his first Filmfare) was a tragic one—the bereaved headmaster of **Saaransh**.

Best Choreographer

The Dancing Queen's crown has been hotly contested for—among stars and choreographers. If there has to be a first among equals, then it has to be the one who has a hat-trick, the maximum awards AND who is the first recipient of the award.

In the first three years of the award itself, Saroj Khan had her threesome by winning for **Tezaab** (*Ek do teen*), **Chaalbaaz** (*Na jaane kahan se*) and **Sailaab** (*Hum ko aajkal hai*).

Over the years, it has been a see-saw battle between her and Farah Khan, with both ladies breaking each other's hat-trick streaks several times.

Did you notice the composition of heroines in Saroj Khan's hat-trick? Madhuri Dixit—2. Sridevi—1. Would you agree that's a fair representation of their standing in the '90s industry? Or wouldn't you? Either way, that can only be a separate chapter.

What's In A Name: 9 Stars Appearing On-Screen With Their Real Names

*A*mitabh Bachchan's Vijay and Shah Rukh Khan's Raj (or is it Rahul?) are two of the iconic names that have become an inseparable part of their star personae. And indeed, many stars have been identified with a character on-screen that has evolved far beyond the running time of the film it is from. For example, Manoj Kumar as Bharat is known far and wide for his patriotic roles (starting with **Upkar** and ending with **Clerk**).

But quite a few of the stars have also been appearing on-screen with their real names. Some are quite famous while some aren't.

Prem Chopra

'Prem naam hai mera, Prem Chopra...'—when he said these lines in **Bobby** with his trademark leer and usual floppiness, he immediately established that he was certainly not the Good Samaritan the eloping couple was hoping him to be. It was not the first time he was appearing on-screen as Prem but it was certainly the most famous, and his track record as an ace bad-man was cleverly brought on with the utterance of his full name.

For the statistically inclined, Prem Chopra appeared as Prem in twenty-four films (out of the 300+ he has acted in) including the recent **Golmaal 3**.

Ranjeet

Just when you thought Prem Chopra was the King of the Look-Ma-same-name game, in walked yet another ace-villain, Ranjeet, and topped him with twenty-three same-named roles (out of his nearly 250 films, till date). For the mathematically inclined, that's a higher strike rate than Prem's.

In 1977, he appeared in two of the biggest hits—**Dharam Veer** and **Amar Akbar Anthony**—with his real name as screen name, establishing himself as one of the top villains of the times. Both were Manmohan Desai-directed blockbusters, which had more stars than anyone could possibly remember. It certainly made the screenwriter's task easier.

Raj Kapoor

And if you have started to think that villains are the usual suspects to saddle unimaginative (read: real) names with, we have Raj Kapoor appearing with his real name in nearly a quarter of the films he acted in. Be it as the perennial do-gooder or the tycoon with a heart of gold, Raj Kapoor was Raj on screen as much as off it. All his iconic roles—most of them his own productions as well—have him as Raj. Starting with **Awara**, **Shree 420** and **Anari**, right down to his magnum opus **Mera Naam Joker**, audiences knew and loved him as Raj. Of his sixty-seven films as actor, seventeen are as Raj, and while many of them are bunched around 1950–51, the aura stayed well afterwards.

Pooja Bhatt

After the hero, it's the heroine.

Pooja Bhatt debuted—literally and figuratively—as Daddy's girl. Her short acting career (twenty-six films) started and (almost) ended with playing characters called Pooja (in about ten of them). If there was a story to be told through the name, there was none—at least in her biggest hits (**Daddy**, **Dil Hai Ke Manta Nahin**, **Sadak**, **Sir**, **Phir Teri Kahani Yaad Aayee**). Whether she played a spoilt brat, a psychotic actress or a reluctant prostitute, Pooja Bhatt was always Pooja. But Anupam Kher— her most frequent screen dad—said it in a variety of ways.

Amitabh Bachchan

Amitabh Bachchan has not appeared as Amit as many times as Vijay. But if Vijay was his angry young avatar, Amit was his sweet, poetic persona. The professor in **Kasme Vaade**, the poets in **Silsila** and **Kabhi Kabhie**, the householder in **Do Anjaane** were all Amits. Of the nine times he played Amit, there were a few action heroes as well (**Parvarish**, **Mahaan** and **Suhaag**) but even they were not the typical angry vigilantes.

In **Benaam**, his name was Amit Srivastava—which is actually his real name because 'Bachchan' was a title taken by his father Harivanshrai, and Srivastava is their original family surname.

Rekha

When Amitabh is here, can Rekha be far behind?

In **Do Anjaane**, Rekha played Amit Roy's wife Rekha Roy, thus making the film one of the very few where the lead pair appears with their real first names. In seven films (out of her total output of 167), Rekha was Rekha—the biggest hit probably being **Rampur Ka Lakshman**.

Sunny Deol

Now, here's a twist.

Here is an actor whose screen name is not his real name. But he has acted in several films with his real name. Sunny Deol was christened Ajay Singh Deol but like most Punjabi boys, he came to be known by his nickname.

He was Ajay the young boxer out to avenge his brother's death in **Ghayal**—the film that launched him as the Angry Young Hulk and set box-office records across his home state. He ended up being Ajay in eight films—**Right Yaaa Wrong** being one of the last.

And by the way, he was Sunny in two of his earliest films as well—**Betaab** and **Sunny**.[69]

Kumar Gaurav

Rajendra Kumar produced his son's lavish debut vehicle—**Love Story**—and keeping in mind that it was a 'home production', the hero's name was his real-life nickname (Bunty) too. The film became a massive hit and the industry celebrated the arrival of a new chocolate-box star. Except that Kumar Gaurav could never replicate the success of his debut.

---

[69] Dharmendra's he-man persona became bigger and bigger till he was referred to as Garam Dharam by the filmi press as well but he was hardly ever named Dharam in his films. Among his many hits, he was Dharam Singh in only **Dharam Veer**.

It may have crossed the mind of someone in superstitious Bollywood that maybe the name 'Bunty' was the lucky mascot and the name was brought back later in a film called **Hai Meri Jaan**. Yes, you are right—that film flopped as well. Sigh.

Aamir Khan

Sometimes, there are no numbers. But a fact has to be recognised for its trivia value.

Aamir Khan appeared in his second starring role with his real name on-screen. In **Raakh**, he played Aamir Hussein, a young man out to take revenge on his fiancée's rapists. The film did not make too much of a mark except that this was the only time—yet—Aamir's screen name was his real name.

QS Cutie: 18 Early Films Of Aamir Khan

Aamir Khan debuted in **Qayamat Se Qayamat Tak** and quickly caught the imagination of teenage girls in the country. He was married by then but that information was kept under wraps to keep his lover-boy image alive.[70]

One of his biggest contributions to Bollywood has been the fact that he brought the work ethic of doing one film at a time and immersing himself into it completely. However, before this 'method' period (which started in the mid-'90s), Aamir Khan had a 'mad' period when he did a series of delightfully crazy films that straddled the entire gamut of box-office performances (super-hit to unmitigated disaster) and critical acclaim (deafening applause to pelting eggs).

Raakh

Aamir Khan's second release[71] was a critical success and a box-office disaster. Aditya Bhattacharya (son of director Basu Bhattacharya) directed this gritty, dark film about a young man hunting down his girlfriend's rapists. Aamir played the young man, assisted by a cynical cop, played by Pankaj Kapur. Teenage girls, who went to see the chocolate-box hero of **QSQT**, were shocked to see him in

---

[70] His wife, Reena Dutt, appeared briefly in the *Papa kehte hain* song, as a giggling teenager at the college party.
[71] His first film as an adult was **Holi**, which never got a theatre release.

this avatar and they quickly went out and warned their friends.

Love Love Love

The usual rich-girl-poor-boy formula paired the hot couple of Juhi and Aamir, but the film sank without a trace. Neither the music nor the treatment of the hackneyed plot could interest audiences. The standard act of hero being upstaged at parties by the brash villain seemed to be a little too jaded by now. They even repeated Dalip Tahil in Aamir's dad's role but it remained a Dud Dud Dud.

Jawani Zindabaad

Noble themes seldom make entertaining movies. But at least they are applauded for their stand. This one—on anti-dowry—got shafted both ways. It was too frivolous for an issue-based film and too serious to be an out-and-out entertainer. Farha starred opposite him, Javed Jaffrey starred alongside and all of them contributed to the abominable wastage of celluloid.

Deewana Mujh Sa Nahin

Aamir Khan's first pairing with Madhuri Dixit and his first (and last) film wearing spectacles bombed spectacularly. He played a fashion photographer to Madhuri's supermodel character, following her devotedly in the total conviction that she would eventually realise that it was match made in heaven while she remained blissfully unaware of his existence. A tremendously bad film later, all got settled in true filmi style.

Awwal Number

This is not an Aamir Khan film, actually. Any film which has Dev Anand cannot be anybody else's. One of the greatest films of the So-Bad-That-It's-Good genre, this cricket film had Aamir as Sunny, who made it to the Indian cricket team. In between, he romanced Ekta (a plump Dev Anand discovery). There was a gossip item that in a scene for which Aamir and Ekta had to roll on the ground, he passed out under Ekta's weight.

Tum Mere Ho

A snake film! Aamir was the son of a snake-charmer and wore strange headgear made of cowries, waistcoats without anything under them and Juhi Chawla all over himself. *Ichhadhari nagin, kabila, inteqam, qurbani* and similar words of the genre were bandied about as Juhi died of a snake bite, was revived, killing the audience in the process. Eventually the film did not survive either.

Dil

Just when his professional obituary was being written, Aamir appeared in this college romance opposite Madhuri Dixit. Their earlier flop did nothing to raise the expectations and neither did the non-entity director-producer. It must have been the lucky tree in Ooty around which the title song was shot that turned this film into a monster hit. The music was a super success, the loud comedy was appreciated in college campuses all over India and the Aamir-Madhuri pairing was fêted as the Next Big Thing.

They have never appeared in a film again together. Yet.

Dil Hai Ke Manta Nahin

Aamir Khan's fabled perfectionism started to show as Pooja Bhatt expressed concern in an interview that she thought he would go from cinema to cinema, seeing if the seats were okay and the ACs were working right!

As Raghu Jaitley—the motor-mouthed reporter, Aamir did a competent job and the film was a runaway success. Nadeem-Shravan's music was hugely popular and the film was re-released with one song added later.

Afsana Pyar Ka

Aamir and the heroine studied in the same college. He irritated her and she challenged him to fight the college boxing champion. Aamir's honourable and valiant behaviour in the boxing ring caused a change of heart... Wait! This is the story of **Dil**.

Well yes, but **APK** has the same story as well! This Aamir-Neelam starrer had at least one very good rain song (*Tip tip tip tip barish shuru ho gayee*) and a convoluted sub-plot about his estranged parents as well. But everybody had this feeling that they had seen the film already.

Isi Ka Naam Zindagi

A Bengali comedy **Banchharam-er Bagan** (Banchharam's Garden) was—for reasons beyond the limits of human comprehension—remade in Hindi. The zamindar's role was reprised by Shakti Kapoor, and Pran played the garden's owner. Aamir was his grandson, a role that was almost insignificant in the Bengali version but expanded miraculously—and needlessly—in Hindi.

Daulat Ki Jung

Sometimes, Hindi film titles tell you the entire story of the film. This was one such title that made the entire star cast, music and direction of the film irrelevant. As per laws of the land, children of business rivals are not allowed to marry unless they endure eighteen reels of terrible pain. What was really unfortunate was that we had to endure the same agony.

Parampara

Yash Chopra's directional venture was a tri-generational saga starring Sunil Dutt, Vinod Khanna and Aamir Khan (as also Saif, as part of the third generation). *Yeh shaadi nahin ho sakti, bhagwaan ko sakshi maan kar tumhe apna loonga, main tumhe jaidaad se bedakhal kar doonga* and million other familiar bombasts exploded as Aamir-Saif appeared towards the second half, while Vinod Khanna romanced Ramya and Ashwini Bhave for the most part of the film.

Jo Jeeta Wohi Sikandar

Riverdale came alive and Aamir Khan played the quintessential Archie to a brilliant soundtrack by Jatin-Lalit. Aamir—in his late twenties—played a schoolboy in white uniform but did not look too out of place. Director Mansoor Khan did an excellent job of getting the angst of the lower middle-class Model School against the rich, spoilt brats of Rajput.

His performance was overlooked by Filmfare which gave Anil Kapoor (for **Beta**, of all things) the prize. And that was the last time we saw Aamir at awards functions.

Hum Hain Rahi Pyar Ke

Aamir Khan was credited with ghost-directing the film, which was officially directed by Mahesh Bhatt (then helming about half-a-dozen films simultaneously, some of which supposedly directed entirely on phone). Since the film was produced by Aamir's father and Aamir was slowly developing an intellectual aura, it was unanimously decided that he be credited for the direction. Whoever directed the film did a competent job of making a nice comedy about Aamir's adventures with his nephews-nieces, a murderous Sindhi creditor and a south Indian lover.

Andaz Apna Apna

In one of the most manic comedies ever, Aamir and Salman were paired for the first—and last—time as two wastrels out to marry heiress Raveena, where they also met her secretary Karishma. Raveena was played by Raveena Tandon and Karishma was played by Karisma Kapoor—or were they? *Mogambo ka bhatija*, *Vasco Da Gama ki gun* and a villain called Teja (who was a twin of Raveena's father) were all in the fray. Confused? Don't be. Leave your brains aside and die laughing.

Aatank Hi Aatank

The Godfather has spawned many copies, none of them probably as bad as this one. Aamir played Michael Corleone, who had to take a break from singing songs with Juhi Chawla to join the family business. Rajnikanth was thoroughly under-utilised as Sonny and Pooja Bedi dropped in as the second lead. Aamir went around with an AK-47 from hotel to hotel, killing his enemies in elevators.

Baazi

Ashutosh Gowariker and Aamir Khan came together for the first time in this cops-and-terrorists tale, with a climax lifted straight out of **Die Hard**. Aamir Khan played Special Branch cop Amar Damjee Rathore and took on several get-ups including that of Julie Braganza, she of silken thighs and cleavage! Heroine Mamta Kulkarni had an inconsequential role but rumours of an affair between the two of them surfaced during the making.

Akele Hum Akele Tum

A remake of **Kramer Vs Kramer**, Aamir Khan played a self-obsessed music composer ignoring his talented wife, Manisha Koirala. The couple fought for custody of their son and the ending was altered to suit Bolly sensibilities. The film had fantastic music (by Annu Malik) and even better digs at the contemporary music scene. Satish Shah played Gulbadan Kumar, owner of a music company and there was a composer-duo (one short and paunchy and the other dapper and French-bearded) called Amar-Kaushik. Basically, the producers—Venus—took a major dig at their biggest competitors.

The other Aamir Khan release of 1995 was **Rangeela**, in which he delivered a fantastic performance, but his transformation to a moody perfectionist was complete. Nowadays, he restricts himself only to the most unusual projects, does some-great-some-record-shattering films, is a whiz at marketing his films and speaks sonorously on the reasons for choosing his films. Maybe an intrepid film journalist should pin him down and ask him to explain the creative rationale behind '*Khambe jaisi khadi hai / Ladki hai ya chhadi hai...*'

Nishabd: 10 Silent Scenes Of Amitabh Bachchan

One of the mandatories of any list of Hindi film trivia is the story how Amitabh Bachchan was rejected in an audition for All India Radio. And also that one of his earlier mentors (Sunil Dutt) did not find the legendary voice attractive enough to give him a speaking part in **Reshma Aur Shera**. While his fabled baritone has always been a huge draw, there are some iconic scenes in which he did not use his magical voice. And said much more than what lesser mortals did with flared nostrils, flaring biceps and bare chest.

Anand

As Anand Sehgal stood at the twilight of his life and sang the melancholic *Kahin door jab din dhal jaaye*, his host—Dr Bhaskar Banerjee—silently walked up the stairs, came behind him and waited for the song to end. Despite the restraint and the measured body language, enough charisma seeped through for a nation to take note of the arrival of the next superstar. Not a very easy task, considering that it all happened when Rajesh Khanna was singing a massive hit.

Deewaar

Vijay Verma rose to the top of the Bombay underworld. And his mentor—*Daavar-saab*—handed over his chair to the heir. As an envious colleague watched in awe, Vijay Verma slowly circled the coveted chair, sat down with an air of finality and then plonked his feet on the table. The *lambi race ka ghoda* had finally come good.

Don

What do you notice when Helen is in a thigh-high slit skirt, dancing away? A lot if the person she is trying to seduce is a smuggler wanted in eleven countries. The gangster did nothing beyond getting dressed in a green shirt and green-and-white check blazer. The subdued lust, the arrogance, the imperious behaviour all shone through as he sauntered around.

SRK did the same scene twenty-eight years later. Did he succeed? Well, as they said, *'Don ko pakadna mushkil hi nahin...'*

Kaala Patthar

Probably the angriest role of the Angry Young Man, this film had quite a few silent passages which spoke more than the entire filmography of Nana Patekar.

One was a scene in which he was confronted with a knife—and he walked up to the goon and gripped the knife at the blade. As the blood trickled through, the pain and the anger on his face was something only he can pull off.

The second one was a sequence of one-upmanship instigated by the garrulous Shatrughan Sinha—who snatched away the light from his beedi. He calmly went up to him, picked the beedi out of Shatrughan's mouth, lit his own, stubbed the other out and walked away.

Yaarana

Emily Post came to *Gangaa-kinare*. *Kisanwa* was being groomed into superstar Kishan by Ram Sethi (a regular feature of many Amitabh Bachchan films). As Kishan failed spectacularly with the fork and knife in a comic mime sequence, he dared his teacher to do a physical equivalent of a tongue-twister.

Slap your knees with both hands. Get your right hand to touch your left ear and left hand to touch your nose. Slap again. Get your left hand to touch your right ear and right hand to touch your nose. Repeat (till your nose turns red with ill-timed slaps). He did it so effortlessly... just as effortlessly, we rolled in helpless laughter.

Satte Pe Satta

A dreaded criminal came out of jail and slowly shuffled towards a waiting car. He had salt-and-pepper hair, eerily light eyes, a gaunt face and the stoop of a burdened man. Also, he was supposed to be identical to a lively, happy man—seen in just the previous scene.

Actors of today would probably starve themselves to achieve that lean and hungry look while the man did it in alternate shifts of shooting with a little help from under-eye make-up, contact lenses and a whole lot of acting talent. And the menace that he exuded when he crouched out of the jail door was not something that comes out of rehearsals. It was pure magic.

Main Azaad Hoon

Azaad tried to bring about a compromise between sugar-mill workers and sugar cane farmers. Admittedly, a difficult task, it came about after a long meeting. And when the farmers asked him to address the gathering, he was too overcome with emotion to speak. He fought back tears, choked a little, smiled a little and raised his right fist in a well-known gesture of inquilaab! The crowd roared in approval.

Sholay

The widow of the Thakur household went around the balcony at sunset—lighting the lamps. A mercenary sat outside his cottage across the courtyard and played a haunting tune on his mouth-organ. On-screen love has never been so understated, yet so eloquent.

The legends abound... it was RD who played the mouth-organ. The lighting of dusk was so delicate that it took a fortnight to shoot the scene. And the players on screen were as much in love in real life. They still are.

Ek Ajnabee

A retired army-man tried to exorcise the demons of his past. He drank heavily to shut out the brutal scenes in his memory. The eternal Hindi film cliché of a troubled man drowning his sorrows was given a soundless dimension as the man drank, cried, contemplated suicide, crumpled up in agony and exhausted himself at the end of it all. One of the longest silent scenes in recent times, any lesser actor would have ended up making it a yawn. He kept you on a gut-wrenching edge.

Shakti

A dreaded smuggler—Vijay—was released from jail for a short while to attend his mother's funeral. His fury at his adversaries' act slowly morphed into grief as he walked into the room and saw the dead body. He eventually knelt down in front of his estranged father and started weeping. The father and son held each other tightly and kept weeping. Two of Hindi cinema's best actors didn't speak a word but said volumes.

Honourable Mention: Sarkar

This film was an ensemble of his moods—angry, amused, frustrated, relaxed, tired, energetic, devastated, victorious, benevolent—almost like the nine rasas and of which Ram Gopal Verma seems to have prepared a slideshow. No one scene stood out. Not one scene was forgettable either. And it all added up to become a textbook on acting.

Amul's tribute to the baap of them all

8

THIS IS THE
BEGINNING

'Don't give away the ending. It's the only one we have.'—Publicity line for **Psycho**

Picture Abhi Baaki Hai: 15 Unusual 'The End's

*I*ndian cinegoers are programmed to jump up like a jack-in-the-box whenever a movie approaches some sort of resolution. Even before the entire cast gets in position for the mandatory family portrait, you have busy souls treading over toes and bumping into seats in their crazed desire to reach the parking lot before anyone else can go there. No Indian ever sees the 'The End' card... or at least, they try their best not to.

If they do succeed, they miss out on some cool endings—which seem to be getting snazzier by the day and sometimes a little quirky even. Before the end-card comes on, there is a lot to say—even if the story is over.

Message

Movies always ended with a 'The End' card—superimposed on hugging siblings, embracing lovers and crying parents. But filmmakers try to give a complete closure... just in case, you thought this was the interval and some explosive plot detail would be revealed later.

Shakti Samanta was a pioneer of this brand of spoon-feeding. After Rajesh Khanna (the son) lovingly hugged Sharmila Tagore (the mother) and touched her feet, we were allowed to leave with an end card which said— '**Aradhana** is complete'.

And when an elderly Rajesh Khanna half-smilingly-half-tearfully waved to Sharmila Tagore (and presumably his shining teeth were symbols of his undying love) we were informed—'This is **Amar Prem**'—as the frame froze.

Sometimes, the message is subtle—especially if the director wants to get a wee bit naughty.

In **Seeta aur Geeta**, the two Hema Malinis dispatched the villains with a mix of whips and tears and married the two leading men (Dharmendra and Sanjeev Kumar). There was a bit of tomfoolery with each of the two men trying to get into the bed of the wrong Hema. Once the confusion was settled, 'The End' came on screen within an inverted red triangle—the familiar symbol for family planning.

Presumably, the director wanted to discourage having twins to scotch possibilities of sequels.

Symmetry

It would be interesting to mention two of Ramesh Sippy's films—**Sholay** and **Shakti**—for an interesting symmetry of their opening and closing scenes.

In **Sholay**, the film opened with a train chugging into a station from which a police officer got off and proceeded on a journey through the ravines to meet Thakur Baldeo Singh. The film closed with a train—carrying the lead pair—chugging out of the same station as the Thakur saw it go off.

Even in **Shakti**, the film opened with a 'toy train' entering a hill-station and a grandson got off, welcomed by his grandfather. And in the closing scene, the same grandson went off by a similar train, seen off by his grandpa.

Intentional? Coincidental?

Bloopers

A very popular concept for end credits all over the world is to show the shooting bloopers from the unused footage. Jackie Chan films are the most famous proponents of this since you sometimes don't realise the intricacy of the stunt till you see the setup and the failed attempts.

The super-popular (though slightly inexplicably so) **Golmaal** series directed by Rohit Shetty follows this format quite religiously. With their spinning cars, stunts atop ferris wheels and timed bum-kicks, it is imperative to know whether they got it right the first time or whether they landed on their bums.

Story Completion

Sometimes, the film ends on a high and there is a need—either for closure or for comic relief—to describe what the main characters went on to do.

In **Rock On!** the futures of the main characters were described through subtitles as a hauntingly beautiful song (about dreams coming true) played on. The band members of Magik and their spouses had started following their dreams and they rocked on.

Rab Ne Bana Di Jodi had a humorous photo album of Suri-ji and Taani-ji's Japanese honeymoon (won in a Sumo-wrestling championship, no less) with their gradually increasing intimacy. Starting with the kimono-clad couple in Japanese tea-rooms, the album ended with them in a bedroom scene just before the U-rated censor certificate could be challenged.

These two films had sure-shot happy endings and no 'spoiler alerts' were required. Ramesh Sharma's critically acclaimed **New Delhi Times** had probably the most damning story continuation but that cannot be revealed without spoiling the suspense.

Cast

Farah Khan has developed and—with three films—patented a completely innovative way of acknowledging the unsung members of her cast. In all her films, the cast and crew appear on-screen with great fanfare, usually jiving to the tune of a hit song.

In **Main Hoon Na**, the crew was at a fair dancing to the tune of *Yeh fizaaein*.

In **Om Shanti Om**, they walked the red carpet for a glitzy premier—but with a twist. The spot boys arrived in a Merc while the director herself got off an auto (when the carpet itself was being rolled back).

In **Tees Maar Khan**, one part of the crew was shown in the 'village' where the film was shot and the others were at the Oscar awards ceremony (where, presumably, the film won handsomely).

Song

The one draw that keeps the audience—or at least, some part of it—glued to the seats is a hit song while the credits roll.

Dibakar Banerjee has perfected this art of creating a huge musical draw with a rocking number to go with the end credits. In **Khosla Ka Ghosla**, it was *Chak de phattey* with the entire cast in a construction ensemble, trying to seal Anupam Kher in a wall *á la* Anarkali. In **Love Sex Aur Dhokha**, the title song—to the accompaniment of cast members in jazzy music video costumes—brought up the end.

A music video by Loki Local to bring proceeedings to an end

This concept of having a music video during the credits is essentially a Hollywood concept, where the poor dears cannot have songs within the movie and place the biggest hit from the soundtrack in the end.

One of the earliest Indian films to replicate this was Kaizad Gustad's **Bombay Boys**, which ended with a rap song by Javed Jaffrey, who enlightened us on the bhais of Mumbai with a music video he featured in as well.

And the way he announced the song was reason enough for a lot of people to stop leaving. *Kyunki... abhi khatam nahin hua, ch*****!!!*

Photographs & Illustrations

I am very grateful to:

- Tanul Bhartiya, Ramkumar Srivatsa (RK) and Jai Arjun Singh, who helped in making some vital connections.
- Ishneet Kaur Monga, who corrected and converted the images to make them suitable for printing.
- Dibakar Banerjee and Kundan Shah, who took time out of their creative pursuits to help out with several pictures.

Images courtesy and copyright

AB Corp Limited
Paa

Dibakar Banerjee Productions
Love Sex Aur Dhokha

Gujarat Cooperative Milk Marketing Federation (www.amul.com)
Advertisements for Amul

Kunal Kundu (http://www.behance.net/kunalkundu/frame)
Illustration of Kishore Kumar

MAD Entertainment Limited
Cheeni Kum

Madras Talkies (www.madrastalkies.com)
Dil Se
Guru

National Film Development Corporation Limited
(www.nfdcindia.com)
Jaane Bhi Do Yaaro

Pritish Nandy Communications
(www.pritishnandycom.com)
Jhankaar Beats
Shabd

Vinod Chopra Films (www.vinodchopra.com)
Lage Raho Munna Bhai
Parineeta

Vinod Chopra Productions (www.vinodchopra.com)
Khamosh

Yashraj Films Pvt Ltd (www.yashrajfilms.com)
Chak De India
Dilwale Dulhania Le Jayenge
Rocket Singh: Salesman Of The Year